GREAT

HOW THE MISSISSIPPI

RIVER

SHAPED ST. LOUIS

CITY

BY ANDREW WANKO

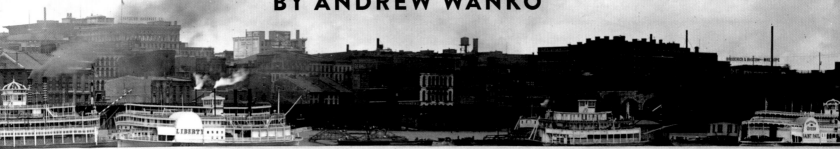

MISSOURI HISTORICAL SOCIETY PRESS

ST. LOUIS

DISTRIBUTED BY UNIVERSITY OF CHICAGO PRESS

SINCERE THANKS TO THE SPONSOR OF THIS BOOK
Mercantile Library and Its Pott Inland Waterways Collections at University of Missouri–St. Louis

AND TO THE SPONSORS OF THE MISSOURI HISTORY MUSEUM EXHIBIT *MIGHTY MISSISSIPPI*

Presenting Sponsor
Bank of America

Lead Sponsors
JSM Charitable Trust
Alberici Corporation
Ameren

Confluence Sponsors
Emerson
Edward Jones
Ken and Nancy Kranzberg
Sam and Marilyn Fox Foundation

Historic Painting Sponsors
Dan and Sondra Ellis
Bellefontaine Cemetery and Arboretum

Conservation Sponsor
William R. Piper

Tributary Sponsors
General Marine Services, Inc.
Grossman Iron and Steel
Missouri American Water
The Cahokia Mounds Museum Society / Cahokia Mounds State Historic Site

ISBN 978-1-883982-95-9
© 2019 by Missouri Historical Society Press

Library of Congress Cataloging-in-Publication Data

Names: Wanko, Andrew, 1986- author. | Missouri Historical Society.
Title: Great river city : how the Mississippi shaped St. Louis / Andrew Wanko.
Other titles: How the Mississippi shaped St. Louis
Description: St. Louis : Missouri Historical Society, [2019] | Includes bibliographical references and index. | Summary: "This
    book examines the importance of the Mississippi River across time and through the lens of a single city: St. Louis. Features
    hundreds of maps, artifacts, and fascinating historic images, spanning back to St. Louis's founding and even earlier"--
    Provided by publisher.
Identifiers: LCCN 2019022194 | ISBN 9781883982959 (paperback)
Subjects: LCSH: Saint Louis (Mo.)--History. | Saint Louis (Mo.)--Description and travel. | Mississippi River--History.
Classification: LCC F474.S257 W36 2019 | DDC 977.8/66--dc23
LC record available at https://lccn.loc.gov/2019022194

Design by Tom White
Infographics by Christopher Brauss of Brauss Creative LLC
Cover image: Night view of Eads Bridge to downtown St. Louis. Photograph by P. R. Papin Photo Company, ca. 1945. Missouri
Historical Society Collections.

Distributed by University of Chicago Press
Printed and bound in the United States by Modern Litho

TABLE OF CONTENTS

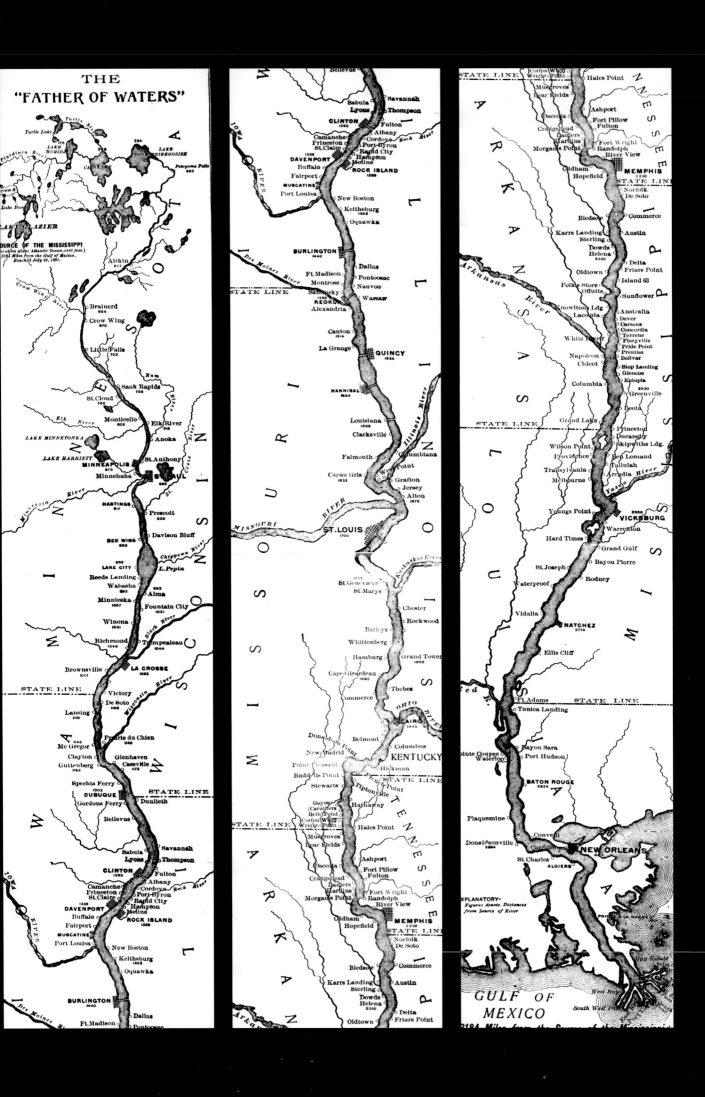

FOREWORD

Even before mapmakers, explorers, and their Old World sovereigns knew much about anything else in North America–a time when California was often depicted on a map as an offshore island and the term *terra incognita* dotted charts of the Arctic and the Southwest alike–people knew about a great flowing waterway in the heart of the continent: the Mississippi River. It was a highway, a boundary, a symbol, a tremendous natural force, a timeless influence on Missouri's long history. The great river and its confluence with the Missouri, Illinois, and Meramec rivers formed a watershed, defining the prehistoric and historic landscape of St. Louis. The river system appeared on maps, more or less accurately, from the Renaissance on. From time to time the stories that the old maps hinted at need retelling. These narratives refocus the region's cultural heritage and landscape on its single greatest resource–the Mississippi River. But so often it is taken for granted. Usually it isn't until the river threatens to wipe out structures and settlements along its banks that we're again reminded what an awesome, powerful force it is.

Great River City: How the Mississippi Shaped St. Louis, Andrew Wanko's creative river history, accompanies an exhibition and programs that are the result of the work and legacies of many people, past and present. The *Mighty Mississippi* exhibition and related programs represent a historic collaboration between the two historical institutions best equipped to tell the story of the Mississippi as it meanders along Missouri's eastern border and weaves in and out of local lore. The Missouri Historical Society and the St. Louis Mercantile Library Association, both established in the mid-nineteenth century, grew side by side in downtown St. Louis for generations. They stood within earshot of steamboat bells and plaintive whistles, of locomotives powering across the newly constructed Eads Bridge, of deckhands' work songs. The Mississippi was a way of life for the Missouri Historical Society and the St. Louis Mercantile Library, just as it was for St. Louis's early inhabitants. Both institutions were established to preserve the heritage of a great mid-continent city and its culture, and we are delighted to again work together to tell a story that has been a major part of our collections efforts for over 150 years. By combining lovingly preserved photographs, art, manuscripts, rare books, and objects–as well as the expertise of our two staffs–we have achieved a rich retelling of the Mississippi's story.

Ironically, the river's ageless quality is the very trait that seems to dull its impact. Every day, people rush across its bridges, leaving rusting industrial structures of the past in their rearview. There are few historical markers to commemorate the extraordinary events that have taken place at the levee. Views from the top of the Gateway Arch stretch out in every direction, but do visitors ever consider the long view backward, the history that this 2,000-mile-long waterway has created? And what of the river itself? This book and the *Mighty Mississippi* exhibit seek to reacquaint modern audiences with the river by celebrating the diverse heritage of the many peoples who have lived along its central course. We also hope to inspire future collecting and preservation efforts. Researchers and the general public alike can explore the river via our institutions' robust digital resources so the Mississippi's story can once again be the heart of St. Louis's story.

We wish to thank the many donors, lenders, and sponsors of this exhibition, and the dedicated staff members of our two institutions who have been deeply involved with this project. For the Missouri Historical Society: Public Historian Andrew Wanko, Curator of Environmental Life David Lobbig, Director of Education and Interpretation Elizabeth Pickard, Managing Director of Museum Services Katie Van Allen, Managing Director of Education and Visitor Experience Nicholas Hoffman, Director of Visitor Engagement and Accessibility Sarah Sims, Youth and Family Programs Manager Lindsay Newton, Director of Community Programs Emily Underwood, and Director of Marketing and Communications Leigh Walters. For the St. Louis Mercantile Library: Curator of the Herman T. Pott Inland Waterways Collection Porsche Schlapper, Mercantile Library Association Endowed Curator of Art Julie Dunn-Morton, and the Oliver M. Langenberg Curator of Reference Services Charles E. Brown.

The many planning sessions and discussions surrounding the Mississippi project have inspired the Missouri Historical Society and the St. Louis Mercantile Library to continue to collaborate and tell the great stories of the St. Louis region by using 300 years of artifacts that are in our care. The enthusiasm, hard work, and dedication to this project have made a profound impact on both of our institutions, and we are proud to share it with you.

Dr. Frances Levine
PRESIDENT, MISSOURI HISTORICAL SOCIETY

John N. Hoover
EXECUTIVE DIRECTOR, ST. LOUIS MERCANTILE LIBRARY
AT THE UNIVERSITY OF MISSOURI–ST. LOUIS

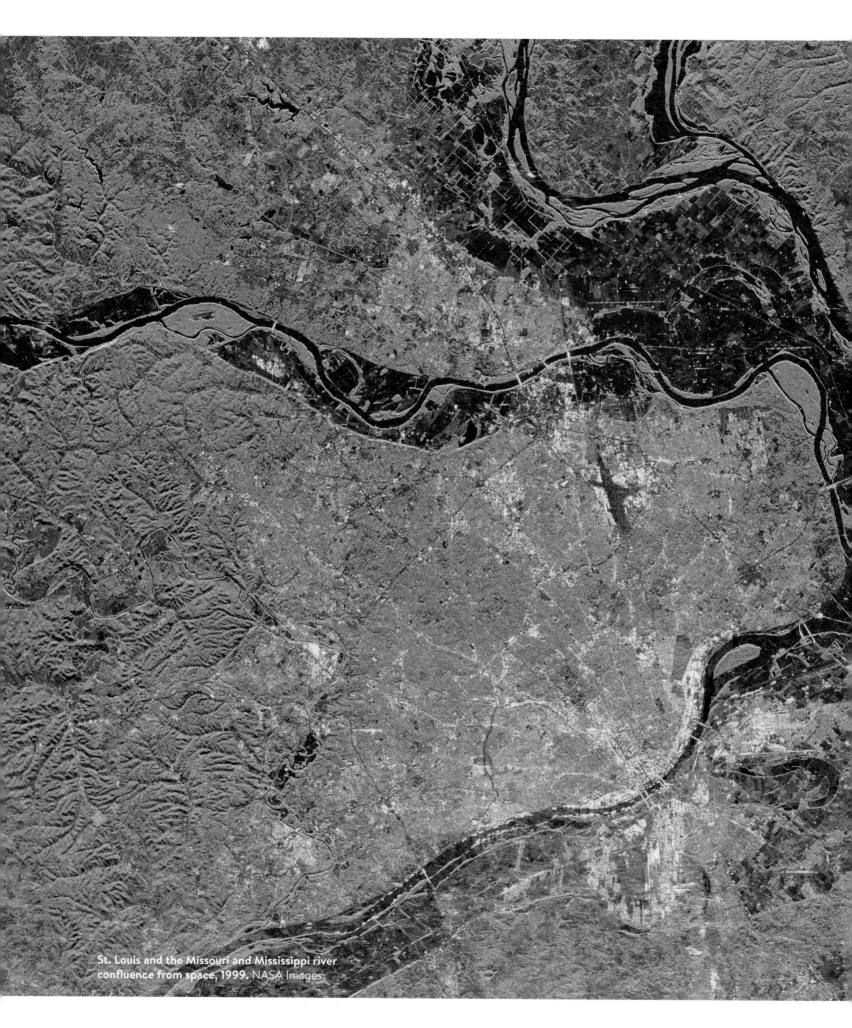

St. Louis and the Missouri and Mississippi river
confluence from space, 1999. NASA Images.

INTRODUCTION

Without the Mississippi River there would be no St. Louis. The river has been vital to the city's life from the moment it was founded in 1764. But as St. Louisans, we have to admit that the river is something we usually forget about from day to day. We drive across its bridges, watch barges drift along its surface, and bring out-of-towners to the 630-foot-tall Arch standing proud on its bank, but overall we don't spend much time pondering how the Mississippi River seeps into our daily lives. This book attempts to remedy that. We'll look back into history at dozens of moments when the stories of the river and the city intertwined and find that the Mississippi has always been more than just water.

St. Louisans of the past witnessed a menagerie of boats traveling up the levee's edge, ranging from fur-trading canoes to a floating McDonald's restaurant. They saw sights they would never forget, like the first locomotive crossing the Eads Bridge, a levee filled with thousands of refugees seeking the city's help, and excursion boats' ballrooms all aglow. They sometimes watched their riverfront descend into violence, like during immigration riots and when "gentlemen" dueled to the death on Bloody Island. They witnessed changes that, today, are difficult for us to truly comprehend—such as on March 10, 1804, when French and Spanish St. Louisans stood by as their town was traded among nations and suddenly realized they were now all "Americans."

Countless works have examined the importance of the Mississippi River in American history but rarely its close relationship to one single city. In this book we'll see how the Mississippi River has been a stage for St. Louis's triumphs, embarrassments, joys, and tragedies—not to mention a source of drinking water, waste removal, and entertainment. As it dives into subjects such as health, urban planning, and racial and ethnic conflict, this book will examine how the river has shaped the lives of millions of St. Louisans. You can still see the marks that some of these moments have left on the city; others have long since washed away. All are proof that both the river and the city will roll on for ages to come.

—Andrew Wanko

1200s:
THE MISSISSIPPI'S FIRST METROPOLIS

Today St. Louis is known as an old river city, but the *first* metropolis on the Mississippi thrived centuries earlier. Cahokia, as the settlement was later named, flourished on the Mississippi's eastern banks between 800 and 1400 AD. Cahokia grew to more than 20,000 inhabitants at its peak around 1200 AD–a bigger population than London, England, had at the time. With an endless supply of river water for large-scale agriculture, it was among the largest urban centers in North America prior to European contact.

Cahokia's inhabitants mysteriously disappeared around 1400 AD, and their wooden city quickly decayed. But they left behind enormous, manmade earthen mounds on both sides of the river. The Cahokia archaeological site contains more than 120 mounds spread across 2,200 acres. The largest of them, Monk's Mound, stretches nearly 1,000 feet long and almost 100 feet high.

Though the Cahokia Mounds site is world famous today, the St. Louis side of the river was also once dotted with mounds. They predated St. Louis by centuries, but as St. Louis industrialized in the mid-1800s, the land they occupied became more and more valuable. The mounds were considered curiosities at best and wastes of space at worst. St. Louisans plowed over them by the dozens. The few voices calling to save the mounds fell on uninterested ears.

Named for its resemblance to the gumdrop-shaped cones of sugar sold at early St. Louis markets, Sugar Loaf Mound is the last remaining Native American mound within St. Louis city limits. It sits atop a south-side bluff overlooking the Mississippi River, and in the 1920s a small frame house was built upon its peak. In 2009 the Osage Nation of Oklahoma purchased the mound site. The Osage Nation has since removed the house, and tribe members are restoring the mound's original appearance.

CAHOKIA OR "MONK'S MOUND," MADISON CO., ILL.

Monk's Mound. Monk's Mound is the largest of Cahokia's more than 120 mounds. At approximately 1,000 feet long and 750 feet wide, it has a larger footprint than any ancient Egyptian pyramid. This 1882 illustration shows the intimidating presence the mounds carried in the eyes of early St. Louisans— and how they were seen as objects of curiosity or even places to build homes.

"Mound City" images, 1818–1870s. St. Louis was home to dozens of mounds through the mid-1800s, and it even picked up the nickname Mound City. Anna Maria von Phul painted these (above) in 1818. Ironically, by the time the postcard (left) promoting the moniker was made, development had destroyed nearly all of the mounds.

Historic locations of the St. Louis mound group. Just north of the original settlement of St. Louis was a group of at least twenty-six Native American mounds. St. Louisans viewed them as objects of curiosity, sketching them, building homes on them, and even placing the city's first water reservoir on top of one.

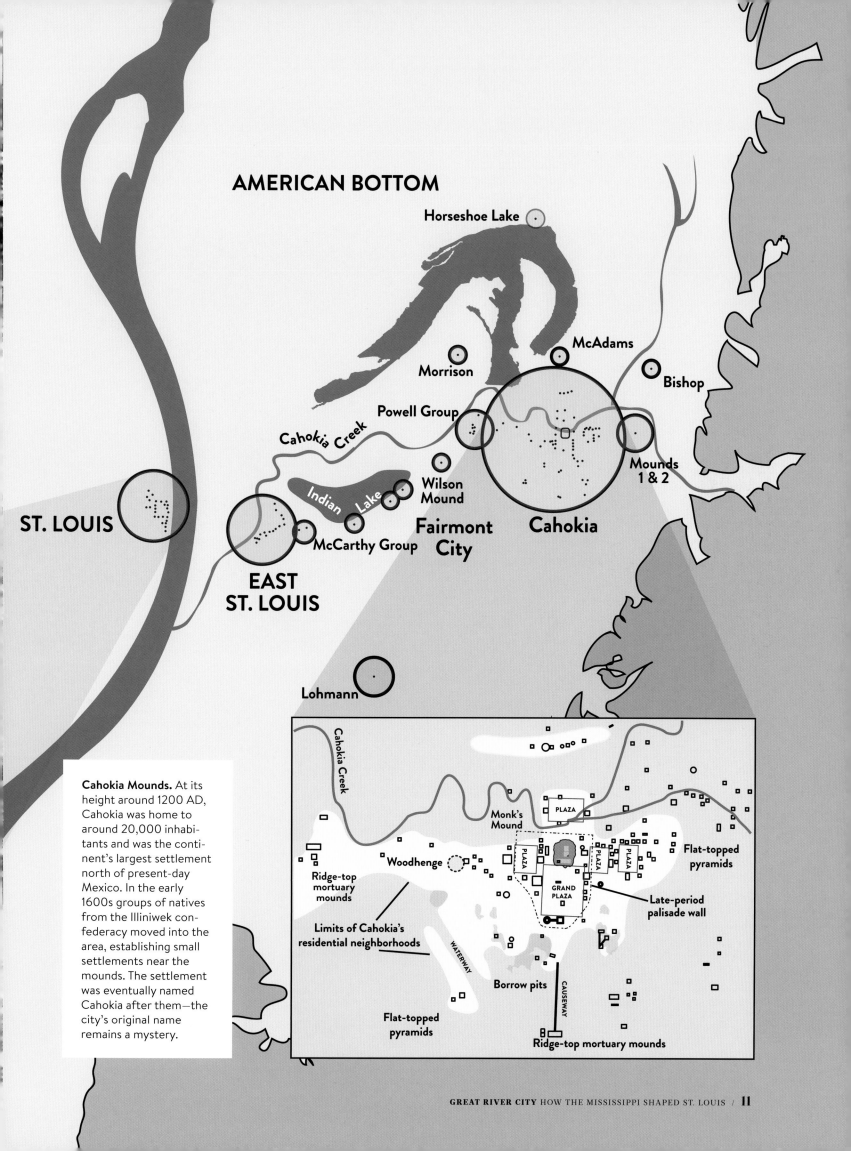

AMERICAN BOTTOM

Horseshoe Lake

McAdams

Morrison

Bishop

Powell Group

Cahokia Creek

Wilson Mound

Mounds 1 & 2

Indian Lake

ST. LOUIS

Cahokia

McCarthy Group

Fairmont City

EAST ST. LOUIS

Lohmann

Cahokia Mounds. At its height around 1200 AD, Cahokia was home to around 20,000 inhabitants and was the continent's largest settlement north of present-day Mexico. In the early 1600s groups of natives from the Illiniwek confederacy moved into the area, establishing small settlements near the mounds. The settlement was eventually named Cahokia after them—the city's original name remains a mystery.

Cahokia Creek

Monk's Mound

PLAZA

Woodhenge

PLAZA

PLAZA

PLAZA

Flat-topped pyramids

Ridge-top mortuary mounds

GRAND PLAZA

Late-period palisade wall

Limits of Cahokia's residential neighborhoods

WATERWAY

Borrow pits

CAUSEWAY

Flat-topped pyramids

Ridge-top mortuary mounds

1852 View of St. Louis, Big Mound at Right (above). Big Mound 1850s–1868 (left and facing). Built between 900 and 1300 AD, Big Mound was known to early French St. Louisans as *La Grange de Terre:* the Earthen Barn. Development crept toward Big Mound until 1868, when the North Missouri Railroad flattened the ancient structure for a railroad line extension. Photographer Thomas Easterly captured the destruction of the ancient site, as well as the St. Louisans who considered it nothing more than a sightseeing opportunity. Big Mound was located in north St. Louis near the present-day inter-section of Broadway and Seventh Street. A small marker now commemorates where it once stood.

1764:
FOUNDING RIVER CITY

From its founding in February 1764, St. Louis was made for river trade. What is now a major American urban center began life as a tiny French trading outpost, created to take advantage of the river system's natural trade highway. France's Louisiana Territory stretched from New Orleans up the Mississippi River's west side to present-day Minnesota, and in 1763 French officials began offering fur-trading monopolies to New Orleans merchants who would settle the territory's upper half. After business partners Pierre Laclède and Gilbert Antoine de Maxent secured exclusive trading rights with Native American tribes along the Missouri River, they suddenly had a potential fortune waiting 1,000 miles away.

In August 1763, Laclède set out to build a fur-trading outpost near the confluence of the Mississippi and Missouri rivers. With him was a crew of men; boatloads of merchandise; and Auguste Chouteau, the fourteen-year-old son of Laclède's love interest, Marie Thérèse Bourgeois Chouteau. That December they spotted the perfect limestone bluff on the river's west bank, 18 miles south of the confluence. They marked some trees at the site, then headed downstream to overwinter at Fort de Chartres. A small group returned to build the outpost.

On February 14, 1764, young Auguste Chouteau arrived with a few dozen men and began clearing trees. They built shelter the next day. Laclède arrived that April, naming the post Saint Louis in honor of Louis IX, the famed medieval king of France. Laclède hadn't planned on building a city, but with all the wealth of the vast western interior of North America floating past, there would soon be one.

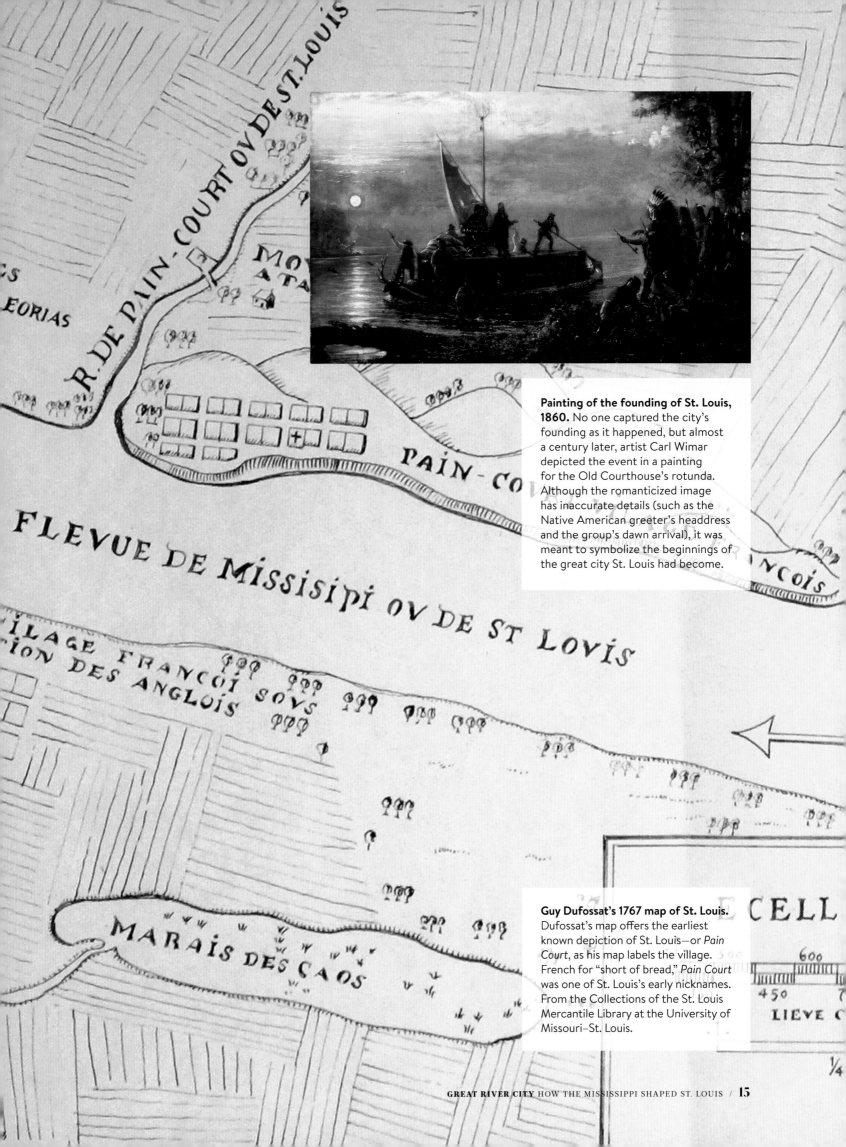

Painting of the founding of St. Louis, 1860. No one captured the city's founding as it happened, but almost a century later, artist Carl Wimar depicted the event in a painting for the Old Courthouse's rotunda. Although the romanticized image has inaccurate details (such as the Native American greeter's headdress and the group's dawn arrival), it was meant to symbolize the beginnings of the great city St. Louis had become.

Guy Dufossat's 1767 map of St. Louis. Dufossat's map offers the earliest known depiction of St. Louis—or *Pain Court*, as his map labels the village. French for "short of bread," *Pain Court* was one of St. Louis's early nicknames. From the Collections of the St. Louis Mercantile Library at the University of Missouri–St. Louis.

St. Louis was founded by an unlikely team: a well-educated thirty-four-year-old businessman from southern France and his common-law wife's fourteen-year-old son.

Pierre Laclède (1729–1778). Born in southern France, Pierre Laclède arrived in New Orleans in 1755 and headed upriver to plant his fur-trading outpost in 1763. Although St. Louis prospered, Laclède ended up penniless and debt ridden. He died returning to St. Louis from New Orleans in 1778. Much of Laclède's life is a mystery to modern historians. There are even suspicions that this image may actually be of a different, unidentified member of the Laclède family.

Laclède family home in Bedous, France, ca. 1950s. Pierre Laclède grew up in this large whitewashed home in the foothills of the Pyrenees Mountains.

Auguste Chouteau (1749–1829). Marie Chouteau's teenage son Auguste accompanied Laclède upriver. Afterward, he and his half-brother, Jean-Pierre Chouteau, thrived as fur traders, building a monopoly with the Osage Nation. The Chouteau family name shows up hundreds of miles from St. Louis—including in Kansas City, which grew from an outpost built by Auguste's nephew François Gesseau Chouteau.

Marie Thérèse Bourgeois Chouteau (1733–1814). Even though her runaway husband Rene Chouteau was still very much alive in the 1760s, Marie Chouteau referred to herself as Veuve (Widow) Chouteau. She became romantically involved with Pierre Laclède, and they entered into a common-law marriage in St. Louis. The matriarch of approximately fifty grandchildren, Marie Chouteau presided over one of the most powerful merchant families in the Mississippi Valley.

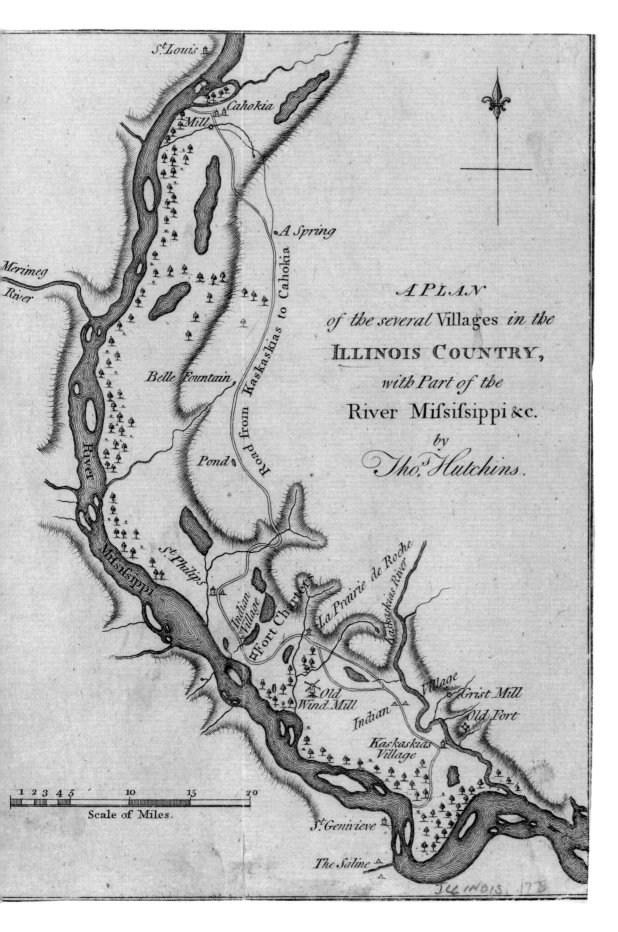

A PLAN
of the several Villages *in the*
ILLINOIS COUNTRY,
with Part of the
River Mifsifsippi &c.
by
Tho.ˢ Hutchins.

St. Louis

Cahokia

Mill

Merimeg River

A Spring

Road from Kaskaskias to Cahokia

Belle Fountain

River

Pond

Mifsifsippi

St. Philips

Indian Village

Fort Chartres

La Prairie de Roche

Kaskaskias River

Old Wind Mill

Indian Village

Grist Mill

Old Fort

Kaskaskias Village

St. Genivieve

The Saline

ILLINOIS, 1773

1 2 3 4 5 10 15 20
Scale of Miles.

St. Louis to Ste. Genevieve, 1770s. St. Louis was one of a handful of French settlements that existed south of the Missouri and Mississippi river confluence, but it was the only one established for trading.

CAHOKIA, 1699. Founded as a Catholic mission post, Cahokia's Church of the Holy Family is the longest continually active Catholic parish in the United States.

FORT DE CHARTRES, 1720. Fort de Chartres established a French military presence in the Upper Louisiana Territory. Pierre Laclède would store his goods here while constructing St. Louis in early 1764.

PRAIRIE DU ROCHER, 1722. This small town sprang up near Fort de Chartres. As it grew, many inhabitants' headed across the river to Ste. Genevieve.

KASKASKIA, 1703. Natives of the Kaskaskia tribe had a small village here, and after French missionaries began living with them, more white settlers followed.

STE. GENEVIEVE, CA. 1750. Ste. Genevieve was the largest settlement by the time St. Louis was founded. Many of its inhabitants worked in salt production and lead mining. After the original village flooded in 1785, the whole town was moved to its present-day location.

1790s:
THE RIVERSIDE VILLAGE

Sitting at the confluence of the Missouri and Mississippi rivers, St. Louis was ideally positioned to grow rich off of furs. As furs poured in from the west and were sent downriver to New Orleans, St. Louis traders became flush with money. St. Louis even picked up the strange nickname *Pain Court*–"short of bread"–because St. Louis residents bought food from surrounding settlements rather than bothering to make it themselves.

Aside from the river connections, there was another reason St. Louis flourished. Unlike many other early settlements in North America, St. Louis maintained respectful relationships with the surrounding native populations. Tribal groups like the Osage controlled vast lands rich with fur-bearing animals, and without strong trade agreements, it was wealth that St. Louis traders had no other chance of accessing. They traded generously, and both parties prospered through cooperation.

With all of this wealth St. Louisans filled their village with orderly, well-constructed homes set in spacious yards. Some of them contained items you would never expect to find in a frontier settlement, such as private libraries, scientific instruments, European paintings, and crystal chandeliers. All of these luxuries pointed back to a single source: Whether it was boating, hunting, or trapping, nearly every colonial St. Louisan was somehow involved in the river's fur-trading system.

The earliest known view of St. Louis, 1817. Drawn for an 1817 banknote, Pierre Laclède's fur storage warehouse and mansion are visible at left, and Fort San Carlos can be seen on the horizon.

St. Louis's *poteaux en terre* homes. Early St. Louisans built houses by driving log posts into the ground in a rectangular outline and filling the gaps between with clay and rubble stone. The exterior was then coated with plaster and whitewashed. This house-building style, called *poteaux en terre*, was unique to the Lower Mississippi River Valley and French Canada.

1. Antoine Saugrain (1763–1820).
Antoine Saugrain was St. Louis's first village physician. His work ranged from performing basic surgeries to supplying the scientific needs for the Lewis and Clark expedition.

THE RIVERSIDE SETTLEMENT
Just 3 blocks wide and 19 blocks long, early St. Louis was made up almost entirely of low-density residences. The linear street grid of square blocks was a copy of the street grid used in New Orleans.

RUE DES GRANGES — BARN ST.
RUE DE L'EGLISE — CHURCH ST.
RUE ROYAL — MAIN ST.

LOMBARD ST.
MULBERRY ST.
CEDAR ST.
PLUM ST.
POPLAR ST.
ALMOND ST.
SPRUCE ST.
MYRTLE ST.
ELM ST.

2. Louis Delisle Bienvenue House, built ca. 1770.
The Bienvenue house survived into the 1860s—albeit in a state of severe decay. At that time it was being used as a shed for a coal seller, and it was torn down by the 1880s.

4. Charles Gratiot (1752–1817).
Wealthy fur merchant Charles Gratiot maintained international ties with London and Montreal. During the Revolutionary War he put up $8,000 (nearly $200,000 today) to finance American attacks on British outposts in the Illinois Territory.

3. Jeanette Forchet (ca. 1736–1803).
By 1800 there were more than 300 black St. Louisans, and about 20 percent of them were free. Jeanette Forchet, who owned land at Second and Plum streets, outlived two husbands, had four children, and likely supported herself as a baker—a dough trough was among the items in an inventory of her possessions (right).

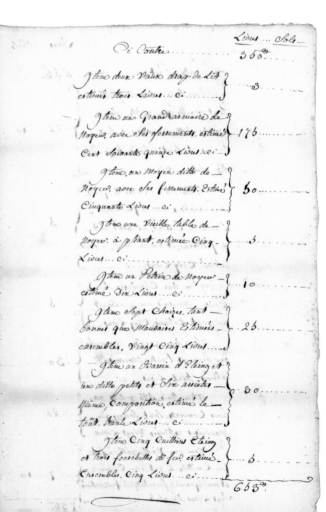

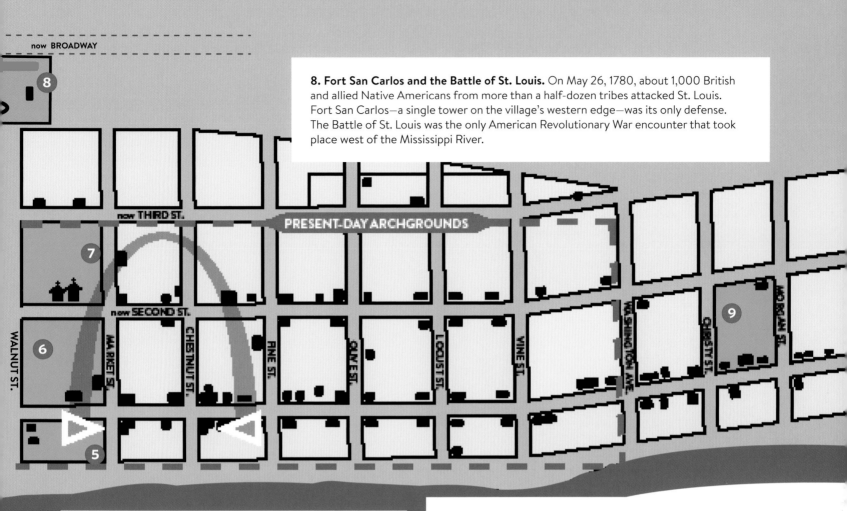

now BROADWAY

8

now THIRD ST.

PRESENT-DAY ARCHGROUNDS

7

now SECOND ST.

WALNUT ST.

6

MARKET ST.

CHESTNUT ST.

PINE ST.

OLIVE ST.

LOCUST ST.

VINE ST.

WASHINGTON AVE.

CHRISTY ST.

MORGAN ST.

9

5

8. Fort San Carlos and the Battle of St. Louis. On May 26, 1780, about 1,000 British and allied Native Americans from more than a half-dozen tribes attacked St. Louis. Fort San Carlos—a single tower on the village's western edge—was its only defense. The Battle of St. Louis was the only American Revolutionary War encounter that took place west of the Mississippi River.

5. The Place Publique. The public plaza offered space for fur trading, public gatherings, and town meetings alongside Laclède's fur-storage warehouses.

9. Jacques Clamorgan (1734–1814). Wealthy black adventurer Jacques Clamorgan, known for his charm and rogue behavior, made a fortune in furs and land speculation. In 1793 he freed his slave Esther to hide land grants in her name. She made the lands profitable, and he tried to take them back, resulting in a court battle. She won several of them.

7. The Laclède/Chouteau Mansion. After Pierre Laclède's death in 1778, Auguste Chouteau made his already massive stone home even bigger. The Chouteau Mansion functioned as St. Louis's hospitality room for visiting dignitaries.

6. The church lot. Constructed in the 1830s, what is known today as the Old Cathedral was actually the fourth church built on this site. The first and second churches (built in 1770 and 1776) would be more accurately described as sheds. The third, a brick church that went under construction in 1818, sat half-finished for years and eventually burned down.

OLD CHOUTEAU MANSION, ST. LOUIS, MO.

Ruins of a Creole house on the river, 1851. By the time photography came about in the early 1840s, most of St. Louis's early Creole structures had been replaced by commercial buildings. On the river bluffs just outside the city, photographer Thomas Easterly took this haunting shot, documenting the weatherworn house of a Creole boatman.

1804:
WASHING AWAY BOUNDARIES

The year 1804 marked the first time St. Louis no longer looked upon a foreign land on the opposite side of the river. The Mississippi's east side (the Illinois Territory) was owned by Britain and then the United States, and its west side (the Louisiana Territory) was traded from France to Spain and then back to France. But in 1803, Napoleon had unexpectedly offered the 828,000-square-mile Louisiana Territory to the United States for just $15 million. In what became known as the Louisiana Purchase, the United States had suddenly consolidated complete control of the entire Mississippi and Missouri river system for the first time.

On March 9, 1804, St. Louisans crowded onto the levee as US Captain Amos Stoddard's boat arrived. For a single day St. Louisans would live beneath the flags of three different countries. Stoddard would accept St. Louis first on behalf of France (Spanish officials still operated St. Louis's day-to-day government, even though the territory belonged to the French) and then the United States. On the morning of March 10, 1804, the United States flag was hoisted permanently over St. Louis, and life would never be the same for the town's French and Spanish inhabitants. They were now all Americans, living beneath a government whose habits, language, and laws were foreign to them.

As these St. Louisans were adjusting to their new world, American explorers Meriwether Lewis and William Clark were on the river's other side at Camp Dubois in Illinois, preparing to venture into a new world of their own. President Thomas Jefferson had charged them with a daunting task: investigate the United States' new territory and carve a path to the Pacific Ocean. They set out in the spring of 1804 and, after two years and more than 8,000 miles of travel, reappeared on the St. Louis levee with journals, animal specimens, and stories of the strange expanse waiting in the far west. In the coming decades the wealth of these lands would turn St. Louis into a frontier metropolis.

Transfer of Upper Louisiana at St Louis, 1804.

Document transferring Upper Louisiana, St. Louis, 1804. The ceremonial transferring of Lower Louisiana took place in New Orleans in December 1803, but it would take many more months before Upper Louisiana was formally transferred to the United States. The day the territory switched from Spanish to French and finally to American hands became known as Three Flags Day. This document authorizing the transfer bears the signatures of US Captain Amos Stoddard; Spanish Lieutenant Governor Carlos Dehault Delassus; and witnesses William Clark, Antoine Soulard, and Charles Gratiot.

Painting depicting Three Flags Day, 1906. As the American flag rose over the city on March 10, 1804, there were mixed emotions. One witness saw French St. Louisans crying "tears of misgivings and regret" as cheers rang "faint and few."

EXPLORING THE MISSOURI AND MISSISSIPPI RIVERS

Setting out from St. Louis in 1804 and returning in 1806, the Corps of Discovery explored thousands of miles on their journey to the Pacific Ocean and back. Meanwhile, Zebulon Pike would journey up the Mississippi River, seeking its source.

TIMELINE OF THE LEWIS AND CLARK EXPEDITION, 1804–1806

1. Fall 1803 to Spring 1804: Camp Dubois
Lewis and Clark establish Camp Dubois a few miles from St. Louis on the Mississippi's east bank. Both Lewis and Clark attend the Three Flags Day transfer ceremony in St. Louis. On May 14, 1804, the expedition sets off.

2. May 1804: La Charrette (60 miles from St. Louis)
On May 25, the Corps pass La Charrette, the last non–Native American settlement on the Missouri River.

3. September 1804: West of present-day Yankton, South Dakota
The Corps study unfamiliar animals (coyotes, antelope) and spend a long day catching a single prairie dog to ship live to President Jefferson.

4. October 1804–April 1805: Fort Mandan
The Corps reach the villages of the Mandan and Hidatsa tribes and build Fort Mandan to overwinter in what is now central North Dakota. Temperatures plummet to forty-five degrees below zero.

5. August 1805: Present-day Idaho
The Shoshone tribe helps the Corps cross the Bitterroot Mountains, and the Nez Perce tribe builds canoes for them. As they push into the Clearwater River, the water's current is in the Corps' favor for the first time.

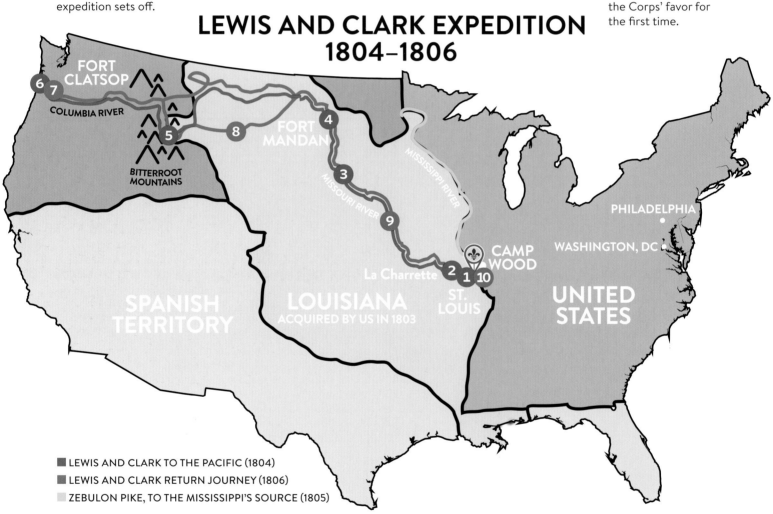

LEWIS AND CLARK EXPEDITION 1804–1806

■ LEWIS AND CLARK TO THE PACIFIC (1804)
■ LEWIS AND CLARK RETURN JOURNEY (1806)
■ ZEBULON PIKE, TO THE MISSISSIPPI'S SOURCE (1805)

6. November 1805: The Pacific Ocean
The Corps reach the Pacific Ocean on November 18. Clark's estimate of their travel distance (4,162 miles) was off by fewer than 40 miles. They cross the Columbia River and build Fort Clatsop.

7. March 1806: The Return Begins
The Corps, thoroughly homesick and out of both whiskey and tobacco, set off for home. They travel for only two months before being stalled by the thick snow still blanketing the Bitterroot Mountains.

8. July 1806: The Split
Past the Bitterroot Mountains, the Corps split in two. Lewis heads up the Marias River and Clark ventures down the Yellowstone River, spreading the Corps across 300 miles.

9. August 1806– September 1806: Headed Home
The expedition reunites on August 12, covering 70 downriver miles a day (more than five times their upriver speed). On September 20 the Corps raise an exuberant cheer at an unfamiliar sight—a domesticated cow.

10. September 23, 1806: St. Louis
On September 23, 1806, the Corps of Discovery arrive in St. Louis. Many people assumed the crew were long since dead, and their primitive, tattered, buckskin clothing shocks those gathered on the levee.

William Clark (1770–1838, below). Lewis invited William Clark, a retired Legion of America lieutenant, to share the Corps of Discovery expedition command. Afterward, Clark became a US Indian Affairs agent and remained in St. Louis for the rest of his life.

Meriwether Lewis (1774–1809, above). Meriwether Lewis joined the military as a teenager and climbed the ranks, eventually becoming an aide to Thomas Jefferson in 1801. When the Corps of Discovery expedition ended, he settled in St. Louis as governor of the Louisiana Territory. His later years were marked by personal and financial breakdown, and on October 11, 1809, Lewis died, likely by suicide.

Zebulon Pike (1779–1813). Just a year after Lewis and Clark headed up the Missouri River, Zebulon Pike was sent up the Mississippi River to find its northern source. Pike's expedition left from Fort Bellefontaine (just north of St. Louis) in August 1805, and by the time his team reached present-day Minnesota, they had struggled through 3 feet of snow and temperatures that congealed Pike's liquor "to the consistency of honey." On February 1, 1806, they arrived at Leech Lake, which Pike claimed to be the river's source. He was only about 40 miles off: Lake Itasca would be identified as the Mississippi's true source in 1832. In July 1806 Pike set out to explore the headwaters of the Arkansas and Red rivers. He attempted to scale the tallest mountain in the Rockies (Pike's Peak) and briefly ended up a prisoner of the Spanish in Santa Fe before returning to the Louisiana Territory in 1807.

Objects from the Corps of Discovery Expedition. Pocket watch and telescope of Meriwether Lewis, long rifle and buckskin journal of William Clark

1817:
THE WIGGINS FERRY COMPANY

Today's drivers can cross the Mississippi River in less than a minute on one of downtown St. Louis's five bridges, but before Samuel Wiggins started his small ferryboat company in 1817, crossing the river was a gargantuan task. When the Wiggins family moved to St. Louis in 1818, future mayor John Darby recalled that ferrying their belongings from one side to the other took three days and more than a dozen trips. With each trip the shouts of muscular ferrymen echoed over the Mississippi as they called to one another and jabbed long poles into the river bottom, inching toward St. Louis and battling the current the whole way.

From small beginnings and a single makeshift raft, the Wiggins Ferry Company would build an empire transporting people to and from St. Louis. By the 1820s, Wiggins had a fleet of ferryboats with names fit for battleships, such *Sea Serpent*, *Rhinoceros*, and *Antelope*. He had even experimented with ferries powered by horses on treadmills. In 1830 Wiggins upgraded to steam power, with the *St. Clair* and *Ibez* ferries making two regular daily river crossings. Winter river crossings in 1839 became easier thanks to the *Icelander* and its pointed, ice-smashing iron hull. Despite some setbacks—including an 1851 ferry explosion and the loss of four boats to an 1864 ice floe—the Wiggins Ferry Company kept expanding along with St. Louis.

By the early 1870s the company was averaging river crossings of 1,500 people, 10,000 bushels of coal, and 750 wagons each day. The company's stock cracked $1 million just as the Eads Bridge, St. Louis's first bridge across the Mississippi River, was rising in the middle of the river. Wiggins cut prices and managed to stay afloat for decades longer, but the ferry business was surviving on borrowed time. When the Municipal (later MacArthur) Bridge opened in 1917 as a toll-free passage, Wiggins was doomed. The last of the Wiggins ferryboats, the *Julius S. Walsh*, stopped running in 1930.

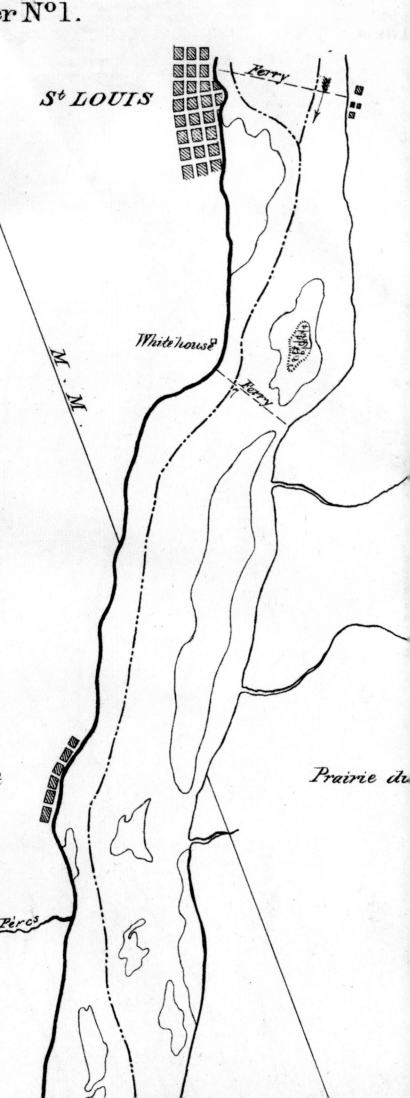

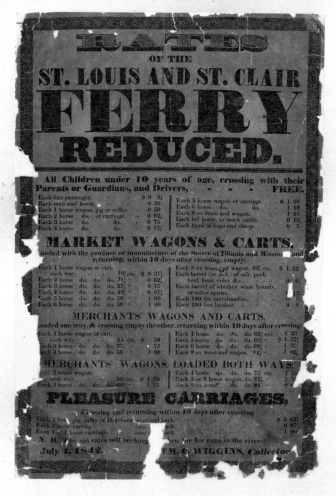

Rates of Wiggins *St. Louis* and *St. Clair* ferries, 1842 (inset). For nearly sixty years Wiggins' ferries transported people and goods across the river into St. Louis. Even after the Eads Bridge opened in 1876, for decades Wiggins remained a cheaper way to make the trip.

1822 map of the Mississippi River near St. Louis (back). From the Collections of the St. Louis Mercantile Library at the University of Missouri–St. Louis.

Painting of St. Louis by Leon Pomarede, 1832. The Wiggins ferries, like the one in this painting, had one platform on each side of the pilot-house. New passengers and cargo loaded onto one side, and outgoing passengers and cargo disembarked on the other.

Ferryboat *Alonzo Church*, ca. early 1900s. The Wiggins ferryboat *Alonzo Church* met with disaster on May 2, 1904. Its upper deck collapsed after hundreds of passengers crowded on to view a naval warship that was visiting St. Louis. More than 70 people were injured, and 1 died. After it was repaired, the boat operated through the 1910s.

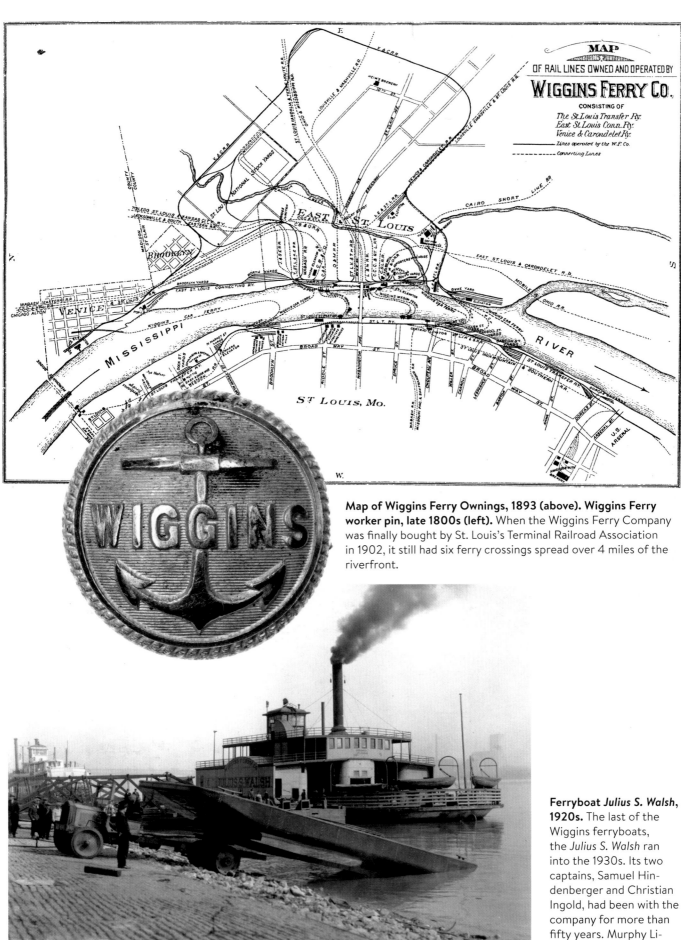

Map of Wiggins Ferry Ownings, 1893 (above). Wiggins Ferry worker pin, late 1800s (left). When the Wiggins Ferry Company was finally bought by St. Louis's Terminal Railroad Association in 1902, it still had six ferry crossings spread over 4 miles of the riverfront.

Ferryboat *Julius S. Walsh*, 1920s. The last of the Wiggins ferryboats, the *Julius S. Walsh* ran into the 1930s. Its two captains, Samuel Hindenberger and Christian Ingold, had been with the company for more than fifty years. Murphy Library Special Collections, University of Wisconsin–La Crosse.

Ferryboat *Samuel B. Wiggins*, early 1900s.
Murphy Library Special Collections,
University of Wisconsin–La Crosse.

"The ferry consisted of a small keel–boat, which was managed entirely by Frenchmen. Every portion of the body—every muscle, in fact—was brought into play; each oarsman seemed to throw his whole soul into the work. The vessel rocked so that the trace-chains at the end of the tongue often dipped into the river . . . meanwhile, the Frenchmen, with great vivacity and animation talked, cursed, and swore in French, 'prenegard,' 'sacre!'—so that the enterprise seemed a dangerous and hazardous undertaking."

—JOHN DARBY'S RECOLLECTIONS
OF CROSSING THE MISSISSIPPI TO ST. LOUIS
ON A FERRYBOAT, 1818

1817:
THE FIRST STEAMBOAT

On August 2, 1817, St. Louisans craned their necks downriver in anticipation. They gasped at the black smoke rising above the tree line long before they spotted the small boat producing it. After a six-week journey from Louisville, Kentucky, the *Zebulon M. Pike*—the first steamboat to make it upriver to St. Louis—had finally arrived. Although they might not have realized it then, they were witnessing one of the most pivotal moments their small town would ever know.

Sitting low and awkward on the Mississippi's turbulent water, the *Zebulon M. Pike* was hardly a grand vessel. Its puny boiler and single smokestack produced a top speed of about 3 miles per hour, and in the river's more turbulent spots the boatmen had to shove the *Pike* forward with long poles. But to awestruck St. Louisans in their frontier village, the *Zebulon M. Pike* was a floating miracle. Using manpower alone to move a boat upriver was exhaustingly difficult, and here was a self-propelling boat that could travel upriver almost as easily as down.

The *Zebulon M. Pike*'s arrival marked St. Louis's first small step into the Industrial Age, the era of rapid technological evolution that was transforming cities across Europe and North America. Steamboats wouldn't be a novelty for long, and St. Louis's levee would quickly fill with huge piles of freight, swarms of laborers, and commercial shipping offices and warehouses. Billowing steamboat smoke would blot out St. Louis's blue skies while the sawmills, ironworks, lumberyards, and paint factories of the boat-building industry added noise and smoke of their own. The arrival of the *Zebulon M. Pike* was the first glimpse of St. Louis's transformation from a fur-trading outpost into a factory town.

***Missouri Gazette* advertisement for the *Zebulon M. Pike*'s arrival, 1817.** This small newspaper column advertised one of the most pivotal moments in St. Louis history. Steamboats would fundamentally change St. Louis, turning the small village into one of the nation's largest cities.

man collected at Cooper's
ELEVEN MEN, perhaps as
...ant, as himself is designing.
...got them to approve of what,
...ps, not one of them under—
... It is a fact there were pre—
at that meeting, but ELEVEN

H.

War Department, June 9, 1817.
THIS IS TO GIVE NOTICE,
...AT seperate proposals will be
...ed at the office of the secretary
...e Department of War, until the
...of October next, inclusive, for the
...y of all rations that may be re
...for the use of the troops of the
...d States, from the 1st day of June,
...inclusive until the 1st day of June,
...within the states, territories and
...s, following, viz

At *Detroit*, Michilimackinac,
...bay, Fort Wayne, Chicago and
...immediate vicinities, and at any
place or places where troops are
...y be stationed, marched or re
...d, within the territory of Michi
...the vicinity of the upper Lakes
...he state of Ohio, and on or adja
...o the waters of lake Michigan

At any place or places where
...s are or may be stationed, within
...ates of Kentucky and Tennessee.

At St. Louis, Fort Harrison,
...Clarke, Fort Armstrong, Fort
...ford, Fort Osage or Fort Clark on
...issouri river; and at any other
...or places, where troops are or
...e stationed, marched or recruited
...n the state of Indiana, and the ter
...s of Illinois and Missouri.

At Fort Montgomery, Fort
...ford, Mobile, Fort St. Philips, N
...ns, Batton Rouge and Fort Clai
...; and at any other place or pla
...here troops are or may be station,
...arched or recruited within the
...ippi territory, the state of Lou
...and their vicinities, north of the
...of Mexico.

At any place or places where
...s are or may be stationed, marched
...cruited within the *District* of
...e and state of New Hampshire.

At any place or places where
...s are or may be stationed, marched
...ruited within the state of Massa
...ts.

At any place or places where
...s are or may be stationed, marched
...ruited within the states of Con
...ut and Rhode Island.

At any place or places where
...s are or may be stationed, marched
...ruited within the state of New
...north of the Highlands and with
...state of Vermont.

At any place or places where
...s are or may be stationed marched
...ruited within the state of New
...south of the Highlands. including
...Point, and within the state of
...Jersey.

At any place or places where
...s are or may be stationed, marched
...ruited within the state of Pennsyl

A: any place or places where
...s are or may be stationed, marched
...ruited within the states of Dela
...Maryland and the District of Co.

A: any place or places where
...s are or may be stationed, marched
...ruited within the states of Virgin

...uplies which may be furnished under
any of the proposed contracts, shall be
issued until the supplies which have been
or may be furnished under the contract
now in force, have been consumed.

GEORGE GRAHAM,
Acting Secretary of War.
8—Oct. 26.

PROPOSALS

For carrying Mails of the United States
on the following Post roads will be received at the General Post office, until
Saturday the 13th day of September
next, inclusive.

IN ILLINOIS AND MISSOURI.

185. From Shawanoetown by United
States Saline, Jordon's, Great Muddy
River, Little Muddy River, Coxe's, on
Beaucoup River, and Kaskaskia to St.
Genevieve once a week, 120 miles.

Leave Shawanoetown every Saturday
at 2 p m and arrive at St. Genevieve the
next Tuesday by 6 p m Leave St. Gen.
evieve every Wednesday at 6 a m and
arrive at Shawanoetown on Saturday by
10 a m.

186. From Smithland, K. by Fort
Massac and Tywappety to Cape Girardot once a week, 73 miles.

Leave Smithland every saturday at 6
a m and arrive at Cape Girardot on sun
day by 3 p m Leave Cape Girardot every thursday at 6 a m and arrive at
Smithland on friday by 6 p m.

187. From Kaskaskia by Prairie du
Rocher, St Philip, Harrisonville, Hercu-
laneum, Cahoka and St. Louis to St.
Charles once a week, 84 miles.

Leave Kaskaskia every wednesday at
6 a m arrive at Herculaneum by 5 p m
arrive at Cahoka on thursday by 2 p m
and arrive at St. Charles on friday by
10 a m Leave St Charles every sunday
at 3 p m arrive at Herculaneum on teus
day by 6 a m and arrive at Kaskaskia
on tuesday by 6 p m.

188. From St. Charles by Missouri
Crossings, St Johns, Price's, Bibbs and
Big Bonne Femme to Howard c h once
in two weeks, 173 miles.

Leave St Charles every other monday
at 6 a m and arrive at Howard c h on
saturday by 6 p m Leave Howard c h
on tuesday at 6 a m and arrive at St.
Charles on friday by 6 p m

189. From St Louis by Herculaneum,
Potosi, St Michaels, Doct. Betie's, Bal-
linger's, Currants, Laurens c h Cadrons
on Arkansaw, Daniels, on Big Rock, to
Arkansas Post office once a month, 546
miles.

Leave St Louis the first friday in each
Calender month, and arrive at Arkansas
Post Office, in 15 days, on friday by 4
p m Leave Arkansas Post Office the
next day saturday at 6 a m and arrive at
St. Louis in 15 days, on saturday by 6
p m.

190. From Cahokia by Madison c h
St Clair and Clinton Hill to Cahokia
once a week, 50 miles—25

Leave Cahokia every thursday at 3
p m and arrive at Clinton Hill on friday
by noon. Leave Clinton Hill every
friday at 1 p m and arrive at Cahokia by
6 p m.

191. From Herculaneum by Mine au
Burton to St Genevieve once a week.
80 miles.

Leave Herculaneum every tuesday at
6 a m and arrive at St Genevieve on
wednesday by 6 p m Leave St. Genevieve every thursday at 6 a m and arrive
at Herculaneum on friday by 6 p m.

192. From St. Genevieve by Big Sha.
wanoe, Little Shawanoe, Cape Girardot
and Winchester to New Madrid once a
week, 115 miles.

Leave St. Genevieve every wednesday
at 6 a m and arrive at New Madrid on

...made in the pay on account of any of
...ror in this respect.

9. The contracts are to be in operation
on the first day of January next: those
numbered 1 to 198 are to end December 31, 1819.

The residue are to end December 31,
1818

Contracts for the routes numbered 2 3
11 15 16 18 48 52 53 57 65 81 93 103 104
119 137 148 149 151 165 166 174 175 170
177 178 180 181 183 184 195 196 197 198
199 200 201 202 203 204 205 206 207 208
and 209, are to be in operation on the
sixteenth day of November next.

RETURN J. MEIGS, Jr.
Post-Master General.
GENERAL POST OFFICE,
Washington City, May 26, 1817

The Steam Boat
PIKE,

Will arrive in a day or two from
Louisville.—This vessel will ply
regularly between that place and
this, and will take in her return cargo shortly after her arrival. Persons who may have freight, or want
passage for Louisville, or any of the
Towns on the Ohio, will do well to
make early application to the master on board. On her passage from
this to Louisville, she will make a
stop at Herculaneum, where Mr.
M. Austin will act as agent, as also
at St. Genevieve and Cape Girar-
deau, at the former place Mr. Le
Meillieur, and at the latter Mr.
Steinbeck will act as agents; with
whom freight for the *Pike* may be
deposited and shipped.

Persons wanting passage in this
vessel will apply as above. She
will perform her present voyage to
and from Louisville in about four
weeks, and will always afford an
expeditious and safe passage for the
transportation of freight or passengers.

Jacob Read, Master.
St. Louis, July 25th. 1817. 60 3t

THE STEAM-BOAT
PIKE,

Will be ready to take in freight to
morrow for Louisville, or any of the
towns on the Ohio. She will sail for
Louisville, on Monday morning the 4th
August, from 10 to 12 o'clock For
freight or passage, apply to the master
on board.

JACOB READ, *Master,*
St. Louis, July 31th, 1817.

A Keel Boat,

Of about 24 tuns burden, rigged
with top and main sails, and entirely complete in all her equipment,
will be sold on good terms. En-
quire of Chas. W. Hunter, near Mr.

Sketch of the *Zebulon M. Pike*. Within fifty years of the *Zebulon M. Pike*'s arrival, St. Louis would be the nation's largest inland port, and more than 4,000 steamboats would cruise the Mississippi River at any given time. This sketch mistakenly identifies the boat's arrival as occurring in 1816.

Arrival of the *Zebulon M. Pike*, *The Pageant and Masque of St. Louis*, 1914. In 1914, St. Louis celebrated its 150th anniversary with a theatrical show called *The Pageant and Masque of St. Louis*. Held on Art Hill in Forest Park, the elaborate performance re-created important events from St. Louis's early years, including the 1817 arrival of the *Zebulon M. Pike*.

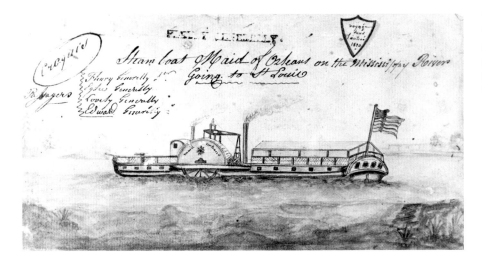

The *Maid of Orleans*, 1820. Noted as "going to St. Louis" on this image, the *Maid of Orleans* arrived just a few years after the *Zebulon M. Pike*. Murphy Library Special Collections, University of Wisconsin–La Crosse.

Packing list of the steamer *Maystown*, 1823. Steamboats carried anything that could be traded or sold. This packing list for the *Maystown* includes books, brandy, indigo, ginger, raisins, shoes, cards, bonnets, coffee, and drugs.

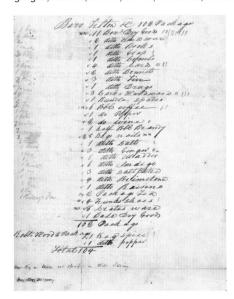

Henry Shreve. In the spring of 1819, Henry Shreve's steamboat *Washington* reached St. Louis. His boat's design—with twin smokestacks, a side paddlewheel, a flat-bottomed hull, and a second deck of passenger rooms—was the basic forerunner of the great river steamers. The city of Shreveport, Louisiana, is named for Henry Shreve. He is buried in Bellefontaine Cemetery in St. Louis.

1818:
A WORLD COLORED BY WATER

In 1818, Anna Maria von Phul stepped onto the St. Louis riverfront with sketchbooks, pencils, and watercolors tucked into her luggage. She had traveled upriver from Lexington, Kentucky, to visit her brother Henry, and though she didn't know it then, this amateur artist would spend the coming weeks creating something extremely valuable for future generations of St. Louisans. Von Phul went on to make some of the earliest known images of St. Louis and the diverse collection of people that the Mississippi River had brought here.

The multicultural, frontier world of St. Louis was a far cry from von Phul's disciplined life among Lexington's upper-class society. She wandered the muddy riverside, quickly discovering peculiar sights like Big Mound, Bloody Island, and a local cave, but her favorite subject seems to have been St. Louisans themselves. Sitting at the confluence of the Missouri and Mississippi rivers, St. Louis was a place of overlapping languages and lifestyles. Its streets were crowded with French socialites, American attorneys, nomadic boatmen, Canadian explorers, free and enslaved blacks, Appalachian hunters, and Native Americans from more than twenty tribal nations. The Mississippi River was the thread that tied their dissimilar lives together.

Anna Maria von Phul's sketches and watercolors may have been just a hobby to her, but they documented many specific details about life in early St. Louis, including clothing styles, transportation, architecture, and its many cultural influences. Von Phul died of fever in 1823, and her artwork disappeared for more than a century before relatives rediscovered it and donated pieces to the Missouri Historical Society in 1953.

A dilapidated Creole home by the riverside, 1818. Factories, warehouses, and steamboats would soon cover this river bluff on the outskirts of St. Louis, but for Anna Maria von Phul in 1818, it was still possible to be alone on the unspoiled edge of the Mississippi.

Anna Maria von Phul (1786–1823). Anna Maria von Phul had ample free time in her young socialite life, and her outlet was painting and drawing. Illustrations of Big Mound, Bloody Island, and "a cave 2 miles from St. Louis" (thought to be English Cave beneath present-day Benton Park) show that she was not afraid to venture beyond the town limits.

She returned to St. Louis to see her brother Henry in 1819 and again in 1821, possibly moving to St. Louis for good that year. Prone to fevers throughout her life, she fell ill while visiting friends in Edwardsville, Illinois, in 1823 and died at age thirty-seven. Her obituary did not mention her art.

A view of a cave 2 miles from St Louis M. T. May 1. 1818.

St. Louis scenes, 1818. Anna Maria von Phul's paintings include unique details of St. Louis life, like the town's mixture of French and American housing, pointed log fences, and watercraft of the Mississippi River.

The people of St. Louis, 1818. Anna Maria von Phul's images of St. Louisans show a spectrum of frontier humanity, ranging from Creole workers to Native Americans to laidback dandies. The young woman dressed in white and holding flowers may be von Phul's sister-in-law, Rosalie Saugrain, seated in her father Antoine's locally famous gardens.

1820s:
BLOODY ISLAND

Keeping one's name in good standing has always been serious business, but in St. Louis in the early 1800s, it could be deadly. For the city's upper-class "gentlemen," any offense to another man's honor could result in a challenge to duel—possibly to the death. The ground for settling scores was a small, tree-covered sandbar in the middle of the Mississippi River. Its name was Bloody Island.

Sitting mid-river just off the St. Louis levee, Bloody Island was assumed to be outside the control of either Missouri or Illinois. (Dueling had been outlawed in both states by 1822.) St. Louisans headed out to Bloody Island to stare down a gun barrel for insults as small as a forgotten party invitation or a sarcastic snub in the newspaper. The actual amount of damage done to one's name was of little concern: A gentleman was supposed to be willing to die to defend his honor, and Bloody Island was where he could prove it.

Better judgment usually calmed the uproar before it escalated into an actual duel, but on occasions when it didn't, it was the talk of St. Louis. Spectators crowded onto the levee, watching as the duelists boarded separate boats and rowed out to Bloody Island. As the gentlemen disappeared into the trees, the anxious crowd could only wait for the crack of gunfire.

By the 1850s dueling had long been sliding out of favor as St. Louis grew larger and its older, established families became less visible. The rise of large political parties made arguing in public more acceptable, and consensus spread that facing death—as one witness stated, "for such a phantom of glory"—was more foolish than gentlemanly. As the romance of dueling faded, a new means of defending one's honor rose in popularity: the ability to sue each other in court.

One of the views from the top of the Mound.

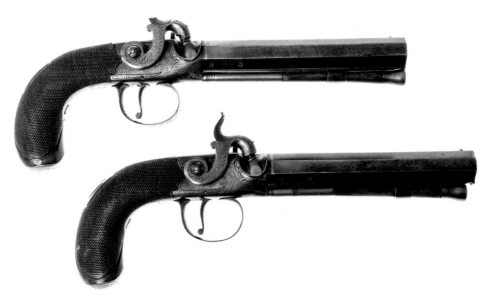

Sketch of Bloody Island, 1818. Bloody Island formed sometime in the late 1790s. Anna Maria von Phul drew this sketch of it in 1818. Just one year earlier Charles Lucas had been killed there in a duel with future Missouri senator Thomas Hart Benton.

Set of matched dueling pistols. Duels by sword were an option for the most old-fashioned St. Louis gentlemen, but Bloody Island's duels were usually fought with a set of matched pistols. Because both parties had the same accuracy, power, and reliability, the identical pistols ensured that "justice" would prevail.

Map of St. Louis, 1853. In the 1850s, Bloody Island stretched roughly from Poplar Street all the way up to St. Louis Avenue. According to this map, it even had a telegraph wire planted on its southern tip.

B. Gratz Brown.

The last Bloody Island duel. On August 26, 1856, Benjamin Gratz Brown and Thomas Reynolds dueled on Bloody Island over the issue of slavery. (Brown favored emancipation, and Reynolds opposed it.) Brown was hit in the leg, causing him to limp for the rest of his life, while Reynolds escaped unhurt. This was the last known duel in Missouri that resulted in bloodshed. The meeting later became known as the Duel of the Governors: Reynolds was elected lieutenant governor of Missouri in 1860, and Brown was elected governor of the state in 1870.

Missouri's anti-dueling statute, 1822. Missouri outlawed dueling in 1822, but in St. Louis it barely mattered. Duelists ignored these laws and were seldom prosecuted because juries were reluctant to convict a man for defending his honor. Public sentiment allowed most duelists off with either a small fine or no punishment at all.

> DUELLING.
>
> CHAP. I.
>
> 13 Dec.1822.   AN ACT more effectually to prevent Duelling.
>
> Preamble.   WHEREAS, experience has evinced that the existing remedy for the suppression of the barbarous custom of duelling is inadequate to the purpose, and the progress and consequence of the evil have become so destructive as to require an effort on the part of the general assembly to arrest a vice, the result of ignorance and barbarity, justified neither by the precepts of morality nor by the dictates of reason: for remedy whereof,
>
>   *Be it enacted by the General Assembly of the state of Missouri,* That any person who shall wilfully and maliciously, or by previous engagement, fight a duel or single combat, with any engine, instrument or weapon, the probable consequence of which might be the death of either party, and in so doing shall kill his antagonist or any other person or persons, or inflict such wound as that the person injured shall die thereof within three months thereafter, such offender, his aiders, abettors or counsellors, being thereof duly convicted, shall be guilty of murder.
>
> Persons fighting duel, and resulting in death, deemed murder.
>
>   [*Sections 2 and 3 repealed after 4th July,* 1825.]
>
> Judges to give this act in charge to grand jury   SEC. 4. *Be it further enacted,* That it shall be the duty of the judges of the circuit courts, at their stated sessions, to give in charge expressly to the grand juries all the laws in force to suppress duelling, also to charge the grand juries to present all persons concerned in carrying, sending or accepting a challenge; and if any person shall be presented in such court, the said court shall proceed to the trial of the same in the same manner as in other penal offences.
>
> Judge or justices to issue warrant agt. persons suspected.   SEC. 5. *Be it further enacted,* That it shall be the duty of the judges of the supreme court, the judges of the circuit courts, the judges of the county courts, and justices of the peace of this state, who have good cause to suspect

Bloody Island's remains, 1920s. Manmade engineering of the river caused Bloody Island to merge with the Illinois shoreline by the 1860s. By 1900 the East St. Louis rail yards and the Eads Bridge stood on its remains.

A SAMPLING OF BLOODY ISLAND GENTLEMEN

"It derives its name from the duels fought there . . . those Honorable Gentlemen whose bodies would look better with a hole through them than their characters to be exposed." –Henry Miller, 1838

FARRAR

BENTON

BARTON

BIDDLE

December 25, 1810:
JAMES GRAHAM AND BERNARD FARRAR

When Dr. Bernard Farrar delivered another man's dueling challenge to attorney James Graham, Graham laughed in his face. Farrar took the insult personally and challenged Graham himself. On Bloody Island they fired three times. Farrar was only hit once, but Graham was hit in the ribs, leg, and right hand. Being a doctor, Farrar raced to bandage the wounds he had just given Graham, but within four months Graham succumbed to his injuries.

August 12 and September 27, 1817:
THOMAS HART BENTON AND CHARLES LUCAS

After a heated exchange following a land dispute trial, attorney Thomas Hart Benton called rival attorney Charles Lucas a "puppy." Lucas, who had previously denounced Benton as a tax avoider, decided the insult was duel worthy. On a damp August morning on Bloody Island, Lucas was hit in the throat and Benton was grazed in the knee, but neither party was killed. Town gossip painted Benton as an enraged madman (after shooting Lucas in the neck, Benton stated he was "not satisfied"), and Benton called for a second duel. This time, only he left Bloody Island alive.

June 30, 1823:
JOSHUA BARTON AND WILLIAM RECTOR

Senator Joshua Barton's first duel, against Thomas Hempstead in 1820, ended without injury, but his next trip made Bloody Island worthy of its name. Barton had criticized William Rector's reappointment as a public lands surveyor, and the volleying newspaper insults escalated into a duel. At the call to fire, Barton was hit and fell dead while Rector escaped unhurt. The duel's implications—that questioning a public official could be silenced by "fear of the pistol"—caused Rector's reappointment to be withdrawn.

August 27, 1831:
THOMAS BIDDLE AND SPENCER PETTIS

In 1831, St. Louis aristocrat Thomas Biddle called Missouri congressman Spencer Pettis "a dish of skim milk." Pettis retorted that Biddle was a "poltroon" (a coward), and then the fight went beyond words. While Pettis slept, Biddle burst into his room and beat him with a rawhide whip. The duel challenge came shortly after. It was fought from the conversational distance of five paces. As the men fired at each other, Pettis ducked into a crouch (a move he worried, as he lay dying, would be considered cowardly), but the shot went through his stomach. Biddle had been hit in the hip. Both men suffered painful, bed-ridden deaths as a result of their wounds.

LUCAS

Articles regulating the terms of a personal interview between Thomas H. Benton and Charles Lucas, Esquires.

1st The parties shall meet at 6 O'clock on the morning of the 12th Ins.t at the upper end of the Island opposite to Madame Roy's.

2.o Each party shall choose and provide himself with a smooth bore pistol not exceeding eleven inches in length.

3 The pistols shall be loaded on the ground by the friends of each party in the presence of both friends and parties if the latter shall require it.

4. The friends of each party shall have the liberty of being armed with two loaded pistols on the ground if they please.

5.o The parties respectively shall be ___
friends of ___
they sha ___
about th ___

Thomas H. Benton Esquire   St Louis August 11th 1817

Sir, I am informed you applied to me on the day of the Election the epithet of "Puppy". If so I shall expect that satisfaction which is due from one gentleman to another for such an indignity.

I am &c

Charles Lucas

1821:
THE MOUNTAIN MEN OF ST. LOUIS

When Lewis and Clark's Corps of Discovery returned to St. Louis in the fall of 1806, they brought back an enticing report: Far up the Missouri River were vast lands, filled with more fur-bearing animals than anyone could dream of. By the 1820s, St. Louis had become both the starting and ending point for any "enterprising young man" trying to make a fortune in the American West.

Waves of trappers decamped from St. Louis, most contracted to a fur-trading company. The three biggest were Manuel Lisa's Missouri Fur Company (founded in 1809); William Henry Ashley's Rocky Mountain Fur Company (founded in 1821); and the American Fur Company (founded in 1808), based in St. Louis but financed by New York multimillionaire John Jacob Astor. By 1830 more than 600 St. Louis mountain men were spread across America's western wilderness.

The lifestyle was not for the faint of heart. Most mountain men lasted only a few years in the wilderness before quitting or dying. They weathered brutal conditions in a world of near-constant isolation, where falling, drowning, freezing, or starving were daily risks. Between 1815 and 1831 nearly 150 trappers were killed in confrontations with Native American groups, on whose lands they were often unwelcome guests. Back in St. Louis, one citizen gloomily noted that "there are more widows in this town than you have ever seen."

Across the early 1800s the mountain men of St. Louis accomplished more than a few gargantuan tasks. They discovered, mapped, and named dozens of rivers, passes, and mountains—overlooking the fact that Native Americans had already done the same. Many of the western pathways they blazed still exist today as trails, roads, highways, and US interstates.

View of St. Louis, George Catlin, 1832. St. Louis's frontier feeling was only amplified by the high numbers of transient fur trappers and mountain men who wandered its streets. Visiting in 1827, Philip St. George Cooke noted, "rowdyism was the order of the day—the predominating influence of the street population of Indian traders and other northwestern adventurers . . ."

Ashley's Hundred. In 1821, St. Louisans William Henry Ashley and Andrew Henry placed an advertisement in the *Missouri Gazette* seeking 100 "enterprising young men" to head west with their Rocky Mountain Fur Company. Over its twelve years of expeditions (1822–1834), the Rocky Mountain Fur Company would produce some of America's most famous mountain men.

FAMOUS ST. LOUIS MOUNTAIN MEN

James Beckwourth. Born a Virginia slave, black mountain man James Beckwourth became a Crow Indian chief, and his life story was the subject of a popular 1856 book.

Jim Bridger. Bridger was among the first white men to see Yellowstone's geysers and the Great Salt Lake. He discovered a south pass that shortened the Oregon Trail by 61 miles.

Robert Campbell. A member of Ashley's Hundred, Campbell invested heavily in St. Louis steamboats and real estate upon his return from the West. His fashionable Lucas Place home is preserved today as the Campbell House Museum.

Hugh Glass. After being attacked by a grizzly bear, Glass was left for dead by his two companions. Legend has it that Glass dragged himself more than 200 miles to Fort Kiowa for medical help.

William Sublette. Sublette took over the Rocky Mountain Fur Company from William Henry Ashley and later helped develop the Overland Trail.

Jedediah Smith. Surviving three attacks by Native Americans and being mauled by a bear, Jedediah Smith became the first American explorer to make it to California from the Southwest.

Map of the American Fur Trade, as conducted from St. Louis, 1807–1843. Library of Congress.

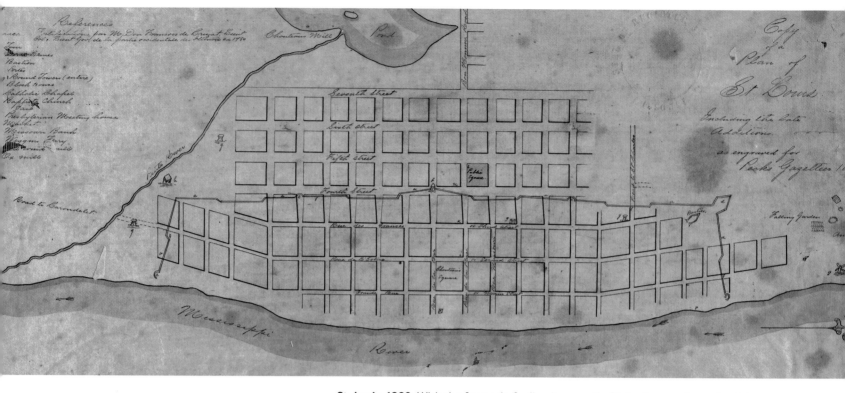

St. Louis, 1822. With the fur trade fueling its growth, St. Louis experienced a string of firsts, including its first newspaper (1808), official boundaries (1809), police force (1809), fire brigade (1810), brick house (1815), brewery (1815), academy of learning (1818), and Baptist church (1818).

Manuel Lisa (1771–1820). Born in New Orleans to Spanish parents, Manuel Lisa arrived in St. Louis in the 1790s. Lisa's Missouri Fur Company challenged established St. Louis fur traders like the Chouteau family, gaining trade monopolies with tribes along the Upper Missouri River. In 1818, Lisa built a rubble stone fur storage warehouse on the St. Louis riverfront. It would come to be known as "the Old Rock House," and over the next 150 years it would be used as a US Army provision house, sail factory, produce store, hotel, saloon, and more. In the late 1950s the Old Rock House was torn down for the Jefferson National Expansion Memorial.

Manuel Lisa's Old Rock House, ca 1940s.

ARTIFACTS OF THE FUR TRADE

Some came to St. Louis to head out into the western wilderness while others wanted to take advantage of the fur trade in different ways. Distilleries, gunsmiths, blacksmith shops, sawmills, and more opened in St. Louis to supply the needs of trappers and traders.

American Fur Company cannon, 1830s. This brass cannon was used by the American Fur Company during its expeditions up the Missouri River from St. Louis. Cannons like this one were mounted on the prow of the company boats and used to repel attacks from Native Americans or to intimidate any hostiles.

Murphy Wagons. At his St. Louis wagon manufacturing shop, Irish immigrant Joseph Murphy built large, sturdy wagons for westward travelers. Murphy wagons had several high-quality touches, like extra-large wheels and joint holes that were burned instead of drilled (to slow rot). St. Louis–made Murphy wagons were sold by the thousands and were durable enough that Murphy received a government contract to build wagons for the US Army.

Beaver felt hat, early 1800s. Fashion drove the demand for animal furs, and beaver pelts were among the most valuable. Beaver felt hats came in a variety of styles and were popular across North America and Europe. This hat was made by R. L. Barrowman, who ran hat shops in both St. Louis and Detroit.

American Fur Company peace medal, 1830s. The American Fur Company—based in St. Louis but funded by New York millionaire John Jacob Astor—handed out these "peace medals" to native tribes they wished to trade with. The medals were used to identify authority figures—in this case, Astor himself.

Hawken rifles. Many trappers set out with goods produced by St. Louis craftsmen. The rifles of St. Louis gunsmiths Jacob and Samuel Hawken became symbols of frontier life. Every gun's barrel had to be shaped, welded, finished, and polished by hand, making a genuine Hawken rifle an expensive prized possession.

1820s:
NOMADS ON THE LEVEE

On any given day in the 1820s, anonymous people could be found roaming around on the St. Louis levee, here one day and gone the next. They were the nomadic boatmen of the Mississippi River, and their home was anywhere along its 2,000-mile path. They worked as freelance freight movers, and their daily lives had little order or schedule. They came and went, shuffling between river towns, hauling cargoes of whiskey, livestock, cotton, furniture, or even enslaved people. They survived on salted meat, alcohol, and coffee, and they rarely bathed–despite living on a river. Most died young, victims of accidents, exhaustion, sickness, drink, or brawls.

These nomads were widely distrusted by St. Louisans–usually for good reason. The boatmen were known to pass off counterfeit money, pickpocket unaware citizens, and steal from unattended piles of goods on the levee. Out on the water they took great pleasure playing games of chicken with St. Louis's colossal steamboats, laughing as the panicked captains cursed them from the pilothouse. They drifted without maps or charts; most knew precisely where they were along the river based on subtle changes in the water's color.

As evening descended upon St. Louis, large groups of boatmen gathered around camp-fires on the levee. Their loud, drunken rituals terrified St. Louisans so much that a night watch of fifty men patrolled the levee just to make sure none of them wandered into town. From a distance, St. Louisans listened in on nightly bouts of "shout boasting," when each boatman took a turn launching into a violent, exaggerated yarn about his prowess, daring any skeptical challengers to fight him. By dawn they would all have their turn proclaiming themselves gods of the Mississippi River.

Flatboatmen Relaxing on Their Cargo, Alexander Anderson, ca. 1820 (above). *Barge on the Mississippi*, A. St. Audelaire, 1832 (below). Dangerous work, heavy drinking, and frequent brawling took many boatmen's lives. In 1826 traveler Timothy Flint wrote, "I do not remember to have traversed this river in any considerable trip, without having heard of some fatal disaster to a boat, or having seen a dead body of some boatman, recognized by the red flannel shirt, which they generally wear."

THE BOATS OF THE MISSISSIPPI RIVER BOATMEN

Keelboats: *Keelboat on the Mississippi River*, Thomas Easterly, 1848. Keelboats reached 50 feet long and carried up to 15 tons of cargo and crews of at least a dozen men. Upstream travel required a clockwork system of boatmen shoving against the river bottom with long wooden poles. Legendary St. Louis fur trader William Sublette "poled" his keelboat up more than 2,000 miles of the Missouri River, inching along at a rate of less than one mile per hour.

Flatboats: *The Mississippi Raft near Port Gibson*, **Nat. Kinsey, 1956.**
These were the "everyman's boat," often built out of scrap wood and wooden pins (rather than expensive iron nails), with a thick coat of tar slathered on the bottom. Flatboats' wide bodies rode high on the water, which kept them above submerged dangers but made them difficult to control. When a wreck was imminent, the helpless crew could usually only watch as the catastrophe unfolded.

Barges: *Bayou Sacre, Louisiana,* **Henry Lewis, 1848.** Barges often looked like floating towns, sometimes complete with pens of pigs, chickens, and cows. Traveler Timothy Flint recalled in 1826, "You can scarcely imagine an abstract form in which a boat can be built, that in some part of the Ohio or Mississippi you will not see, actually in motion."

1830s:
THE AMERICAN NILE

In the mid-1800s the Mississippi River was often branded as the American Nile. The analogy compared the two rivers favorably–focusing on their endless length, abundant fertility, and importance to commerce–but beneath the grand resemblances, the two rivers also shared a repugnant history. For the enslaved blacks of pre–Civil War America, the Mississippi was the successor to the Nile found in the biblical book of Exodus–a river symbolizing oppression, fear, and captivity. Slavery was the foundation of the American South's economy, and the Mississippi River was its highway. Connected by the river to both the North and the South, St. Louis saw the spectrum of the nation's race issues unfold on its riverfront.

By 1830 one in seven St. Louisans was an enslaved person, and many of them told of treatment that was just as brutal as in the Deep South. In 1836 and 1837 the back-to-back mob murders of Francis McIntosh and Elijah Lovejoy (a mulatto steamboat worker and an abolitionist newspaperman, respectively) portrayed St. Louis as a lawless, divided place. Though St. Louis saw slavery's despair, it also saw flourishing resistance. By the 1830s dozens of freedom suits–in which enslaved black persons sued their owners, claiming wrongful captivity–were being filed in St. Louis. The most famous of them, *Dred Scott v. Sandford*, became a national headline that polarized anti- and pro-slavery factions around the country.

Each event that rippled through St. Louis pointed toward the wider division surrounding slavery in the United States. The issue would ultimately lead to the American Civil War, which ripped the country in half in 1861. When full abolition of slavery was declared and the Confederacy surrendered in 1865, as many as three-quarters of a million people had been killed in battle. For St. Louisans who had spent decades watching both sides of this tension develop, the terrible war could hardly have been a surprise.

The Madison Henderson Gang, 1841. In April 1841 the Madison Henderson Gang—a group of three free blacks led by an escaped slave—was convicted of robbing a St. Louis bank and killing two clerks. Their mid-river hanging on Duncan's Island was a public spectacle that took place in front of more than 20,000 people. Residents from nearby towns like Alton were offered chartered boat trips that advertised good sight lines. The Madison Henderson Gang episode embodied a rising fear among St. Louis's white society: that the river econonmy connecting the North and the South allowed free blacks and loosely watched enslaved people to mix in dangerous ways.

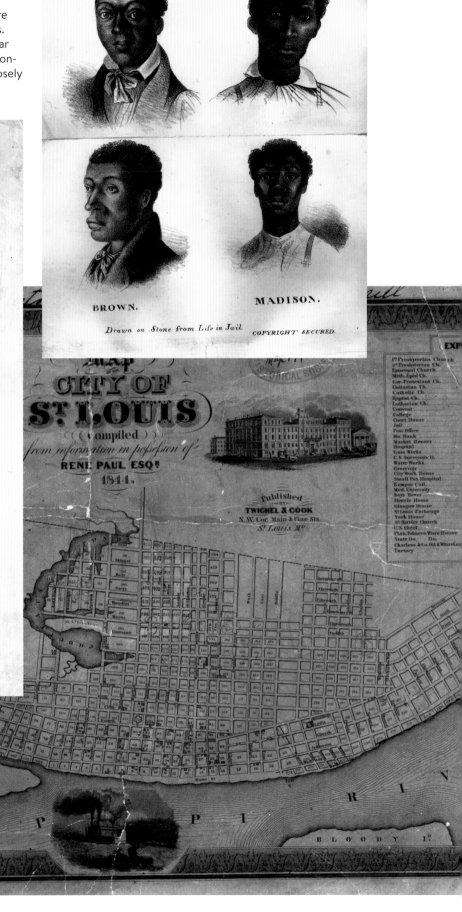

SEWARD. WARRICK.

BROWN. MADISON.

Drawn on Stone from Life in Jail. COPYRIGHT SECURED.

1841

FOR SAINT LOUIS!

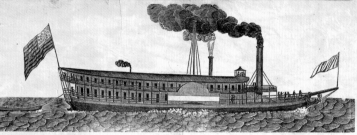

The Regular Steam Packet

EAGLE!

THE undersigned, having chartered the above Steam-boat, for the purpose of accommodating all the citizens of ALTON, and the vicinity, who may wish to see the

Four Negroes Executed,

At St. Louis, on *FRIDAY NEXT*, would inform the public that the Boat will leave this place at SEVEN o'clock, A. M., and St. Louis at about FOUR, P. M., so as to reach home the same evening.

The Boat will be repaired and fitted up for the occasion; and every attention will be paid to the comfort of Passengers.

FARE FOR THE TRIP TO ST. LOUIS & BACK
ONLY $1 50 !!!

The Negroes are to be hung on the point of *Duncan's Island*, just below St. Louis. The Boat will drop alongside, so that ALL CAN SEE WITHOUT DIFFICULTY.

For Passage, apply to

W. A. Wentworth,
P. M. Pinckard.

ALTON, JULY 7, 1841

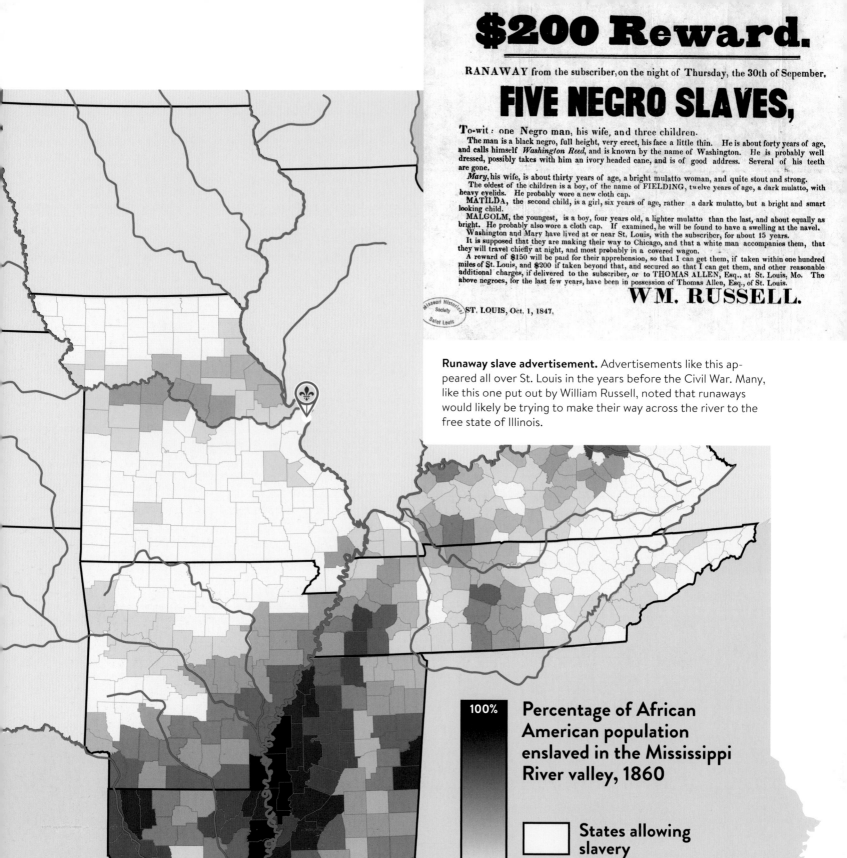

Runaway slave advertisement. Advertisements like this appeared all over St. Louis in the years before the Civil War. Many, like this one put out by William Russell, noted that runaways would likely be trying to make their way across the river to the free state of Illinois.

100%

Percentage of African American population enslaved in the Mississippi River valley, 1860

0%

States allowing slavery

Free states and territories

Slavery along the Mississippi River. While far more enslaved people were held captive in Southern states along the Mississippi River, Missouri represented some of slavery's northernmost reaches. Stretching west from St. Louis along the Missouri River was Missouri's "Little Dixie," and by 1831, one in seven people living in St. Louis was enslaved.

The Francis McIntosh tree, 1836. This map was meant to illustrate the destruction caused by the 1849 fire on the St. Louis riverfront, but far beyond the levee's torched blocks, the map tells of another terrifying burning. Although this map shows the McIntosh tree as a green, vibrant monument to the abolitionist cause, the real tree was nearly dead by the 1850s, carved up beyond recognition by the pocketknives of those who wanted a souvenir.

Burning of McIntosh at St. Louis, in April, 1836.

The murder of Francis McIntosh, 1836. On April 28, 1836, Francis McIntosh, a free mulatto steamboat worker from Pittsburgh, was arrested on the St. Louis levee after deputies claimed he interfered in the apprehension of another worker. The deputies taunted McIntosh, who panicked, pulled a knife, and stabbed both men. A surging crowd broke into the St. Louis jail, dragged McIntosh into the street, chained him to a large tree near Seventh and Chestnut streets, and set him on fire. St. Louis newspapers denounced the lynching as "savage barbarity," but a grand jury found it to be an unpunishable "act of the populace."

The murder of Elijah Lovejoy, 1837. Outspoken abolitionist Elijah Lovejoy covered the lynching of Francis McIntosh in his newspaper, the *St. Louis Observer*. Seven months later he was himself a target when a pro-slavery mob broke in and trashed his press building. Lovejoy moved his business across the river to Alton, in the free state of Illinois, but his press was smashed three more times. Lovejoy resorted to hiding his press in the warehouse of a wealthy supporter, but on the night of November 7, 1837, a mob set it ablaze. When Lovejoy fled the building, he was shot and killed.

THE PRO-SLAVERY RIOT OF NOVEMBER 7, 1837. DEATH OF REV. E. P. LOVEJOY.

List of rules from Bernard Lynch's slave pen (left)

Iron ankle fetter with key

Moneybox used by Bernard Lynch

Bernard Lynch's slave pen, 1850s. The "pen" of Bernard M. Lynch (who may be standing among this group of men) served as a marketplace for the storage, trading, and buying of human beings. Lynch's line of work won him many public enemies, although many of his accusers often also indirectly benefited from the institution of slavery. Lynch operated in St. Louis until September 1861, when he left to join the Confederacy. Little is known about the rest of his life.

FREEDOM SUITS

Between 1814 and 1861, St. Louis courts saw more than 300 freedom suits, in which enslaved persons sued their owners for their freedom. Among the most famous were those of Dred and Harriet Scott and Lucy Delaney.

Dred and Harriet Scott. Dred and Harriet Scott won their freedom in the St. Louis Circuit Court in 1846, but the decision was reversed by the Missouri Supreme Court in 1852. On March 6, 1857, the United States Supreme Court ruled against the Scotts, declaring that black slaves were not US citizens and therefore had no constitutional rights. The publicity of this infamous decision further polarized anti- and pro-slavery factions around the country.

Lucy Delaney. Lucy Delaney's mother, Polly Berry, had been born free in Illinois but was then kidnapped and sold into slavery in Missouri. Polly sued for her own freedom in 1839, and while the case was still pending, sued on behalf of Lucy in 1842. Both women were eventually judged free. Much later in life Lucy Delaney wrote and published *From the Darkness Cometh the Light*, the only known first-person account of a freedom suit.

Petition of Winny, the first freedom suit heard by the Missouri Supreme Court, 1818.

1837:
LEE'S PLAN TO TAME THE MISSISSIPPI

It's a strange twist of history that if the future general of the Confederate army hadn't taken on the unruly Mississippi River, there might not be a St. Louis today. Back in 1837, decades before the Civil War, Robert E. Lee was a young engineer, and St. Louis was facing a huge problem: The Mississippi River was shifting course and leaving the city behind. It was Lee's job to force the two back together.

By its very nature the Mississippi River doesn't like to be still, and by the mid-1830s its channel had started to wander away from St. Louis toward the Illinois shore. As the Illinois side got faster and deeper, the St. Louis side filled with sediment. St. Louis officials pleaded for the federal government's help, and Congress assigned the task to Robert E. Lee, who was anxious to get out of his paperwork-filled office job in Washington, DC.

The plans Lee developed called for two half-mile-long manmade dikes that would block the river's push toward Illinois and force its current back toward St. Louis. Once the dikes were in place the river would do the rest, and silt and debris would accumulate on the Illinois side. The idea was simple, but building the dikes was no small task. Each would require 200 60-foot-tall wooden pilings to be driven into the riverbed with thousands of tons of sand and stones filled between them.

The genius of Lee's plan was evident after just six months, when river soundings found that the St. Louis side had already deepened by 13 feet. The impressive project saved the city. Although his later military career overshadowed the engineering work of his youth, Robert E. Lee was heralded in St. Louis as a hero for decades to come. Looking out at the steamer *Robt. E. Lee* as it sat on the St. Louis levee in 1870, Mayor John Darby said, "My mind reverted back to the fact that but for him, there would have been no deep water in the place where she ran."

> ## " The dearest and dirtiest place I ever was in. . . . Our daily expenses about equal our daily pay."

—ROBERT E. LEE, WRITING FROM ST. LOUIS, 1837

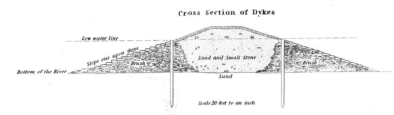

The dike between Illinois and Bloody Island (above). Lee sank two rows of 60-foot-tall wooden pilings in Bloody Island's east canal, dropping one every 5 feet across the 1,000-foot-wide opening. Workers heaped brush outside the pilings and filled the space between with stones and sand. The river would do the rest, accumulating silt and debris for years to come, until Bloody Island merged with the Illinois shore.

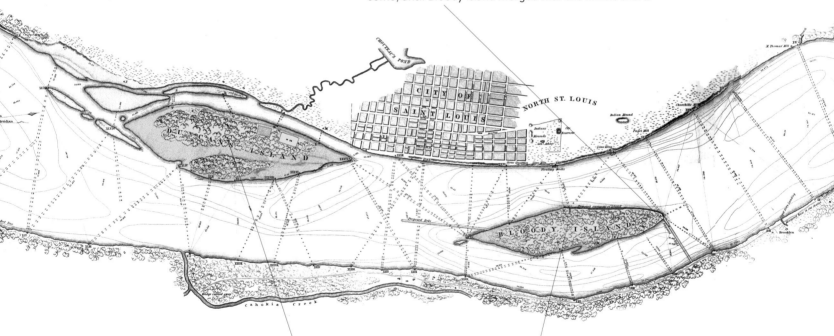

Map of the Lee Plan, 1837. The Lee Plan marked the first human attempt to control the Mississippi River at St. Louis, a fight that has not let up since.

Duncan's Island. Duncan's Island, a product of the Mississippi's shifting course, stretched 200 acres, complete with groves of cottonwood trees and rows of corn cultivated by the island's namesake Mr. Duncan. The city contracted with a man named John Goodfellow to try and haul the island away one cartful of sand at a time, but the only thing that disappeared was the $12,000 the city paid him.

Fortifying Bloody Island. Without further reinforcement, the river's immense force would have washed away Bloody Island's silty land. The western face of Bloody Island was staked with wood pilings, ending with another humanmade dike sticking far into the river, which was designed to toss the current toward St. Louis. As a result, Bloody Island later merged with the Illinois shoreline, and Duncan's Island dissolved completely.

Dike building on the Mississippi, 1940s.
The construction techniques used in
Lee's dike in the 1830s were still being
used over a century later. Image from the
Collections of the St. Louis Mercantile
Library at the University of Missouri–
St. Louis.

**Wing dike on the Mississippi, ca. late
1800s.** During low water in 2012, a dike
similar to the one built by Robert E. Lee
was exposed near the confluence of the
Missouri and Mississippi rivers. The tops
of the pilings are all that remain visible
above the accumulated sediment. Image
courtesy David Lobbig.

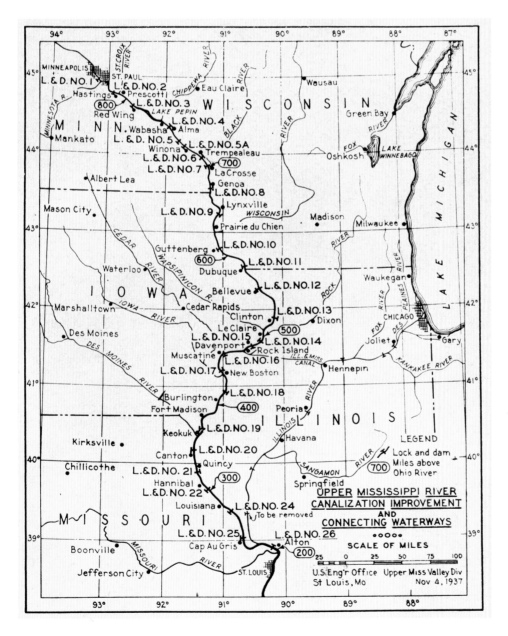

Controlling the Mississippi today.
In 1930, Congress authorized a series of locks and dams to permanently control the flow and water level of the Upper Mississippi River. The last and lowermost, Lock 27 in Granite City, Illinois, was finished in 1953. US Army Corps of Engineers.

1840:
TOURISTS AND ENTREPRENEURS

As St. Louis transitioned from a frontier town into a river metropolis, entrepreneurs and tourists boarded steamboats to see it for themselves. Some came to make a quick buck off the new opportunities in the growing city, and others came out of curiosity. Within just a few years of each other, two prominent visitors would leave St. Louis with drastically different opinions of the city. One would make beautiful pictures depicting St. Louis as a riverside paradise, and the other would despise St. Louis and just about everything in it.

In 1839, John Caspar Wild arrived in St. Louis to make money in a way no one ever had before: by drawing the city. That a professional artist assumed there would be enough prosperous residents with money to buy artwork was a testament to St. Louis's wealth. The eight city views he produced show St. Louis vibrant and alive with dramatic sunlight washing over the city's proudest buildings. In the eyes and artistic hands of John Caspar Wild, St. Louis was a utopia.

Another visitor found this "outlandish corner of the world" to be a far cry from Wild's idyllic images. While touring North America, English author Charles Dickens took a steamboat to St. Louis in 1842. Dickens was disgusted by the Mississippi River, calling it "a slimy monster hideous to behold," and he was equally unimpressed by St. Louis. Aside from enjoying his lodgings at the Planter's House Hotel, he pitied St. Louis's "crazy old tenements," "progressing" riverfront, and "vulgar people." He insisted his next visit would be only in "troubled dreams and nightmares."

Both John Caspar Wild and Charles Dickens experienced St. Louis during a time of great transition. In the early 1840s the city's population hovered around 20,000 people, but by the end of the decade that figure more than quadrupled. Had Wild or Dickens returned, neither one of them would have recognized much of the place they had described in drawing and word just a few years before.

John Caspar Wild's St. Louis, 1840.
Some of the earliest St. Louis places we recognize today, like the Old Courthouse and the Old Cathedral, had just been constructed when artist John Caspar Wild visited in 1840. These were among the first professional images ever made of St. Louis, and their creation says something important about the wealth of the growing settlement: Its inhabitants had enough money to afford pretty pictures.

John Caspar Wild's view of the levee, 1840. In contrast to Dickens's writings, John Caspar Wild's images presented St. Louis at its finest. One of his eight views shows the St. Louis levee, as if the viewer had just stepped off a steamboat. The levee's flurry of movement stretches into the distance, as barrels are rolled onto steamboats and crowds converse about shipments and prices.

AMERICAN NOTES

FOR

GENERAL CIRCULATION.

BY CHARLES DICKENS.

IN TWO VOLUMES.

VOL. II.

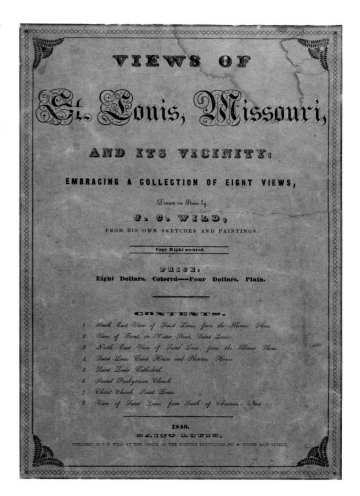

LONDON:
CHAPMAN AND HALL, 186, STRAND.

MDCCCXLII.

Charles Dickens. The Mississippi River and St. Louis were two of many disappointments Dickens experienced on his 1842 tour of North America. The Mississippi's "liquid mud" made Dickens's skin crawl, and he considered riverside cities like St. Louis to be lawless "investment bubbles" waiting to burst "to many people's ruin." He seemed particularly dismissive of St. Louis, writing, "It is not likely to ever vie, in point of elegance or beauty, with Cincinnati." Wikimedia Commons.

Boz

66 Thank Heaven I have escaped from St. Louis: during the time that I remained in that city, I was, day and night, so melting away that I expected . . . to become a tributary stream to the Mississippi. . . . I hate the Mississippi . . . I cannot help feeling a disgust at the idea of perishing in such a vile sewer, to be buried in mud, and perhaps to be rooted out again by some pig-nosed alligator."

—FREDERICK MARRYAT, *A DIARY IN AMERICA*, 1839

66 The lofty spire and dusky walls of St. Louis Cathedral on rounding a river bend, opened upon the eye, the gilded crucifix gleaming in the sunlight from its lofty summit; and then the glittering cupolas and church domes, and the fresh aspect of private residences. . . . For beauty of outline in distant view St. Louis is deservedly famed."

—EDMUND FLAGG, 1838

John Caspar Wild, *South East View of St. Louis from the Illinois Shore,* 1841

1841:
THE MISSOURI LEVIATHAN

Tales of fantastical creatures have always flourished in the Mississippi River valley, but in 1841, Albert Koch had a new one for St. Louis. He claimed to have discovered the bones of an enormous tusked beast "yet to be discovered by science," and St. Louisans would be the first to lay eyes on it. He called it the Missouri Leviathan, or the Missourium.

Fossil hunter Albert Koch was a man equal parts amateur archaeologist and vaudeville promoter who operated a hall of wonders called the St. Louis Museum on the city's riverfront. He had followed a lead to the Pomme de Terre River in central Missouri, where he actually did uncover the real bones of a prehistoric mastodon. But as Koch reassembled the skeleton–adding bones from his St. Louis Museum stockpile to fill in "missing" parts–he quickly convinced himself that he had dug up something new and extraordinary.

Despite looking like a land-dwelling mastodon or elephant, Koch claimed the Missouri Leviathan was aquatic and once lived in Missouri's river systems. He proclaimed it was covered in alligator-like armor plating and had outward pointed tusks for sweeping away downed trees in the river. The Missouri Leviathan was an instant hit in frontier St. Louis, but Koch had even bigger plans, and he took the skeleton overseas to strike it rich in London.

London's well-educated naturalists were suspicious of Koch's Missouri Leviathan and his wild claims, but their skepticism only stoked public interest. In 1843, Koch made a deal to sell the Missouri Leviathan skeleton to the British Museum for the enormous sum of $2,000, plus an additional $1,000 annually for the rest of his life. (Koch lived another twenty-two years.) He would go on to create another fanciful skeleton, this one of a sea serpent he called the Hydrarchus. The British Museum eventually reassembled the bones into an accurate mastodon skeleton, and it can still be seen today in London's Natural History Museum.

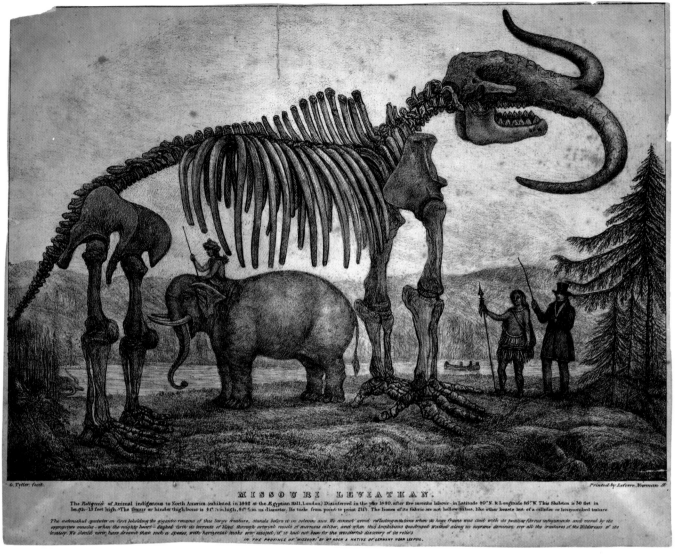

G. Tytler, fecit.

MISSOURI LEVIATHAN.

Printed by Lefevre, Newman St.

The *Reliquiæ* of Animal indigenous to North America (exhibited in 1842 at the Ægyptian Hall, London) Disinterred in the year 1840, after five months labour—in Latitude 40° N. & Longitude 95° W. This Skeleton is 30 feet in length—15 feet high.—The femur or hinder thigh bone is 4 ft. 7 in. high, 6 ft. 5½ in. in diameter. Its tusk from point to point 21 ft. The bones of its fabric are not hollow tubes, like other beasts but of a cellular or honeycombed texture.

The astonished spectator on first beholding the gigantic remains of this large creature, stands before it in solemn awe. We cannot avoid reflecting on a time when its huge frame was clad with its positive fibrous integuments and moved by its appropriate muscles—when the mighty heart—dashed forth its torrents of blood through arterial vessels of enormous calibre, and when this Amphibious Quadruped walked along its supreme dominion, over all the creatures of the Wilderness of its locality. We should never have dreamt there such a species, with horizontal tusks ever escaped, if it had not been for the wonderful discovery of its relic's.

IN THE PROVINCE OF "MISSOURI" BY Mr KOCH A NATIVE OF GERMANY NEAR LEIPSIG.

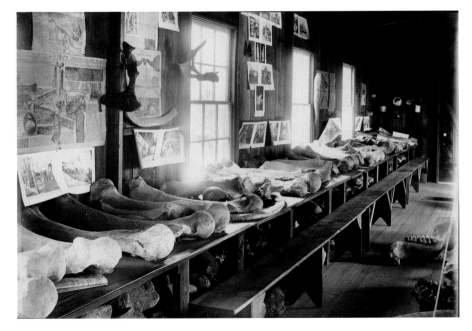

Illustration of the Missouri Leviathan. Koch believed his Missouri Leviathan behaved like a hippopotamus, holding its breath for long periods of time as it walked on the river bottom. He displayed the Missouri Leviathan in his St. Louis Museum, where other attractions like wax figures, stuffed birds, and a man who imitated animal calls were suddenly lackluster opening acts in comparison.

Mastodon bones from Kimmswick, ca. 1900. Actual Ice Age monsters that once stomped around the St. Louis region include mastodons, mammoths, and giant sloths. Around the turn of the twentieth century, many bones were excavated near Kimmswick, and in 1976 the site became a Missouri state park.

DESCRIPTION

OF THE

MISSOURIUM,

OR

MISSOURI LEVIATHAN.

SECOND EDITION, ENLARGED.

LOUISVILLE, KY.
PRENTICE AND WEISSINGER, PRINTERS.
1841.

Description of the Missouri Leviathan. While reassembling a skeleton, Koch made a shocking "discovery"—the beast's tusks were not straight like an elephant's but curved around toward the back of the head, facing away from each other. Koch settled on this "correct and indisputable" conclusion because one of the tusks was sticking out this way when he dug up the bones. University of Pittsburgh Library System.

Mastodon skeleton, London's Natural History Museum. After Albert Koch sold the Missouri Leviathan to the British Museum, Richard Owen, the museum's superintendent, reassembled it into an anatomically correct mastodon skeleton. It stands in the main hall of London's Natural History Museum, where it is seen by millions of people every year.

Skeleton of Koch's Hydrarchus. After selling his Missourium to the British Museum, Koch created another sensation with his Hydrarchus, a purported 114-foot-long sea creature. By the time this image was published in 1901, it was well known that the Hydrarchos was a fakery. A Harvard zoology professor called it a "bad piece of patchwork."

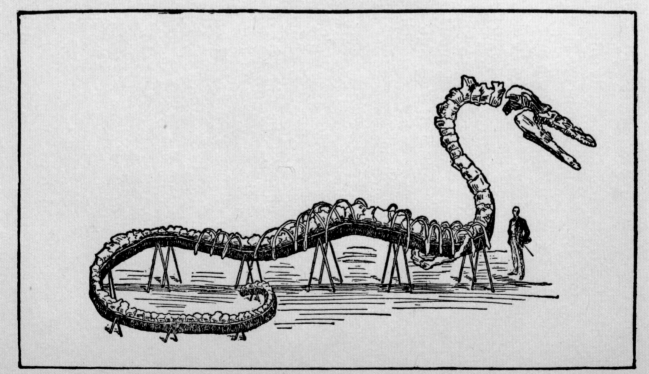

Fig. 11.—Koch's Hydrarchus, Composed of Portions of the Skeletons of Several Zeuglodons.

1842:
DIGGING UP THE RIVER'S GRAVEYARD

Today we envision Mississippi River steamboats as timeless and graceful, but most of them suffered early and violent ends. Frail wooden steamboats regularly exploded, caught fire, or were ripped open by submerged trees. When they sank, they took fortunes of valuable cargo with them. In 1842, twenty-two-year-old St. Louisan James Eads would invent a way to collect the Mississippi's buried treasure.

Eads was working as a ledger keeper on the steamboat *Knickerbocker* when the boat smashed into a sunken tree. Eads survived the accident, and once back on dry land in St. Louis, he couldn't stop thinking about the goods and wealth trapped in boats beneath the murky water. He drew up plans for a wreckage salvage boat, complete with hoisting chains, pumps to remove river sediment, and a diving bell that could scour the river bottom.

Made from a tar-coated whiskey barrel with one end removed, the diving bell was a claustrophobic's nightmare. Dangling lead weights pulled the bell to the riverbed, and with only a thin air-supply hose to keep him alive, the blind diver shuffled across the river bottom's unstable sand. The diver would feel around for pieces of steamboat wreckage, then winch them up to the surface to be examined.

Eads made more than five hundred trips to the river bottom in his diving bell; few others were willing to attempt the dangerous but rewarding work. The 1849 St. Louis fire, which sank twenty-three steamboats just off the levee, provided Eads with a grand finale of salvage work, and by 1853 he retired from river diving a wealthy man. Even though his salvaging days were over, Eads never could have guessed the other ways his life would forever be linked to the Mississippi River.

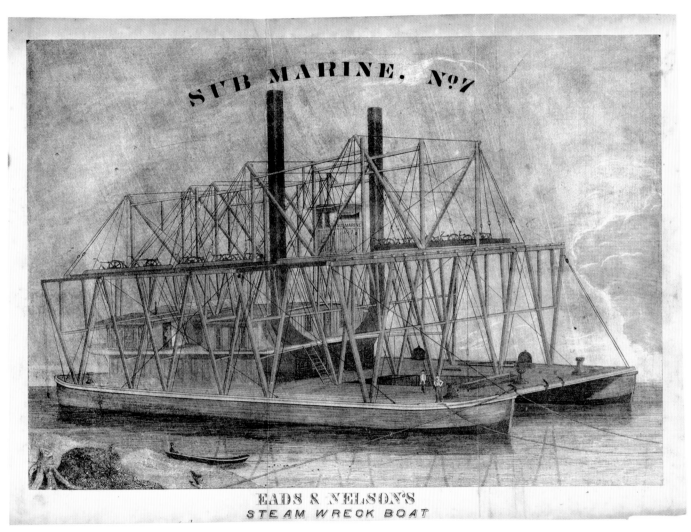

SUB MARINE. N°7

EADS & NELSON'S
STEAM WRECK BOAT

James Eads's submarine, 1858. It seemed unlikely that young Eads would be able to secure an investor for his untested and expensive invention, but to his surprise, shipbuilders Calvin Case and William Nelson were impressed enough to take the risk. James Eads's wreckage salvage boat featured twin pontoons with a winch between them to crank up recovered cargo or entire sections of downed boats.

James Eads, 1860s. From the moment he arrived in St. Louis, James Eads had known steamboat disaster. While moving to the city on the steamer *Carrolton* in 1833, his family lost everything they owned when the boat caught fire and sank.

Steamer *Calypso* sunk in ice at St. Louis, 1865. Boats were sure to be lost any time the Mississippi froze over. The *Missouri Republican* reported that an 1856 freeze saw more than 100 steamers "torn away from shore as easily as if they had been mere skiffs. . . . All their ample fastenings were as nothing."

Snags, 1899. River workers called submerged trees "snags"—a deceptively tame nickname for the danger they posed. Snags often bobbed just beneath the Mississippi's surface, threatening to rip through steamboats' fragile wooden underbellies. Invented by Henry Shreve in 1829, snag boats scoured the river, winching downed trees to the surface where they could be cut up. From the Collections of the St. Louis Mercantile Library at the University of Missouri–St. Louis.

1849:
WHEN THE RIVER BROUGHT RUIN, PART 1

Riverboats brought St. Louis endless prosperity throughout the early 1800s, but on May 17, 1849, St. Louisans learned just how quickly these same boats could take it away. Around 10:00 p.m. a small fire broke out on the steamboat *White Cloud* as it sat at the St. Louis levee's north end. The boat's mooring ropes quickly burned through, and it became a drifting fireball, spreading flames as it bumped into nearby steamboats. It wasn't long before the levee's towering piles of cargo—and then the first buildings—caught fire.

Volunteer fire companies tried desperately to contain the inferno, but St. Louis's tiny water reservoir emptied quickly. Minutes turned to hours, and winds whipped the blaze as deep into the city as Third Street. With no other options, firefighters resorted to a new tactic: blowing up entire blocks of buildings to create a firebreak. The drastic measure saved the city but had a tragic price. When a gunpowder barrel exploded prematurely, Fire Captain Thomas Targee became the first known fireman killed in the line of duty in the history of the United States.

Over the course of the night the Great St. Louis Fire reduced twenty-three steamboats and fifteen city blocks to ash and rubble, resulting in more than $6 million in total damages. The wreckage was shoved into the river, extending St. Louis's levee further outward. Many blamed the incredible damage on the narrow streets and dense wooden buildings along the St. Louis riverfront. The city passed a new building code requiring all replacement structures to be masonry construction, and St. Louis would rebuild itself with the deep red brick it is now famous for.

As St. Louis recovered from the May 1849 fire, another terror swept through the city that summer. It, too, started at the river's edge.

Aftermath of the Great Fire of May 17, 1849. The fire burned for ten hours and jumped across fifteen blocks of the riverfront. By the morning of May 18, 1849, the city had lost 23 steamboats and 430 buildings, resulting in $6 million in damages. The Old Cathedral's spire stood tall over the destruction. The block where it's located was one of few along the riverfront to emerge entirely unscathed.

THE GREAT ST. LOUIS FIRE OF MAY 17, 1849

1. FIRE BEGINS ON THE STEAMER *WHITE CLOUD*

2. FIRE SPREADS TO NEARBY STEAMER *EDWARD BATES*, WHICH BREAKS FREE AND DRIFTS DOWNSTREAM

3. DENSELY PACKED STEAMBOATS CATCH FIRE, SPREADING FLAMES TO LEVEE CARGO AND BUILDINGS

4. A SECOND SECTION OF THE CITY CATCHES FIRE

5. LOCATION WHERE FIREFIGHTER THOMAS TARGEE WAS KILLED

6. THE OLD CATHEDRAL, THE ONLY RIVERFRONT BUILDING TO SURVIVE THE FIRE STILL STANDING TODAY

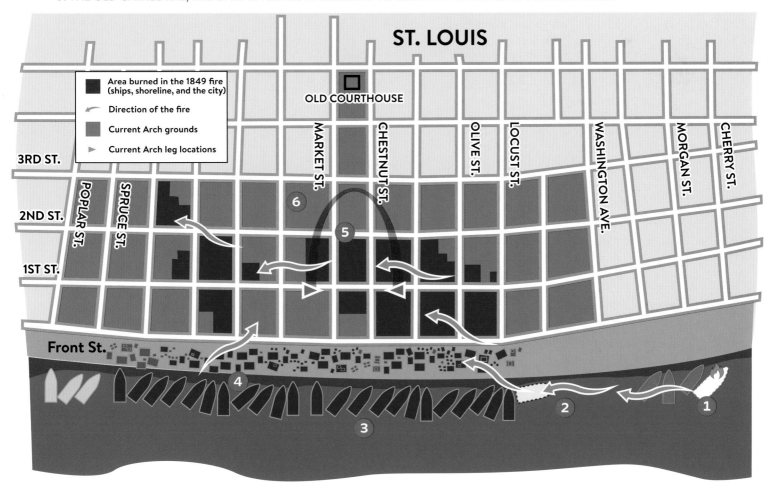

ST. LOUIS

Area burned in the 1849 fire (ships, shoreline, and the city)

Direction of the fire

Current Arch grounds

Current Arch leg locations

OLD COURTHOUSE

3RD ST.

2ND ST.

1ST ST.

POPLAR ST.

SPRUCE ST.

MARKET ST.

CHESTNUT ST.

OLIVE ST.

LOCUST ST.

WASHINGTON AVE.

MORGAN ST.

CHERRY ST.

Front St.

The Great Fire of May 17, 1849. The fire started on the riverfront's north end and worked its way south until the first buildings caught fire at the foot of Locust Street. Volunteer fire companies desperately tried to battle the blaze, but St. Louis's small water reservoir was quickly drained.

Captain Thomas Targee. Through his efforts to create firebreaks by blowing up standing structures, Thomas Targee is credited with saving much of St. Louis. Tragically, he was killed when a gunpowder barrel exploded prematurely as he placed it in Phillips Music Store at Second and Market streets. He is the first known fireman killed in the line of duty in US history.

Fire Engine Dinkey, 1852 (above). Mid-1800s water bucket (right). St. Louis Volunteer Fire Department parade uniforms and helmets, 1840–1860 (below). Before the first paid fire department was established in 1857, all firefighting in St. Louis was done by volunteer fire houses located throughout the city. During the 1849 riverfront fire, firefighters were armed with only hand reels, hose carts, and leather-lined buckets. The city's undersized reservoir quickly ran out of water, and firefighters resorted to blowing up unburned structures to create firebreaks.

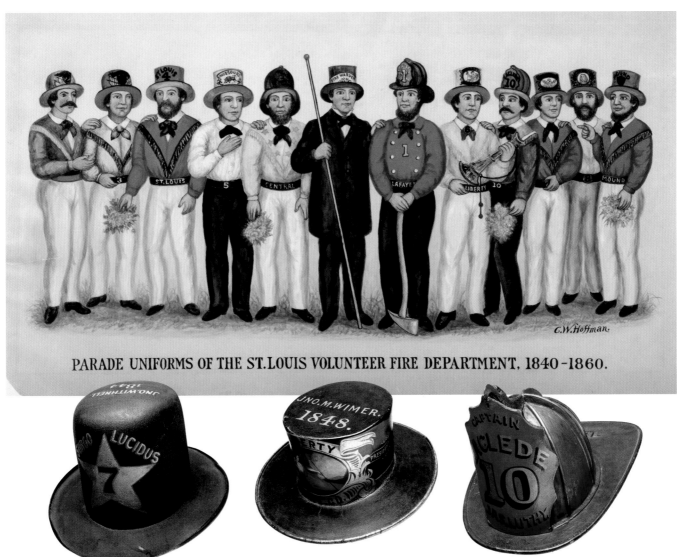

PARADE UNIFORMS OF THE ST. LOUIS VOLUNTEER FIRE DEPARTMENT, 1840-1860.

1849:
WHEN THE RIVER BROUGHT RUIN, PART 2

The fire of May 1849 torched the St. Louis riverfront just as an even deadlier problem was silently arriving via steamboat. Thousands of migrants came to St. Louis in 1849, and some carried with them a microscopic bacterium that would ravage the city. The earliest cases of cholera appeared in January 1849, and after simmering through the spring, an epidemic erupted. Within three months St. Louis physicians tallied more than 4,500 official deaths. The actual number might have reached twice that amount: Cholera over-whelmingly killed lower-class St. Louisans, whose deaths frequently went unrecorded.

Watching family members who seemed healthy at breakfast fall dead by dinner, St. Louisans had no idea what they were up against. Following popular theory, citizens in 1849 widely believed that cholera came from "miasmas," invisible, poisonous fogs floating through the city's air. Miasmas didn't actually exist, but the theory's believers blamed the plague on stagnant pools of water, dead animals, factory pollution, and even "unclean" immigrant foods like sauerkraut.

The real problem facing St. Louis wasn't poisonous fogs; it was waste removal. Cholera is transmitted through bodily fluids, and St. Louis had no sewer system in 1849, so peo-ple threw their waste out into the streets. Cholera-infected waste mixed into the city's ponds and wells, creating new victims, who would in turn create more cholera-infected water. As St. Louisans lit bonfires around the city to ward off the miasmas, they remained oblivious to the danger waiting in their drinking glasses.

In late July 1849 the number of cholera victims fell drastically, for reasons that are still uncertain. Perhaps with so many deaths and people fleeing the city, the cholera epidemic had simply run its course.

Quarantine Island, *Map of the City of St. Louis, Missouri, and Vicinity*, J. H. Fisher, 1853. Arsenal Island, which sat midriver at the foot of Arsenal Street, was renamed Quarantine Island at the epidemic's peak. All incoming steam-boats underwent cholera inspections, and those passengers showing symptoms were held on Quarantine Island until they recovered or died. In the 1860s dike construction along the St. Louis river-front shifted the river's currents and washed away Quarantine Island.

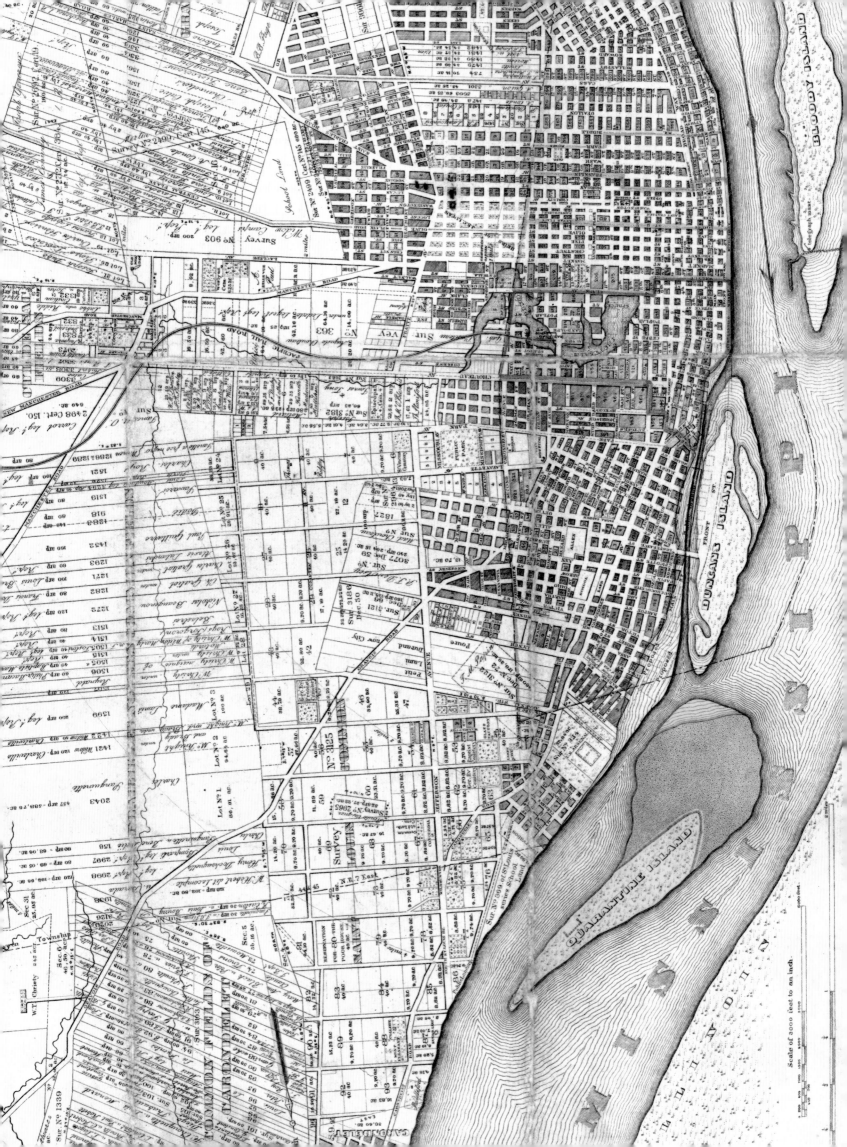

Cholera remedies, 1850. No one knew how to avoid contracting cholera in 1849. Bitters—a strong alcoholic concoction made of herbs, bark, and fruit—were promoted as a cholera preventative, and others believed that cholera could be treated by smelling horse urine, bloodletting, and all-meat diets. This cartoon of a decked-out "Cholera Preventative Woman" pokes fun at the numerous folk remedies and best guesses about how cholera was spread. Library of Congress.

Vibrio cholerae (magnified). It takes about 10 million individual *Vibrio cholerae* bacteria to infect an adult human, but a glass of water could hold twenty times that amount—without even appearing cloudy. The ingested bacteria burrow into the small intestine's mucus lining, resulting in convulsive diarrhea that quickly dehydrates the individual.

Bottle of bitters, mid-1800s.

Chouteau's Pond after its draining, 1850s. Many early St. Louisans daydreamed away their afternoons on the shores of Chouteau's Pond, a natural-sinkhole-turned-lake that stretched for ten blocks along the southwest side of the city. As St. Louis industrialized in the 1840s, the former "beautiful fairy lake" became a "natural slop-bowl." The putrid pond was one of many blamed for the 1849 cholera epidemic, and it was drained soon after.

Pierre Chouteau tombstone, Calvary Cemetery. Cholera decimated working-class St. Louis, but in the end, it knew no class boundaries. Pierre Chouteau Sr. of St. Louis's wealthy founding family died at the height of the epidemic in July 1849.

Joseph Mersman. Among the cholera epidemic's witnesses was whiskey rectifier Joseph Mersman, who arrived in St. Louis in February 1849. He recorded that chaotic summer in his journal, including the fact that both he and his business partner contracted the disease. Remarkably, they survived.

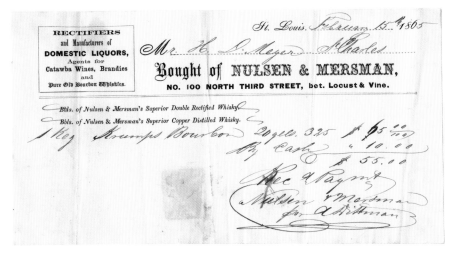

1850:
THIRTEEN BLOCKS, A WORLD APART

By 1850 many upper-class St. Louisans looked onto the city's teeming riverfront with nothing but distrust. Their scattered mansions had plenty of room to spread out along the riverside a decade earlier, but now factories, row houses, and working-class laborers all crept in on the wealthy's domestic tranquility. Fears only grew after the 1849 fire and cholera epidemic, both of which began at the river's edge. The rich were looking for an escape, and siblings James and Anne Lucas were building one far away from the levee.

Near the city's outskirts at Thirteenth Street, the siblings converted a twenty-acre tract of pastureland into Lucas Place. It was the first St. Louis residential street that had rules controlling development, and it quickly became the city's most extravagant address. The street's residents included industrialists, the founder of Washington University's School of Law, two St. Louis mayors, and the governor of Missouri. Land-use restrictions built into Lucas Place's lots guaranteed that no smoking factories, dirty tenements, or rowdy saloons could ever spring up next door. To further ensure that the crowded city would stay comfortably in the distance, Lucas Place had a block-wide park that cut it off from Locust Street farther east.

Lucas Place marked a change in the way St. Louis society interacted with the river and one another: Those with the means fled the city, while the less wealthy remained glued to the riverside. But as the city continued growing, the riverfront eventually caught up to Lucas Place. The last house went up in 1877, and by the early 1900s, Lucas Place reverted back to Locust Street. Its rich denizens had left for new private streets farther west, each more exclusive and distant from the river's edge than the last.

View of St. Louis, 1854. From Lucas Place.

① LARKIN HOUSE
② GEN. HARNEY'S HOUSE *(formerly owned by Louis R. LeBeaume)*
③ FIRST PRESBYTERIAN CHURCH
④ UNION METHODIST CHURCH
⑤ SECOND PRESBYTERIAN CHURCH

⑥ MISSOURI PARK
⑦ HIGH SCHOOL
⑧ HENRY KAYSER'S HOUSE
⑨ THOMAS GRATTY'S HOUSE

Looking toward the St. Louis riverfront from Lucas Place, 1854. Lucas Place boasted freestanding mansions, spacious yards, tree-lined sidewalks, and private security patrols, all of which were non-existent on the riverfront. A century before the 1950s—often considered the golden age of suburbia—Lucas Place's design was among the earliest examples of suburban expansion found in the United States.

John How, 1515 Lucas Place. John How had just finished three terms as the mayor of St. Louis (1853–1857) when he built this 20,000-square-foot home. James Lucas liked the home so much he moved in after How died.

Robert Campbell, 1508 Lucas Place. The first house built on Lucas Place is today the only one left standing (its address is now Locust Street). Robert Campbell, who had already made a fortune in the fur trade, bought the house in 1854. His family occupied it until the 1930s, when almost all of the other Lucas Place mansions had been torn down for warehouses and parking lots. In 1943 it was reopened as the Campbell House Museum.

Sarah Collier, 1603 Lucas Place. For a time the richest resident of Lucas Place, Sarah Collier was the widow of industrial giant George Collier, who manufactured white lead for paint. Collier's mansion was meant to replicate the Renaissance villas of Florence, Italy.

Henry Kayser, 1420 Lucas Place. St. Louis's first city engineer, Henry Kayser helped Robert E. Lee survey and improve the St. Louis levee. He also designed the city's first plumbing and sewage systems.

VIEW ON LUCAS PLACE.

ENGRAVED EXPRESSLY FOR THIS WORK FROM A PHOTOGRAPH BY BROWN.

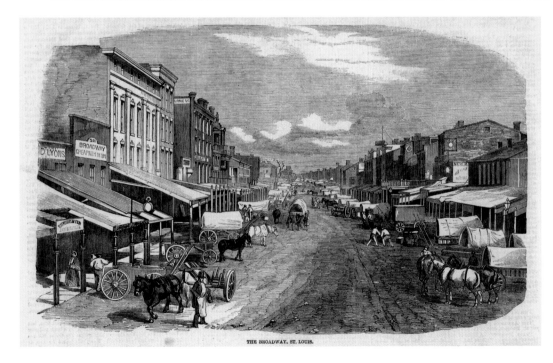

THE BROADWAY, ST. LOUIS.

Different worlds—Lucas Place and Broadway (Third Street), mid-1800s. Lucas Place spread out from Thirteenth to Sixteenth streets. To the east, the crowded city stretched all the way to the river's edge. One world was filled with velvet furniture, greenery, and chirping birds, the other with rattling machinery, smokestacks, and shouting crowds.

1850s:
LIFE ON A ST. LOUIS STEAMBOAT

Around 3,000 steamboats made regular stops at St. Louis in the mid-1850s, and taking a ride on one became a rite of passage for any self-proclaimed adventurer. These floating tourists came to see the American landscape that lay beyond the boat's decks, but life onboard also captured their attention. It was perfectly normal to find English aristocrats mingling with German socialists, temperance reformers bumping into cheerful drunks, and Minnesota farmers swapping advice with Louisiana fishermen. Riverboats' decks buzzed with life. Fiddlers provided the soundtrack, political rivals debated the day's hottest topics, and poker games devolved into rolling brawls.

Inside a steamboat's lavish cabin, whiskey-fueled passengers were known to shout across tables, spit on the floors, and attack meals like predatory animals. Steamboat carpets absorbed the brunt of this debauchery. English novelist Frances Trollope wrote in 1832, "But oh! That carpet! I will not, I may not describe its condition. . . . Let no one who wishes to receive agreeable impressions of American manners, commence their travels in a Mississippi steamboat." During an "ever-to-be remembered" trip from Louisville to St. Louis in 1843, famed naturalist John James Audubon watched in shock as a waiter apathetically sloshed the contents of used drinking cups right onto the cabin carpet.

Plenty of travelers noted how lives and worlds collided on a Mississippi steamboat's upper decks, but life on the lower decks was a world they usually overlooked. As the nightly escapades raged on inside the cabin, other poor passengers—usually Irish or African American—curled up on the lower decks, bracing themselves against the cold night air. They squatted in empty spaces around the cargo and were cursed at by the steamboat deckhands simply for being in the way. The famous luxury of Mississippi River steamers didn't apply to them. They were entitled to a trip between two stops and little else.

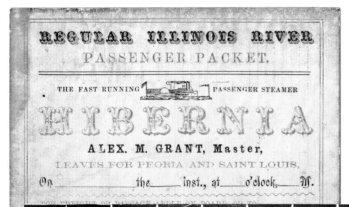

REGULAR ILLINOIS RIVER
PASSENGER PACKET.

THE FAST RUNNING PASSENGER STEAMER

HIBERNIA

ALEX. M. GRANT, Master,

LEAVES FOR PEORIA AND SAINT LOUIS.

On the inst., at o'clock, M.

ST. LOUIS AND ALTON DAILY PACKET.

FARE—ONE DOLLAR!—EITHER WAY!!

FOR FREIGHT OR PASSAGE, APPLY ON BOARD.

EAGLE.

STEAMER EAGLE:

A. REED, Master.

REGULAR SAINT LOUIS AND NEW ORLEANS PACKET!

In connection with all Roads terminating at St. Louis and with the Illinois Central R. R. from Cairo.

FOR MEMPHIS & NEW ORLEANS

The New and Elegant 1852

Passenger Steamer,

NEW ORLEANS PACKET

GLADIATOR.

GLADIATOR!

JOHN KLINEFEL. A. DOHRMAN, Clerk,

st., at o'clock, M.

AGENT.

REGULAR NAPLES PACKET

For ALTON, JERSEY LANDING, GRAFTON,
HARDIN, FLORENCE,
FARROWTON, Harris' Landing,
COLUMBIANA, GRIGGSVILLE,
MONTEZUMA, Perry and Naples.

Str. BELLE OF PIKE,

RIDER, Master.

WILL LEAVE AS ABOVE

On Mondays, Wednesdays and Fridays, at 4 P. M.

FREIGHT RECEIVED AT WHARFBOAT AT ALL TIMES.

Also in connection with Toledo, Wabash & Western Railroad, taking freight for Mount Sterling, Versailles, Jacksonville, Springfield, Decatur, Lafayette, Fort Wayne, Toledo and all stations East and West. Through receipts given to all points as above, at the Naples Pack wharfboat, foot of Spruce Street, or at Office, No. 6 S. Commercial St.

ST. LOUIS. **C. S. ROGERS.**

TENNESSEE RIVER.

REGULAR

St. Louis and Tennessee River Packet,

FOR CAIRO, PADUCAH, BIRMINGHAM,

JACKSONVILLE, CLIFTON, EASTPORT, WATERLOO,

TUSCUMBIA AND FLORENCE.

The Light Draught Passenger Steamer

DAVID WATTS,

DAVID W. CHAPMAN, Master. R. A. DARST, Clerk.
02

FOR IDAHO AND THE GOLD MINES!

For Fort Benton, Helena, Virginia and Bannock Cities, Deer Lodge, Kercheval, Mouth of Muscle Shell and all Points in the

MINING DISTRICT!

The New and Elegant Light Draught Passenger Steamer

IRON CITY!

P. BISSELL, MASTER,

J. H. OGLESBY, - - - - - Clerk,

IN CONNECTION WITH

Steamers PETER BALEN & GOLD FINCH,

WILL LEAVE AS ABOVE

ON OR ABOUT MARCH 28.

For freight or Passage, having splendid accommodations, ply on board or to

M. S. MEPHAM & BRO.

63 & 65 Locust Street, ST. LOUIS.

St. Louis steamboat advertisements, mid-1800s. Steamboat departure and arrival times were rough guesses at best. If light on freight or passengers, captains often just waited around. Traveler E. W. Gould recalled, "I have . . . known Ohio River boats [to] lie at St. Louis with steam up and all the appearances of starting in an hour—lay there five or six days. . . ."

Interior of the steamer *Great Republic*, 1870s (left). **Advertisements for the *Grand Republic*.** The central halls of steamers like the *Great Republic* were famously opulent, as were the individual passenger cabins lining them. The *Great Republic* ran the rivers from 1866 to 1871, when the boat was sold and remodeled into the *Grand Republic*. Measuring 340 feet long, the *Grand Republic* was among the largest boats on the Mississippi and, according to this flyer, even boasted an enclosed skating rink. It burned on the St. Louis riverfront in September 1877.

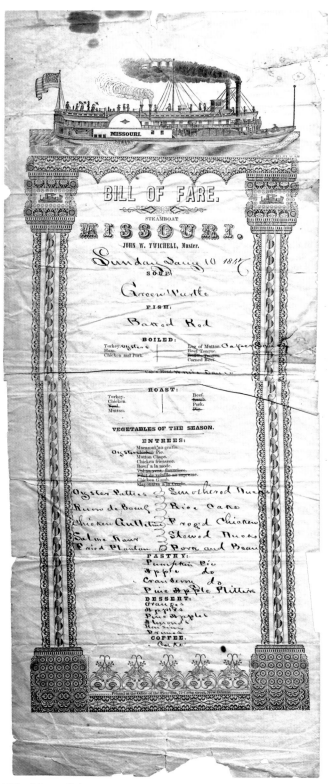

Bill of fare of the steamer *Missouri*, 1847. Steamer menus were lavish. This menu includes riverboat specialties like turtle soup, oyster pie, and boiled calf's head jelly.

Steamer *Charles P. Chouteau*, 1870s. River travelers were often astonished at how much cargo steamboats could hold. The *Charles P. Chouteau*, which ran a regular route between St. Louis and New Orleans, is seen here loaded with more than 8,000 bales of cotton.

Lower-deck passengers, 1870s. While the cabins of Mississippi River steamboats were famously opulent and rowdy, poor passengers spent their trip on the bottom deck, squeezing in among the animals and cargo.

Unloading a steamboat in East St. Louis, 1882. Steamer *Trudeau* at St. Louis, 1880s. Crew members known as "roustabouts," who were usually African American, lived on the bottom deck of the boat and loaded and unloaded cargo at every port.

"We reached St. Louis about 9 o'clock . . . I felt very dull and sluggish. . . . This is one of the effects that traveling on steamboats will have on a person used to active exercise; The table is fitted with the luxuries of life, and all things fitted up in an inviting manner; you sit down with a great variety before you; you are well paying for it and have every encouragement to eat . . . thus time is too frequently spent on board the steamers . . ."

—HENRY B. MILLER, 1838

The steamer *Mayflower*, packet boat from St. Louis, 1855

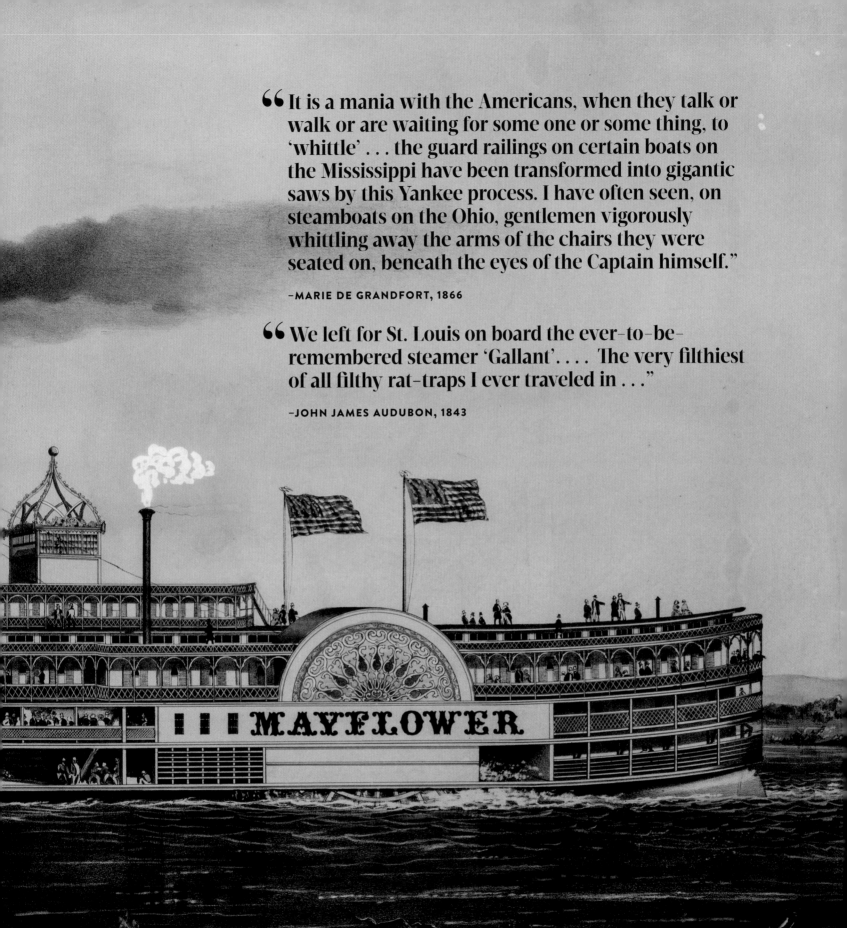

> "It is a mania with the Americans, when they talk or walk or are waiting for some one or some thing, to 'whittle' . . . the guard railings on certain boats on the Mississippi have been transformed into gigantic saws by this Yankee process. I have often seen, on steamboats on the Ohio, gentlemen vigorously whittling away the arms of the chairs they were seated on, beneath the eyes of the Captain himself."

—MARIE DE GRANDFORT, 1866

> "We left for St. Louis on board the ever-to-be-remembered steamer 'Gallant'. . . . The very filthiest of all filthy rat-traps I ever traveled in . . ."

—JOHN JAMES AUDUBON, 1843

MAYFLOWER

1852:
"DREADFUL EXPLOSION AND LOSS OF LIFE"

On the evening of Saturday, April 3, 1852, the steamer *Glencoe* puttered up to the St. Louis levee after a long journey from New Orleans. The boat's passengers crowded the upper decks, eager to catch their first glimpses of St. Louis or to once again see home. But just as the boat reached the foot of Chestnut Street, disaster struck. All three of the boat's high-pressure boilers simultaneously exploded, sending a deafening rain of shrapnel and flames ripping across the St. Louis sky.

Steamboat explosions were a horrific but regular occurrence in mid-1800s river cities. The fastest steamboats made the most money, and the boiler operators–usually untrained young men who drank often and heavily–knew plenty of tricks to push safety's limits. Boiler safety valves were tied down, firewood was coated in tar or resin, and chunks of lard were thrown in to make the fiercest burn possible. The muddy river water used to build steam created other explosive situations. Sediment-clogged boiler pipes meant uneven heating, and the frigid river water warped the boilers' scalding-hot metal skin.

We'll never know what combination of factors brought about the *Glencoe*'s fiery end in 1852. The boat's burning remains drifted out mid-river, illuminating a terrible scene on the St. Louis levee. Jagged iron and wood had sprayed in every direction, shattering windows and leaving casualties, in the words of the *Missouri Republican*, "so shockingly disfigured or torn to pieces that all recognition was out of the question."

Later that same week, steamboat tragedy again appeared in the local papers. The steamer *Saluda* had left St. Louis the day before the *Glencoe* exploded, and it met the same horrible fate on Friday, April 9, near Lexington, Missouri. At least six known steamboat explosions happened on the St. Louis riverfront: the *Liberator* (1826), the *Charilton* (1837), the *St. Charles* (1844), the *Glencoe*, the *Kate Kearney* (1854), and the *Henry Dickerson* (1865). Dozens more happened mid-river on trips to or from St. Louis.

EXPLOSION OF THE GENERAL BROWN.

EXPLOSION OF THE BEN FRANKLIN, 1836.

EXPLOSION OF THE GLENCOE.

EXPLOSION OF THE STEAMER LOUISIANA.

Illustrations of steamboat explosions, including the *Glencoe*, from *Disasters on the Western Waters*, 1856. According to the *Missouri Republican*, the *Glencoe*'s explosion shattered windows all across the levee, and the brick buildings themselves seemed to "reel under the force of the concussion." St. Louisans in distant corners of the city thought they were experiencing an earthquake. Casualties were found blown onto the upper decks of nearby steamboats, and bricks were found as far away as Third Street. The newspaper openly admitted the loss of life could not be "correctly ascertained."

The *Kate Kearney*, 1853. The year after this photo was taken, the *Kate Kearney* exploded on the St. Louis levee. The huge firewood stacks on the boat's lower level give an idea just how much fuel steamboat boilers devoured. Murphy Library Special Collections, University of Wisconsin–La Crosse.

The explosion of the *Moselle*, 1838. Captain Isaac Perrin was determined to beat his own record—making it from Cincinnati to St. Louis in two days and sixteen hours—and he stoked the *Moselle's* boilers to an incredible heat. The boat had barely left Cincinnati when all four boilers simultaneously exploded. Half of the 280 passengers were killed, including Captain Perrin, who was found blown onto the riverbank.

EXPLOSION OF THE MOSELLE.

Steamboat boiler under construction, late 1800s. High-pressure boilers could hold up to 150 pounds per inch of pressure—but only when careful attention was paid to construction. Most 1800s boilers were hastily built, resulting in weak spots and poorly sealed joint lines that were disasters waiting to happen. Murphy Library Special Collections, University of Wisconsin–La Crosse.

The explosion of the *Sultana*, 1865. The horrific pinnacle of steamboat explosions was the *Sultana*, which ran a regular route between St. Louis and New Orleans. Built to carry 376 passengers, in April 1865 the boat was loaded with nearly 2,000 former Union prisoners of war, plus another 300 in crew and passengers. The boat's strained boilers exploded just north of Memphis. With an estimated 1,800 deaths, the *Sultana* explosion was the worst maritime disaster of the nineteenth century. Library of Congress.

1852:
MISSISSIPPI RIVER PANORAMAS

The world saw the Mississippi River as a source of excitement, danger, and adventure, and by the early 1850s, panoramas were bringing the river to the world's front door. One of the most popular art forms of the mid–1800s, panoramas were paintings done on a colossal scale, often stretching across rolls of canvas hundreds of yards long. St. Louis theaters hosted traveling panoramas of Venice, ancient Jerusalem, and the Garden of Eden, but no other splendor compared to the mighty Mississippi River. At least five different Mississippi River panoramas were created, all of them by artists who had lived in St. Louis. They toured North America and Europe, captivating audiences with depictions of river cities like St. Louis that were equal parts fact and fiction.

When a Mississippi panorama visited St. Louis the thrill was incomparable–even though it purportedly showed the very same river that ran past the city's doorstep. The enormous painting–executed in overly vibrant colors so that the audience could see by dim gaslight–slowly unrolled across a stage as a narrator guided the viewer through each exciting scene. It was a 2,000-mile-long river adventure condensed into a two-hour show, and the audience never knew what might come next.

The five Mississippi River panoramas mesmerized audiences through the 1850s, but the art form would quickly fall out of popularity. The rise of photography and new types of theatre gave people other ways to see the world, and the outbreak of the Civil War destroyed the touring circuits that panorama promoters relied on. Because panoramas were as much tools designed to make money as they were works of art, the canvases were reused, cut up, sold, or simply disintegrated after years of shows. Only one of the five Mississippi panoramas survived: John J. Egan's 348-foot-long *Panorama of the Monumental Grandeur of the Mississippi Valley* now lives in the Saint Louis Art Museum collections.

CARONDELET or VIDE-POCHE.
MISSOURI.

CARONDELET oder VIDE-POCHE.
(Die leere Tasche) MISSOURI.

H.Lewis pinx.

Lith. Jnst Arnz & Cᵒ Düsseldorf

St Louis

View of Carondelet and *View of St. Louis*, **Henry Lewis, 1857.** Artists who created panoramas made long journeys to sketch the river's scenery, then transferred those sketches onto the panorama's giant canvas. St. Louis artist Henry Lewis painted the fourth major Mississippi panorama, finishing it in spring 1849. Lewis sold the tattered painting in 1857 after nearly a decade of shows, and it was never seen again. He compiled the sketches he used to create the panorama in a book called *Das Illustrirte Mississippithal* (*The Valley of the Mississippi Illustrated*), including these views of Carondelet and St. Louis.

Mr. BANVARD exhibiting and explaining his MAMMOTH PANORAMA OF THE MISSISSIPPI, before the **Queen**, **Prince Albert**, the **Royal Children**, and the **Court**, at St. George's Hall, Windsor Castle. At the Close of the Exhibition, HER MAJESTY was pleased to bestow upon Mr BANVARD a distinguished mark of her Royal Approbation.

WILL OPEN MONDAY EVENING, February 9th, 1852

AT THE

ASSEMBLY ROOMS,

GEORGE TAVERN, NORTH SHIELDS.

MR. BANVARD

Has the honor of announcing that his GIGANTIC, ORIGINAL, MOVING PANORAMA of the

MISSISSIPPI

MISSOURI AND OHIO RIVERS,

THE SAME THAT WAS EXHIBITED BY ROYAL COMMAND, BEFORE THE

QUEEN AND COURT, AT WINDSOR CASTLE,

Will be exhibited, as above

FOR FIVE DAYS ONLY.

Positively closing Friday Evening, February 13th, 1852.

Exhibition on Monday, once only; in the Evening at half-past 8 o'clock. On Tuesday and Wednesday, twice each day; at 2 and half-past 8 o'clock. And on Thursday and Friday, THREE TIMES A DAY; at 2, half-past 6 and half-past 8.

Doors Open half an hour previous.

NOTICES OF THE PRESS.

The Panorama of the great American Rivers, by BANVARD, has left this town for South Shields, where we have no doubt it will produce the same feeling of excitement and wonderful interest it did while in this town, where some thousands visited the exhibition daily.—*Newcastle Journal.*

BANVARD'S PANORAMA OF THE MISSISSIPPI.—This extraordinary and magnificent picture on the canvas of which are elaborated with consummate skill the landscapes, rivers and forests of 3,800 miles, is now being exhibited in Newcastle, and will probably soon be in Sunderland. The bold projecting bluff, the deadly swamp, the pretty village, the minor and the major towns built on hill side or plain, the little craft and the big, floating on the breast of the waters, the deer on the bank, the flying herds of hunted buffaloes scouting the plain, and the myriad varieties of plant, shrub, flower, and tree glide past as if nature herself were before the eye. Some portions really grand, and extort from the audience bursts of admiration. Such are the gulf, the glorious sunset on the Ohio, the night scenes, the forest on fire at night. The time required to witness the exhibition is enlivened at intervals by a lady playing on a piano forte.—*Sunderland News.*

BANVARD'S ORIGINAL PANORAMA.—This beautiful work of Art gives a clear representation of the great rivers of the far west, the forests and plantations which adorn their banks, and the singularly-built steamboats and other craft which are seen floating on their surface. The descriptive lecture of the painting, given by Mr. Banvard, is very interesting and humorous. The lady who presides at the piano possesses great ability, and her performances form an important feature in the entertainment. We are happy to find that up to the present period the Panorama has been very numerously attended, at which we are not surprised. The fact is, that such is the extent of the picture, and so numerous and interesting are the objects delineated, that a spectator cannot fully appreciate the exhibition after a single visit.—*Newcastle Chronicle.*

BANVARD'S PAINTING OF THE MISSISSIPPI.—This Noble Panorama, familiar either by observation or report, to all lovers of art, in this country, has been attended in Shields by increasing and admiring audiences daily, and we could confer no greater favour upon any person of taste and intelligence than induce him to pay a visit to Mr. Banvard while amongst us. Without any exaggeration or puff it is the finest scenic representation ever shown in Shields, and as an original production of a man of high genius unique.—*North and South Shields Gazette.*

The painting occupies about two hours in passing before the audience, during which time so varied and beautiful is the Scenery, it is with difficulty that the Spectators can convince themselves that they are not actually sailing along these mighty rivers. This will be the only opportunity in this town of seeing the "GREAT ORIGINAL."

Admission :—RESERVED FRONT SEATS, 2s. MIDDLE SEATS, 1s. BACK SEATS, 6d.

Children under 12 years of age and Schools half-price to the Front and Middle Seats.

John Banvard's Mississippi panorama, 1852 (above). Portrait of John Banvard, 1840s (top facing). John Banvard presented his Mississippi River panorama—which was falsely advertised as 3 miles long—to England's Queen Victoria. Banvard weaved in tales of comedy and terror as the panorama moved and a piano punctuated the journey's highs and lows. During a failing tour of the American West, Banvard ended up in the lonely frontier settlement of Watertown, South Dakota, where he died broke in 1891. Among his few possessions was the dusty, rolled-up panorama of the Mississippi. His family threw it out.

BANVARD.

John J. Egan's *Panorama of the Monumental Grandeur of the Mississippi Valley* (following page). In 1852 amateur archaeologist Wilson Dickeson commissioned John J. Egan to create a 348-foot-long panorama. It traveled around the United States, accompanied by selections from Dickeson's 40,000-piece relic collection. Egan sought to hold the audience's attention by constantly changing the weather, including thunderstorms, snow flurries, a tornado, and a spring rainbow. Now housed in the collections of the Saint Louis Art Museum, Egan's work is the only known surviving panorama of the Mississippi River. John J. Egan, *Panorama of the Monumental Grandeur of the Mississippi Valley*, ca. 1850; distemper on cotton muslin; 90 in. x 348 ft; Saint Louis Art Museum, Eliza McMillan Trust 34:1953.

MONUMENTAL GRANDEUR

OF THE

MISSISSIPPI

VALLEY!

NOW EXHIBITING FOR A SHORT TIME ONLY,

WITH SCIENTIFIC LECTURES ON

American Ærchiology.

Dr. Dickeson, late Professor in Philadelphia College of Medicine ; Member of the Academy of Natural Sciences, and Fellow of the Royal Society of Copenhagen, &c., &c., will Lecture THIS EVENING on the

ANTIQUITIES & CUSTOMS OF THE UNHISTORIED INDIAN TRIBES,

who dwelt on this Continent 3,500 years ago, and also on the leading peculiarities in the construction of those *Mounds, Tumulii, Fossas*, &c., with the Geology, Mineralogy and Botany of this beautiful country.

Dr. D. has devoted twelve years of his life in these investigations, having in that time explored the whole Valley of the Mississippi, and opened over 1,000 Indian Monuments or Mounds, and has now a collection of 40,000 *relics* of those interesting but unhistoried Native Americans.

During the entertainment, the Doctor will unroll a most magnificent *Scenic Mirror*, covering 15,000 feet of canvass, illustrating the Monumental Grandeur of the Valley, with the splendid scenes that occur upon the *Father of Rivers*

His Lecture, which accompanies each moving of the Tableaux, abounds in invaluable information, and is worth alone, double the price of admission.

THIS GORGEOUS PANORAMA,

WITH ALL THE

ABORIGINAL MONUMENTS

Of a large extent of Country, once roamed by the RED MAN, was painted by the

Eminent Artist I. J. EGAN, Esq.,

AND COVERS OVER 15,000 FEET OF CANVASS !

It has been pronounced by our Celebrated Artists to be the most

FINISHED AND MAGNIFICENT PICTURE

Ever presented to

THE AMERICAN PUBLIC.

Each View and Scene is taken from DRAWINGS MADE ON THE SPOT, by

Prof. M. W. DICKESON, M. D.,

Who spent TWELVE YEARS of his Life in opening

Indian Mounds.

SECTION I.

Marietta Ancient Fortification—A grand view of their Walls, Bastions, Ramparts, Fossa and Walls, with the relics therein found—Circleville Aboriginal Tumuli—Cado Chiefs in full costume—Youths at their War Practice—Hanging or Hieroglyphical Rock—Colossal Bust at low water mark, used as a metre by the Aborigines—Portsmouth Aboriginal Group in a Storm—Cave in the Rock, Stalagmitic Chamber and Crystal Fountan, Desecated and Mummied Bodies in their burial places—Magnificent effect of Crystalization—Terraced Mound in a snow storm, at sunset—Twelve gated Labyrinth, Missouri—Indians at their piscatory exploits.

SECTION II.

Bon Hom Island Group—Distant view of the Rocky Mountains—Encamping Grounds of Lewis and Clark—Louisiana Swale Group, with extensive Wall—Lakes and Sacrificial Monuments—Natchez Hill by Moonlight—Indian Encampment—Distant view of Louisiana—Indians preparing supper—The Tornado of 1844—Destruction of Indian Settlements—Horrid loss of Life—Louisiana Squatter pursued by Wolves—Humorous Scene—Prairie with Buffalo, Elk, and Gigantic Bust on the ledge of a Limestone Rock—Spring Creek, Texas—Fort Rosalie—Extermination of the French in 1729—Grand Battle Scene—Mode of Scalping.

SECTION III.

Chamberlain's Gigantic Mounds and Walls—Natchez above the Hill—Indians at their Games—Baluxie Shell, Mounds—Ferguson Group—The Landing of Gen. Jackson—Lake Concordia and Aboriginal Tumuli—Huge Mound and the manner of opening them—Cado Parish Monument—De Soto's Burial at White Cliffs—Mammoth Ravine—Exhuming of Fossil Bones—Temple of the Sun by sunset.

Exhibition to commence at 8 every evening, and at 3 o'clock every Wednesday and Saturday afternoon.

Admission - - - - - - - - - -	25 cents.
Children under 12 - - - - - -	12½ "

During the week a FREE ENTERTAINMENT will be given in the Afternoon, for the examination of the *Indian Museum*.

PRINTED AT THE MERCURY OFFICE—NEWARK, N. J.

1854:
THE LEVEE'S NEW FACES

Immigrants crowded the decks of arriving steamboats in the early 1850s, but some St. Louisans glared back coldly in return. Famine in Ireland (1845–1849) and political upheaval in Germany (1848) sent thousands of Irish and German immigrants flocking to St. Louis. The 1850 city census revealed the massive scale of the in-bound migration boom: St. Louis's population had experienced a five-fold increase in ten years, jumping from 15,000 to nearly 80,000 people.

As a response, an aggressive political movement called nativism began gaining ground in St. Louis and many other major cities nationwide. Nativists blamed immigrants for crime, overcrowded tenements, disease, political corruption, and the downfall of American morals. They considered themselves patriots and called their political party the Know–Nothings, for the response members were expected to give when asked about party activities. Although immigrants and nativists generally kept to their own circles, they couldn't help but cross paths on the bustling St. Louis riverfront—sometimes with violent results.

During an election on August 7, 1854, a standoff between Irishmen attempting to vote and nativists trying to scare them away erupted in violence. What started as a small scuffle descended into a riot that engulfed the levee for three days. Nativist mobs prowled the streets, clashing with groups of Irish beneath a hail of rocks and bottles. By the riot's end, 10 people were killed and more than 100 Irish businesses and boarding houses were burned. Unfortunately, St. Louis's nativist riot was just one of many in the United States, and similar outbreaks of violence followed in Cincinnati (1855), Louisville (1855), Baltimore (1856), Washington, DC (1857), New York City (1857), and New Orleans (1858).

St. Louis levee, 1852. The German and Irish immigrants who made their way to St. Louis were escaping problems in their home countries. Potato blight in Ireland killed 1 million people and caused 1 million more to leave the country. Meanwhile, a failed 1848 political revolution in Germany sent thousands of working-class and intellectual Germans fleeing to US shores.

IMMIGRANT ST. LOUIS

German and Irish immigrants moved into very different roles in St. Louis. The mostly rural Irish immigrants took industrial labor jobs and lived in close quarters, largely on St. Louis's north side. The Germans, who were often trained professionals from educated backgrounds, dominated trades like journalism and brewing, and they lived in small pockets spread throughout the city.

Schnaider's Beer Garden, 1880. Nativists railed against the "blasphemous" German habit of drinking beer on Sunday, seeing it as a breakdown of St. Louis's morality. Germans fired back, claiming beer gardens offered the perfect rest for the Sabbath and calling nativists' Sunday "the day of gloom."

St. Patrick's Day Parade, 1874. Every St. Patrick's Day the streets of north St. Louis filled with throngs of Irish celebrants. St. Patrick's School (the building at center in this image) at Seventh and Biddle streets was a cornerstone of the Irish community.

WEEKLY AMERICAN.

BY J. M. JULIAN & CO. ST. LOUIS, MISSOURI, FRIDAY MORNING, JULY 22, 1846. VOL. II.—NO. 31.

[Columns of small newspaper text, largely illegible, including sections titled "TERMS OF THE WEEKLY AMERICAN," "Inducements to Immigration," and "News from Oregon."]

SAM'S PRINCIPLES!

He is satisfied that in a few years the foreign vote will exceed that of the natives, if foreigners are allowed, as heretofore, to become voters in five years, and that a bad use may be made of the power.

He thinks the time has come to establish, upon a firm basis, the principle that *"None but Americans shall govern America!"* and that no man can be regarded as an American *unless born on the soil.*

He is willing, however, that all persons of foreign birth who have *already been declared citizens* under our laws, and *all who are now here* with intention to become citizens, *shall be regarded as Americans, and as such entitled to all the rights and privileges of American citizenship.*

He thinks that adopted citizens ought not to be elected to office until after the Naturalization Laws are repealed, for it would not look well for those who have become citizens under those laws to be instrumental in the repeal thereof. As soon as those laws are repealed, (which SAM says will happen in 1856 or 1857,) every man who is a citizen, either by birth or by law, shall have equal rights and privileges.

He will not support—*but will oppose as enemies of Republicanism*—any man or set of men, whether *Baptists, Methodists, Presbyterians, Episcopalians, Catholics,* or any other denomination, who claim for their church or association, by divine right—or any other right—*authority or control over temporal affairs, and seek to unite Church and State.*

religious belief men have, or how they carry it ... confined to religious affairs and does not teach ...

honest and well disposed refugees from foreign ... il, to our broad, fertile and happy land, *and will ... rivilege which American citizens enjoy, except ... the affairs of our Government.*

...ues; is death on all demagogues; hates office ...arty hacks; detests nullification and secession; ...—looking forward, with calm assurance, to ...nies of America shall be in the hands of those ...hrig'd, the control of those destinies.

SAM.

Nativism. The St. Louis newspaper *Weekly American* was associated with the nativist Know-Nothing Party. Under the slogan "None but Americans Shall Govern America," this 1853 nativist broadside titled "Sam's Principles!" demands that only those with "birthright" should be eligible for political positions.

198   BOARDING   198

At No. 198, Corner of Fourth Street and Franklin Avenue.

DANIEL DAVIES

Can accommodate a few gentlemen with the best the market affords, at his residence, as above.

TERMS VERY MODERATE,

☞ BUT PROMPT PAYMENT WILL BE INVARIABLY DEMANDED. ☜

Advertisement for boarders, 1845. Finding housing was difficult for immigrants in St. Louis. Many became "boarders," renting a bed in a private home.

The Mullanphy Emigrant Home. St. Louis mayor and philanthropist Bryan Mullanphy created the Mullanphy Emigrant Relief Fund in 1849 to help the poor Irish immigrants arriving at St. Louis's doorstep. The Mullanphy Emigrant Home provided empty-handed immigrants with food and shelter.

1855:
THE BIG DRAIN

Today we take it for granted that waste and rainwater disappears down sewers and ultimately joins the Mississippi River, but in the 1850s the city didn't have sewers–and that was a big problem. Rainwater often lingered on the city's unpaved streets for days or weeks, leaving stagnant, swampy pools and dunes of mud that shut down St. Louis traffic. Something had to be done, and city engineers turned to Mill Creek, a natural depression just south of central St. Louis that ran from the Mississippi River all the way to Grand Avenue. There, they built the city's first sewer. Work began on the 5-mile-long, 20-foot-wide sewer in 1855, but it would be nearly four decades and $3 million later before it was finally finished in 1889.

The Mill Creek sewer's long construction process was filled with problems. Beyond Fifteenth Street there was little natural bedrock to build on, and near the riverfront, sewer workers had to tunnel through layers of limestone. Workers spent much of their time unclogging portions of the sewer they had already finished, thanks to the St. Louis factories that dumped in huge loads of garbage, ash, and grease, with no concern for where it ended up. Multiple collapses followed violent thunderstorms, including a nearly 300-foot-long section in July 1880, and a collapse in April 1882 that flooded fifteen low-lying city blocks.

But the Mill Creek sewer's biggest catastrophe came in 1892, just three years after the city celebrated its completion. Whenever the Mississippi River rose, high water blocked the sewer's outlet and trapped volatile gas inside. On the afternoon of July 26, 1892, a tavern keeper at Fourth and Chouteau walked down to his cellar with a lit candle. The candle ignited a bomb of trapped sewer gas that was seeping through the basement floor drain, and the resulting explosion ripped a 350-foot-long canyon down Chouteau Avenue, toppled buildings, and killed four people. Miraculously, the sewer remained in service–the explosion blew all the debris outward–but repairs took another seven months.

The St. Louis sewer system, 1949. The Mill Creek sewer drains more than 6,400 acres; its basin covers downtown St. Louis to Forest Park and parts of north city and south city. In 1855 a huge proportion of St. Louis's factories, businesses, and 100,000 residents were located within this area. From the Collections of the St. Louis Mercantile Library at the University of Missouri–St. Louis.

Mill Creek and Chouteau's Pond, 1852.
For nearly a century, Mill Creek Valley had been dammed up to create Chouteau's Pond. The pond turned rancid as St. Louis industrialized, and it was permanently drained in the early 1850s. The dam is visible at Ninth and Poplar streets in this 1852 map, and the flow line of Mill Creek snakes beneath the street grid, emerging near the foot of Park Avenue.

Mill Creek sewer under construction near Tenth Street, 1868. The Mill Creek sewer had a 20-foot-wide opening and required structural walls nearly 6 feet thick. St. Louis's natural bedrock formed its base, and where there was no stable bedrock to be found, 9-inch square timbers were used.

Mill Creek pumping station, 2019. The Mill Creek sewer remains a vital part of St. Louis's sewer system. Today, waste water can be pumped out so that volatile gases do not accumulate.

1856:
THE ICE GORGE

During the very coldest winters St. Louisans waited anxiously for that special moment when the Mississippi River would disappear. The river didn't technically go anywhere—it was just hidden beneath a solid surface of ice that could measure up to 3 feet thick. St. Louisans took to the ice in droves, delighting at the peculiar sensation of walking on the water. But while the frozen Mississippi amounted to curious entertainment for some, for others it spelled disaster.

When the river froze over during the bitterly cold month of December 1855, newspapers nicknamed it the ice gorge. An expansive ice sheet fused St. Louis to the Illinois shore, and just like every other time the river froze, city officials begged St. Louisans to stay off of it. Their pleas went ignored, and thrilled St. Louisans came out by the hundreds for ice parades, mid-river bonfires, and carriage rides. They set up makeshift businesses on the new frozen real estate, including bowling alleys, skating rinks, pop-up saloons, and gambling houses. Farther from the levee, brewery workers chopped away large chunks of river ice to pack into their beer cellars.

The ice revelers disappeared as the weather warmed up, and that's when catastrophe struck. On February 27, 1856, some St. Louisans noticed that a few of the docked steamboats had been nudged up onto the levee's dry cobblestones. It was the first sign of the slow-motion disaster to come. The sheet of river ice was breaking up and moving, dragging more than 100 steamboats along with it. St. Louisans gathered on the riverfront, listening to the eerie snaps and booms as the ice's powerful force crushed one boat after another. The ice piled up into a jagged wall along the riverfront, twisted pieces of steamboats mixed throughout. As the blackened piles of slushy ice melted away, they left behind a graveyard of pulverized boilers, mangled brass chandeliers, crunched china, and splintered bedframes.

MISSOURI.—DESTRUCTION OF MISSISSIPPI STEAMBOATS BY AN ICE-JAM AT ST. LOUIS, DECEMBER 12TH.—FROM A SKETCH BY A. GORDON.

Ice Bridge Over the Mississippi at St. Louis, 1873 (above) and *Destruction of Steamers at St. Louis*, 1877 (left). Depending on your relationship to the river, the ice was either exciting or disastrous—as these two illustrations show. 1873 image from the Collections of the St. Louis Mercantile Library at the University of Missouri–St. Louis.

The 1887 freeze. The ice gorge of 1887 destroyed dozens of steamboats. Small rescue boats made rounds to the trapped steamers, picking up stranded crewmembers and taking away whatever valuables they could.

The Winter Carnival at St. Louis, Frank Leslie's Illustrated Newspaper, 1864. The Mississippi still occasionally freezes at St. Louis today, but a century's worth of river controls have made the river much narrower, deeper, and faster than it was in the late 1800s. Back then, it was apparently quite common—the ice was thick enough for St. Louisans to walk across the river in at least eight of the years between 1870 and 1885.

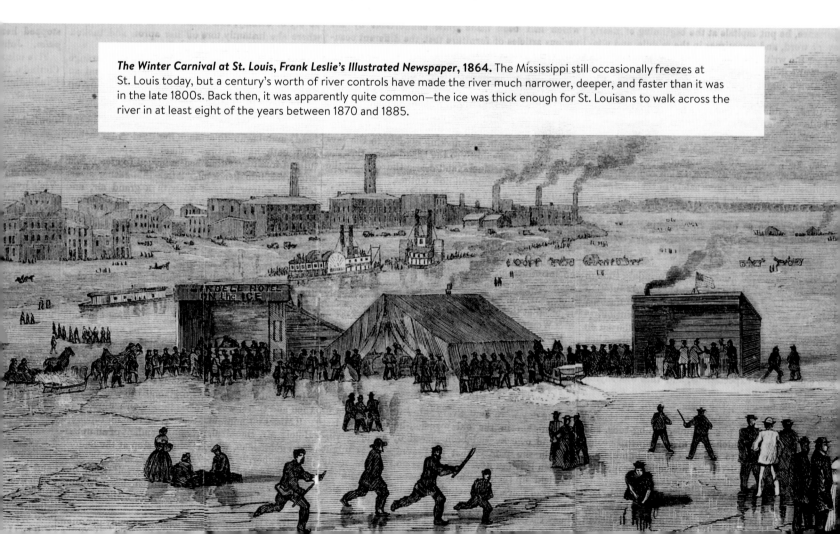

ICE GORGE ON THE MISSISSIPPI RIVER, ST. LOUIS, MO.

The frozen river, early 1900s.
St. Louisans couldn't resist feeling the frozen river beneath their feet—especially after photography became widespread and they could snap a photo of themselves doing it. The frozen Mississippi was a novelty even worthy of a postcard for those who couldn't see it for themselves.

> **"Yesterday I went in company with some Ladies and Gentlemen, and we walked over on the ice to the Illinois shore. Don't be alarmed, for the ice is 5 or 6 inches thick and they are constantly passing over with horses and loaded sleighs. Indeed while we were on the ice, a man passed us with a sleigh load of coffee in sacks at a full gallop. The river is covered with skaters cutting all sorts of capers."**
>
> –J. F. SOWELL, 1845

The Frozen Mississippi at St. Louis, 1875

"It was somewhat surprising to learn that for a rather long time in the winter, the river south of St. Louis can become closed by ice. There are, of course, years in which shipping is not stopped for a single day, but in other years the river can remain shut for as much as two and a half months."

—NICHOLAS MOHR, 1883

1859:
THE ST. LOUIS LEVEE, BORN AGAIN

When St. Louis botanist George Engelmann stood on the city's lively riverfront in the late 1850s, he couldn't believe his eyes. Less than a decade earlier the 1849 fire had left everything around him in ruins, and here was a brand-new city filled with more boats and people than ever. "St. Louis," he wrote to a Boston acquaintance, "is the center of North America, if not the world and of civilization! We burn one third of our steamboats, destroy one tenth of the wealth of our citizens in one night, kill one tenth by cholera . . . all only to show how much we can stand without succumbing."

Surveying the levee's endless storefronts, towers of merchandise, and smoke-belching steamboats, it seemed as though the fire were nothing more than a bad dream. The riverfront buildings were now taller and denser than what had been lost, and every day as many as 170 gingerbread-trimmed steamboats crammed against the levee's cobblestones. The wall of boats could stretch more than 5 miles long from end to end.

Though the levee powered St. Louis's growth, visible changes were also taking place far beyond it. St. Louis's city limits pushed all the way out to Grand Avenue in 1855, and new neighborhoods were under construction along the river's edge to the north and the south. New developments and horse-drawn omnibus lines shot out west in uneven bursts, and the riverfront's towering steamboat smokestacks were suddenly matched by new church spires, opulent theaters, and luxurious hotels. By 1859 the city's population had boomed to nearly 150,000 residents–around twenty times the population it had been two decades earlier. All of this growth had its origins in the riverfront.

St. Louis levee, 1860s. Though the riverfront had regained its place as the city's
commercial heart, it wasn't the only thing
growing in St. Louis. New public parks,
residential neighborhoods, rail lines,
schools, and industries were appearing
around St. Louis during this era. All of the
growth was fueled by the river economy.
Library of Congress.

"No city in the world offers to the gaze of the spectators such a vast assemblage of steamboats . . . these steamers are but frail affairs; and just one hour of an Atlantic storm would be sufficient to make wrecks of all that ever plied or ever will ply upon the drumly bosom of the 'Father of the Waters.'"

—CHARLES MACKAY, 1859

"... you have no idea at the East what the Mississippi is to the West; It is the ocean, the great highway of commerce ..."

—ST. LOUIS CIVIL WAR NURSE EMILY ELIZABETH PARSONS, 1863

Birds-eye view of St. Louis, 1859

1861:
OVER THERE

Every city built on a riverbank looks across the water onto something else. St. Louis's "over there" was a place vital to the city's success, but it was also a place that was used, abused, and misunderstood. There had been settlement on the Illinois bank of the river since as early as the 1790s, when James Piggott opened a ferry service (which later became Wiggins Ferry) and a few small houses popped up nearby. The settlement was formally named Illinoistown in 1817, but in April 1861, a new name appeared on the map: East St. Louis. The name change emphasized a growing reality–that this side of the river was intricately tied to St. Louis.

East St. Louis was St. Louis's industrial back yard: a city-sized workshop of smokestacks, train yards, and factories that, thanks to the river, was sure to remain conveniently distant from St. Louisans' daily lives. The cheaper land on the Illinois side could be bought in huge, unregulated parcels perfect for massive industries like the St. Louis National Stockyard Company, which processed more than 50,000 animals a week at its 160-acre site on East St. Louis's northern edge. East St. Louis became the machine that powered St. Louis's life, producing more than 5 million annual tons of soft coal that was consumed as fuel for St. Louis's homes, businesses, and factories.

East St. Louis's massive success as an industrial center is also where the story of its modern crisis begins. Though it had for years enjoyed many opportunities for employment, by the 1950s its jobs were quickly drying up as deindustrialization took hold in older cities across America. The city's coming decades descended into a free-fall of factory closings, abandonment, and population decline. The city's 2018 population estimate sat below 27,000–a staggering drop of more than 65 percent from its high of 82,000 in 1950.

Countless St. Louisans have grown up with a fear of ending up on "that side of the river," their worries driven by hearsay and labels like "the most dangerous place in America" or "the nation's most distressed small city." Such terms undermine East St. Louis's rich history and the inventors, politicians, musicians, and athletes who have emerged from its streets. East St. Louis's past–as well as its future–is far more complex and interesting than any simple label allows.

St. Louis and East St. Louis, 1870. By 1865, Bloody Island had so fully merged with the Illinois shoreline that East St. Louisans were platting houses on it. That year, the first ever census of Bloody Island revealed 800 people lived there.

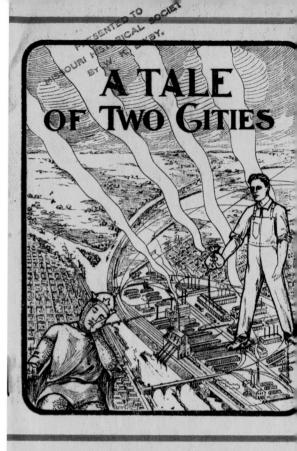

Flooding in East St. Louis, 1903 (above and below). East St. Louis's low-lying riverfront was occupied by vast train yards that were prone to flooding whenever the river rose. In early June 1903 water toppled the city's makeshift levee, causing millions of dollars in damages and displacing thousands of people.

A Tale of Two Cities, **1910s.** This pamphlet produced by the East St. Louis Association of Commerce depicts the city as an industrious, prosperous revenue source trying to gain the attention of the sleeping royalty of St. Louis.

East St. Louis, 1920. By the early 1900s, East St. Louis was one of the largest industrial centers in the United States, with a web of train tracks from all over the eastern United States converging on its riverbank.

1861:
MARK TWAIN IN ST. LOUIS

Though he's inseparably linked to the Hannibal, Missouri, of his youth, Samuel Clemens may not have become Mark Twain without a chance encounter with a St. Louis steamboat pilot. Living on a Mississippi riverboat was Samuel Clemens's "one permanent ambition" as a young boy in the 1840s, but as he entered his teenage years he instead found himself working as a disenchanted printer's apprentice. Fed up, he boarded the steamboat *Paul Jones* in 1857, planning to find adventure in South America. But once aboard the steamboat, dreams of his childhood came rushing back.

Clemens struck up a conversation with the boat's pilot, Horace Bixby, and convinced Bixby to take him on as a cub apprentice and teach him the art of steamboat piloting. For the next five years St. Louis would be his home base, where he soaked up the Mississippi's floating and transient human world. River life left him feeling "acquainted with all the different types of human nature that are to be found in fiction, biography, or history."

Clemens had his dream job, but when the 1861 outbreak of the Civil War shut down river traffic, he was forced to walk away from it. After he left St. Louis that year, he would never see the city as Samuel Clemens again. Through the late 1800s the prolific writings of Mark Twain—a pen name derived from the call of a Mississippi boatman—would become the defining voice of the Mississippi River's age of empire. Twain later recalled that any "well-drawn character" of his fiction was a second meeting, having first "met [the character] on the river."

Locations both known and unknown contributed to Mark Twain's unique literary inventions, but few places had the impact that St. Louis did. Writing to his mother and sister from San Francisco in 1866, Twain says of an unnamed book's remaining pages, "The last hundred will have to be written in St. Louis, because the materials for them can only be got there."

Samuel Clemens's steamboat pilot's license, 1859. After two apprenticeships under pilot Horace Bixby, Samuel Clemens's boyhood dream came true when he received his pilot's license in April 1859. Clemens loved working as a steamboat pilot, but he never made it past a second-class pilot's license before the Civil War shut down river traffic. From the Collections of the St. Louis Mercantile Library at the University of Missouri–St. Louis.

Samuel Clemens, age fifteen. As a young printer's apprentice, Clemens already showed the personality that would later define his writing. His makeshift belt buckle, made of printing-press type, displays his name. Wikimedia Commons.

Mark Twain in St. Louis, 1902. In the early 1900s, St. Louis named its harbor boat after Twain. Twain returned to St. Louis periodically throughout his life, including an 1883 trip where he wrote of how the city barely resembled the place he recalled from his youth. He is seen here with St. Louis mayor David R. Francis, dedicating a plaque on the boyhood home of children's author Eugene Field.

1860s:
IRONCLADS AND FLOATING HOSPITALS

When the Civil War split the nation in two in the spring of 1861, the Mississippi River was no longer just a waterway; it was a crucial military asset. Sitting on the river just beyond the Southern-controlled Lower Mississippi, St. Louis quickly became one of the Union's most important strategy centers.

With their so-called Anaconda Plan, the Union navy planned to encircle the South by water, strangling the Confederacy by cutting off shipping ports along the Atlantic seaboard, the Gulf of Mexico, and the Mississippi River. Oceangoing ships could handle the coastal takeover, but there was no "river navy" at the ready to take the Mississippi's entrenched Confederate cities. The Union turned to St. Louis inventor James Eads, who built a fleet of ironclad gunboats at his shipyards just south of St. Louis in Carondelet and at Mound City, Illinois. These seven ironclads formed the heart of the Mississippi River Squadron and would see nearly a dozen battles on the Lower Mississippi and its tributaries.

St. Louis's river position made it a supplier of boats and other weaponry that pushed the war forward, but it also became the fallback city for the war's horrifying human toll. The Civil War's brutal battles resulted in thousands of wounded, and as smaller hospitals downriver quickly filled, many patients were sent upriver to St. Louis on board hospital steamers. By 1864 the city had cared for more than 60,000 people, housed among at least a dozen makeshift hospitals.

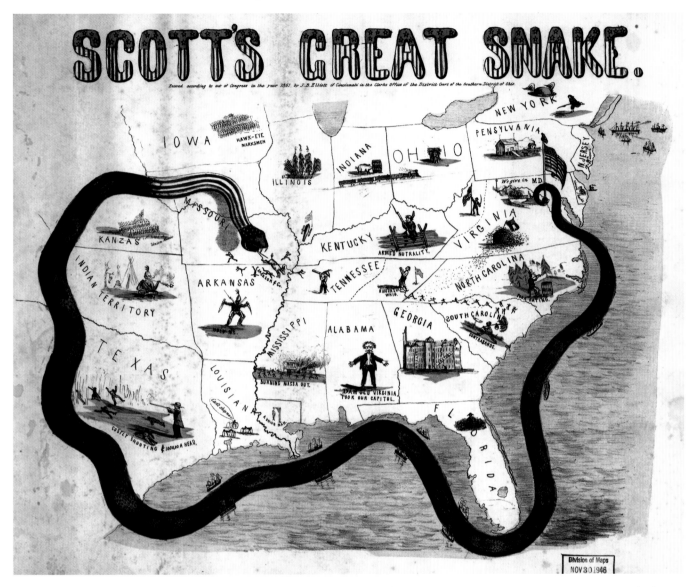

The Anaconda Plan, 1861. US Army Commander Winfield Scott suggested that the Union use its naval superiority to strangle the South economically, blocking its seaports and Mississippi River ports. With no way to import or export goods, the Anaconda Plan would squeeze life from the rebellion. Library of Congress.

UNITED STATES MISSISSIPPI GUN-BOATS BEING BUILT AT CARONDELET, NEAR ST. LOUIS, MISSOURI.
[Sketched by Alexander Simplot.]

Ironclads under construction at Carondelet, 1860s. Connected to the South by the Mississippi River, St. Louis would become one of the most important northern strategy centers of the Civil War's western front.

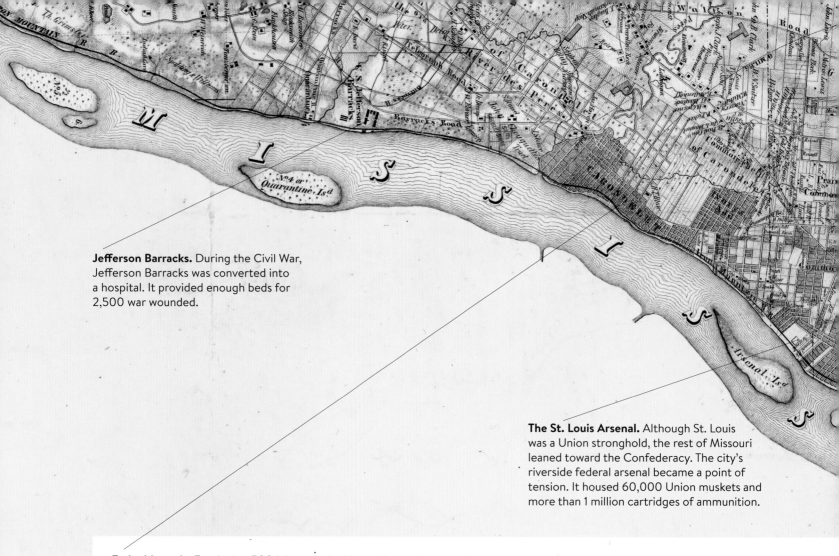

Jefferson Barracks. During the Civil War, Jefferson Barracks was converted into a hospital. It provided enough beds for 2,500 war wounded.

The St. Louis Arsenal. Although St. Louis was a Union stronghold, the rest of Missouri leaned toward the Confederacy. The city's riverside federal arsenal became a point of tension. It housed 60,000 Union muskets and more than 1 million cartridges of ammunition.

Eads shipyards. Employing 500 laborers, the Union Marine Works in Carondelet ran twenty-four hours a day. James Eads built four of the initial seven Union ironclad gunboats there (the *Carondelet*, the *St. Louis*, the *Louisville*, and the *Pittsburgh*), and the other three (the *Cincinnati*, the *Mound City*, and the *Cairo*) were produced 100 miles downstream at Mound City, Illinois.

James Eads's patent model for improved turrets for war vessels, 1862. Eads patented numerous inventions related to his government contract for ironclad gunboats.

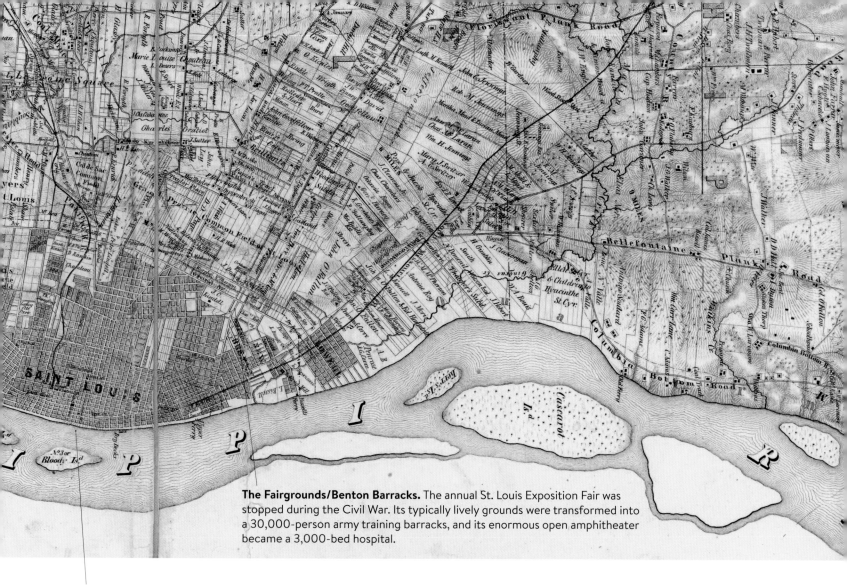

The Fairgrounds/Benton Barracks. The annual St. Louis Exposition Fair was stopped during the Civil War. Its typically lively grounds were transformed into a 30,000-person army training barracks, and its enormous open amphitheater became a 3,000-bed hospital.

Floating hospital *Red Rover*, 1864. With nearly all commercial river traffic halted, hospital steamers were among the only boats on the Mississippi River during the Civil War. On arrival in St. Louis, stretcher carriers hauled bloodied, bandaged men up the levee to the city's makeshift hospitals.

U.S. Hospital Ship Red Rover Act. Vol Lieut Wᵐ R Wells. 1864.

The Interior of a Sanitary Steamer.

TIMELINE OF THE MISSISSIPPI RIVER SQUADRON

1, 2. Building the gunboats. Naval Commander John Rodgers visited with James Eads in May 1861, presenting plans drawn up by engineer Samuel Pook for a squadron of ironclad river gunboats. Eads took the job, building four boats at Carondelet and the other three near Cairo, Illinois. From February 1862 to the spring of 1864, the Mississippi River Squadron battled its way down the Mississippi River valley.

USS *Cairo* (right). Each gunboat was 175 feet long and had a 35 degree slope both above and below the waterline to minimize the damage done by enemy fire. Each ship was wrapped in 2.5-inch-thick iron plating and weighed more than 600 tons. The iron plating was so effective in thwarting attacks that during tests conducted at the Carondelet shipyards, a cannonball fired from 100 yards away exploded on impact.

6. Island Number Ten, spring 1862 (left)
The Confederate forces abandon their position at Columbus, Kentucky, and retreat to Island Number Ten near New Madrid, Missouri. Under the cover of a violent thunderstorm, the ironclads *Carondelet* and *Pittsburgh* dash past the island to surround the dug-in Confederates, who surrender soon after.

8. Memphis, June 1862 (below)
The Mississippi River Squadron crushes Confederate forces in a lopsided defeat witnessed by many Memphis citizens. The Union victory leaves Vicksburg, Mississippi, as the river's only remaining Confederate stronghold.

9. Arkansas Post, January 1863
The Union's combined river and land assault on Arkansas Post results in the surrender of 5,500 Confederate troops.

St. Louis

1 **Carondelet**

3. Fort Henry, February 1862
The squadron arrives during winter floods, and the Confederate force's poorly located fort falls in just over an hour.

4. Fort Donelson, February 1862
The Confederate forces of Fort Donelson rain artillery on the exposed river squadron, forcing them to retreat. Despite this, the Confederates mistakenly believe they face a massive Union land force and suddenly surrender. The Mississippi River Squadron heads back to the Mississippi River and advances south.

OHIO RIVER

Mound City, IL **2**

ILLINOIS

TENNESSEE RIVER

CUMBERLAND RIVER

Columbus, KY **5**

MISSOURI

ARKANSAS

KENTUCKY

TENNESSEE

6

3 **Fort Henry**

4 **Fort Donelson**

Island No. 10

7. Fort Pillow, May 1862
Ram ships from the Confederate River Defense Fleet sink the ironclads *Cincinnati* and *Mound City*, but the rest of the Union fleet makes it past. Both boats are later raised and brought back into action.

5. Columbus, Kentucky, February 1862.
The Confederacy strings a mile-long chain across the river at Columbus, Kentucky, halting Union advances. Forts Henry and Donelson on the Ohio River were the Mississippi River Squadron's first Confederate targets.

Fort Pillow **7**

Memphis, TN **8**

TENNESSEE

MISSISSIPPI

River blockade chain links. Controlling the Mississippi River was so important that Confederate forces near Columbus, Kentucky, literally strung a giant chain across the river in an attempt to keep the Union out. Each of these links is nearly a foot long.

ARKANSAS RIVER

MISSISSIPPI RIVER

Arkansas Post **9**

ARKANSAS

LOUISIANA

10. Vicksburg, Mississippi, March–July 1863
On the night of April 16, 1863, Confederate sentries spot Union gunboats sneaking past Vicksburg, and the river erupts in a massive firefight. The gunboats' successful passage allows the Union army troops to cross the river and surround the city. After six weeks of constant bombardment, the starving, ruined city of Vicksburg surrenders.

10 **Vicksburg, MS**

1868:
THE MISSISSIPPI RIVER'S FUTURE GREAT CITY

St. Louisans have always talked big about their city, but one St. Louisan looked upon the budding metropolis and the huge river flowing past its doorstep and decided it was destined to become the most incredible city the world had ever seen. That man was Logan Uriah Reavis, and his books *A Change of National Empire* and *St. Louis: The Future Great City of the World* laid out St. Louis's unstoppable glory in grandiose detail.

Published in 1868, *A Change of National Empire* demanded the nation's seat of government relocate from Washington, DC, to St. Louis, "the point of radiation at the center of ten thousand miles of navigable rivers." His follow-up work, *St. Louis: The Future Great City of the World*, published in 1870, went a step further, claiming that St. Louis would not just be the nation's next capital but a new benchmark of world civilization. He effortlessly wrote off any other American city as the "future great," including New York ("a barren, rocky island"), Chicago ("a swampy prairie"), and Washington, DC ("a flat, sterile, uninteresting region").

Reavis wasn't alone in his desire to place the nation's capital on the Mississippi's banks. Three capital-relocation bills appeared before Congress in the late 1860s, and even the most unlikely supporter–the *Chicago Tribune*–ran an 1869 article praising regional rival St. Louis as the ideal spot for the nation's capital. In October 1869, Reavis hosted a capital-relocation convention at the St. Louis Mercantile Library. Although twenty-one state and territory representatives attended the convention, little was ultimately accomplished. Reavis's books were published in English and German in multiple editions, but it's uncertain how much of an impact they had. Their opinions seem to have gained just as many detractors as supporters.

***Central Magazine* cover, 1874.** When Logan Uriah Reavis looked at St. Louis, he saw river and rail connections, a rapidly increasing population, and what he called the city's "all-pervading zeal." The final chapter of his book *A National Change of Empire* predicted that within five years, the president of the United States would deliver his speeches from the new seat of government in the Mississippi Valley.

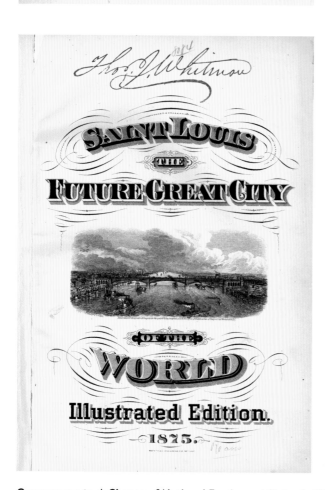

A CHANGE

OF

NATIONAL EMPIRE;

OR

ARGUMENTS IN FAVOR OF THE REMOVAL

OF THE

NATIONAL CAPITAL FROM WASHINGTON CITY

TO THE

MISSISSIPPI VALLEY.

(Illustrated with Maps.)

BY L. U. REAVIS.

Fair St. Louis, the future Capital of the United States, and of the Civilization of the Western Continent.—JAMES PARTON.

There is the East, and there is India.—BENTON.

ST. LOUIS:
PUBLISHED AND FOR SALE BY J. F. TORREY, BOOK AND NEWS DEALER.
1869.

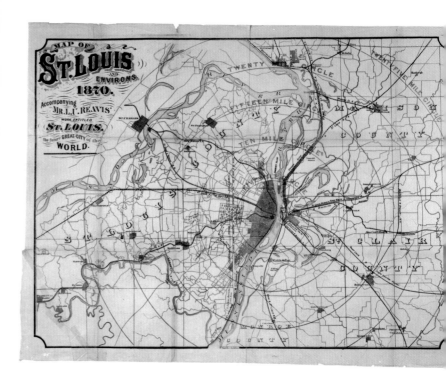

Cover pages to *A Change of National Empire* **and** *St. Louis: The Future Great City of the World.* **Map included with** *St. Louis: The Future Great City of the World,* **1870. Logan Uriah Reavis, ca. 1870.** Logan Uriah Reavis's writings are full of logical leaps, assumptions, and prophecies, but he also made many insightful points. He predicted that the end of slavery would fundamentally change the migration patterns and economy of the United States, and he contemplated how cities would become intricately tied to one another as transportation became faster and more reliable.

Capital relocation. Logan Uriah Reavis hosted a capital-relocation convention at the St. Louis Mercantile Library in October 1869. Twenty-one state and territory representatives (although none from an Atlantic state) spent three days discussing their capital-moving views and vowed to vote against any improvement spending on the existing capital. Although excitement in the room was high, the convention accomplished little for the cause.

The Million Population Club, 1910. Later St. Louisans carried on the fascination with St. Louis's "future greatness." Just like Reavis, the St. Louis Million Population Club—a group that wanted to see 1 million residents within the St. Louis city limits—never quite reached its goal. While the metro region soared past 1 million, the city peaked at 856,000 in the 1950 census.

ST. LOUIS MERCANTILE LIBRARY HALL.

NATIONAL BALLOON RACES. INDIANAPOLIS MOTOR SPEEDWAY. Sept 17- 1910. "CIRKUT PHOTO" by BRETZMAN.

1870:
"THE
SOCIAL EVIL"

Drunkenness, gambling, and cold-blooded murder were regular scenes on the post–Civil War St. Louis riverfront, but no crime or vice provoked public outrage quite like prostitution. Brothels filled the levee blocks of Almond and Poplar streets and Christy Avenue, and many St. Louisans predicted that the city would soon drown in a wave of immorality. But in 1870 some St. Louis civic leaders decided to try something radical: Rather than continue fighting a hopeless battle against "the social evil," they would legalize it.

On July 9, 1870, the St. Louis City Council enacted the Social Evil Ordinance, which legalized and regulated prostitution in the city. All prostitutes could go about their line of work as long as they registered with the city and passed a required monthly medical test. Politicians initially championed the Social Evil Ordinance as a progressive solution, but within weeks, the system started to unravel. Police gave up on street-level enforcement of the ordinance, registrations plummeted, and corruption ran rampant. One account tells of a prostitute presenting a medical examination certificate that was dated three weeks in advance. The social evil seemed worse than ever.

In September 1873 prominent Unitarian minister and Washington University founder William Greenleaf Eliot filed complaints against Eliza Haycraft and Kate Clarke, two of St. Louis's best-known madams. His suit claimed that while St. Louis might let them do their "poisonous" business, they were still breaking Missouri state laws against operating brothels. The resulting newspaper headlines brought out an array of prominent St. Louisans who rallied behind Eliot's movement to once again outlaw prostitution.

On March 30, 1874, the Missouri Supreme Court ruled that St. Louis could no longer attempt to regulate prostitution, and the city nullified the failing Social Evil Ordinance. After its four-year experiment with legal prostitution, the city was back where it started. Down on the riverfront, it was probably just another day at the brothels.

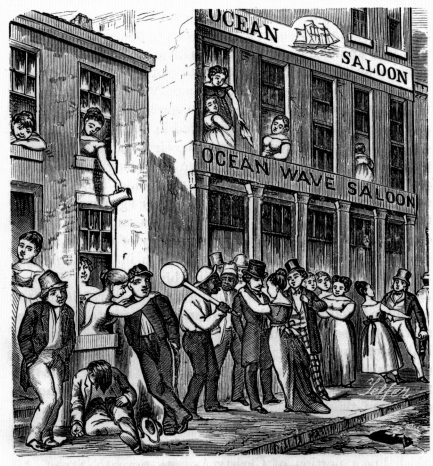

A Scene on Almond Street, from *A Tour of St. Louis,* **1878.** Almond Street, on the St. Louis riverfront's south end, was the levee's vice district from the 1830s on. These "fallen women" bore all of society's blame for prostitution. The men who regularly visited brothels were considered morally upstanding citizens who had been tricked by evil females or were victims of their own excessive sexual appetites.

SCENE ON ALMOND STREET.

The Social Evil Hospital, built in 1872. The Social Evil Hospital opened as a quarantine site for registered prostitutes who failed the required monthly medical examinations. In 1874 the Social Evil Hospital was turned into the Female Hospital for new mothers. It was the birthplace of Freda McDonald, better known to the world as Josephine Baker. The city razed the building in 1915, and the bare land where it stood became Sublette Park.

"The slums of Christy Avenue and Almond and Poplar Streets. . . . The luckless stranger who falls into these social pits may consider himself quite fortunate if he gets out without broken bones."

—A TOUR OF ST. LOUIS, 1878

> " The girls sat with opulent bosoms in the lace curtained windows, or leaned in the doorways, calling the males, joking, flattering, naming the price . . . [below] them plodded a stream of rivermen, back from a week's voyage."

—ORRICK JOHNS ON VALENTINE (PREVIOUSLY ALMOND) STREET, 1883

St. Louis, late 1850s. Whether due to the artist's judgment or just coincidence, this view of St. Louis shows the two ends of the central riverfront shrouded in darkness. Christy Avenue and Almond and Poplar streets—where prostitution flourished—were a shadow land for many St. Louisans.

"Selling Her Picture" (above) and "An Orgie in the Wine Room" (below right), 1875. Cartoons like these let St. Louis's "upstanding" citizens get a glimpse of the kind of debauchery taking place on the levee's streets—that is, if those citizens weren't secretly visiting those districts themselves.

A SCENE AT A FREE-LOVE MEETING.

THE above is an interesting scene at Lize Haycraft's mansion on Poplar street, during a Free-Love meeting that took place there lately.

Eliza Haycraft. Prostitute, madam, and brothel manager Eliza Haycraft was known as the Queen of Almond Street. She was also a generous philanthropist to working-class St. Louis, and when she died in 1871, thousands of St. Louisans lined downtown streets for her funeral.

Almond and Poplar streets, in *Pictorial St. Louis*, 1875. Prostitution grew through the 1850s and 1860s, but the problem exploded after the Civil War. Newspaper accounts and guidebooks warned "greenies," as they called naïve newcomers to the big city, to stay away from the riverfront blocks like Poplar and Almond streets.

1870s:
RIVERS BENEATH ST. LOUIS

St. Louis's rainwater flows through creeks, streams, and sewers on its journey to meet the Mississippi, but some of it takes hidden routes resulting in fascinating changes in the city's physical landscape. The limestone underneath St. Louis erodes as water moves across it, and over thousands of years that erosion has created holes of varying sizes beneath city streets. This pockmarked landscape is known as karst topography. Two of its trademark features–sinkholes and caves–would change St. Louis in surprising ways.

Early French St. Louisans nicknamed their town's sinkholes *entonnoirs* (funnels) for their ability to collect and drain water. These sinkholes came in shapes and sizes ranging from shallow, bowl–shaped dips in the land to jagged canyons deep enough to expose bedrock. As St. Louis expanded throughout the 1800s, the sinkholes were both a resource and a problem. Many late–1800s families had no access to waste removal, so these sinkholes served as convenient substitutes. Appallingly, they also functioned as some St. Louisans' regular source of drinking water.

The caves crisscrossing beneath St. Louis streets played an even bigger role in the city's life. Sometimes stretching miles long, the caves were used by everyday St. Louisans for endless purposes, including mushroom farms, illegal distilleries, and makeshift club–houses. Some were turned into beer gardens and concert halls, which offered priceless summer relief in a time before air conditioning. But these all paled in comparison to the caves' importance to the St. Louis brewing industry. Without the caves' size and temperature, brewers like Anheuser–Busch and Lemp never could have made St. Louis one of the lager beer capitals of the world.

Men standing around a large sinkhole, early 1900s. Often filled with stagnant, festering water, thousands of sinkholes were condemned each year as public nuisances. As St. Louis neighborhoods developed, the vast majority of sinkholes were backfilled to make level ground for homes, businesses, and factories.

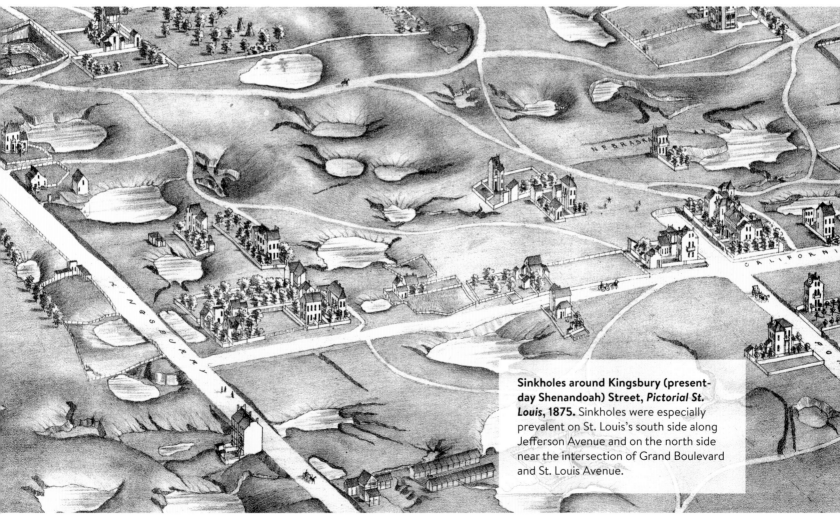

Sinkholes around Kingsbury (present-day Shenandoah) Street, *Pictorial St. Louis*, **1875.** Sinkholes were especially prevalent on St. Louis's south side along Jefferson Avenue and on the north side near the intersection of Grand Boulevard and St. Louis Avenue.

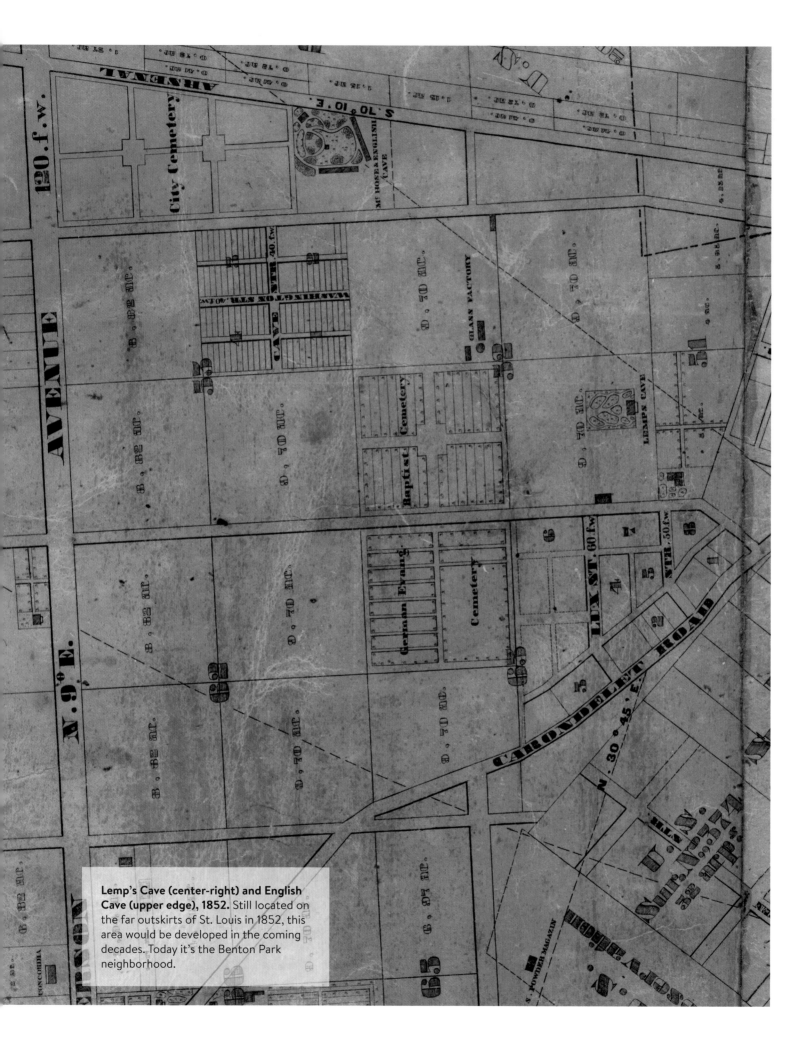

Lemp's Cave (center-right) and English Cave (upper edge), 1852. Still located on the far outskirts of St. Louis in 1852, this area would be developed in the coming decades. Today it's the Benton Park neighborhood.

English Cave (above left), 1840. Ezra English (above), 1850s. Located beneath present-day Benton Park, English Cave—opened by Ezra English in 1826—was one of St. Louis's earliest subterranean pleasure spots. The cave was last used in 1897 as a wine cellar, and its entrance was sealed soon after. Through the 1970s, Benton Park's serene lake repeatedly drained overnight when cracks opened into the cave below.

The Lemp Brewery, 1870s. In the 1840s grocery store owner and brewer Adam Lemp discovered a cave south of St. Louis along Carondelet Road (present-day Broadway). He began using it as a natural refrigeration source for his lager beer, and soon he started constructing a new brewery complex above. By the 1870s the Lemp Brewing Company was one of the largest breweries in the nation. Its cave system held more than 50,000 barrels of beer and included a tunnel that led directly to the basement of the Lemp family's nearby mansion.

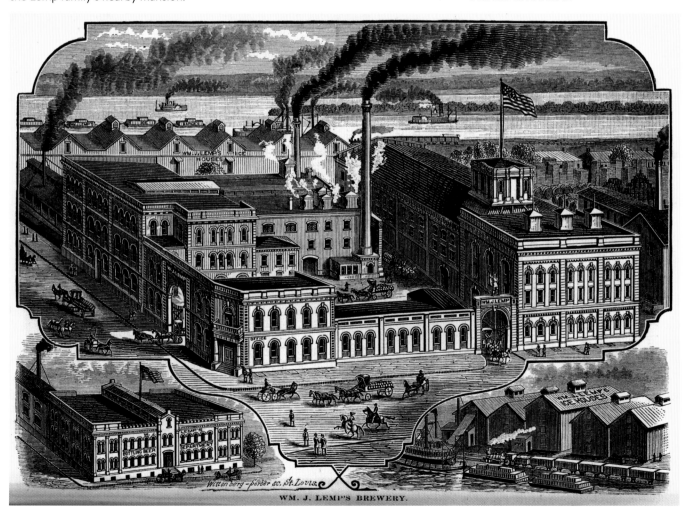

WM. J. LEMP'S BREWERY.

A picnic at Cliff Cave, 1891. Found south of St. Louis at the base of a towering river bluff, Cliff Cave has nearly a mile of surveyed passageway. It was used as a resting spot by Native Americans, fur trappers, and Civil War soldiers before 1868, when the Cliff Cave Wine Company walled off the front and used it as a wine cellar. (The wall's ruins are visible at left in this photo.) The area surrounding Cliff Cave opened as a public park in 1977, but the cave's entrance has since been permanently gated off to protect the colonies of bats that live inside.

Carondelet Park, 1920s. This park contains one of today's best examples of the city's sinkhole landscape. When the park opened in 1876 its natural terrain remained largely unaltered. More than a dozen sinkhole depressions can still be seen, and two of the biggest were even intentionally expanded: Permanently filled with water, they are known today as Boathouse Lake and Horseshoe Lake.

Uhrig's Cave, 1860s. In 1852 brewers Ignatz and Joseph Uhrig bought the southeast corner of Jefferson and Washington avenues for what was beneath it. At its peak in the 1880s, Uhrig's Cave held 3,000 spectators and featured the novelty of electric lighting. But the cave's appeal soon dwindled, and various revival schemes—including a skating rink, a bowling alley, and a mushroom farm—all failed. Subsequent development left much of Uhrig's Cave in disarray or buried.

Cherokee Cave, 1950s. Hand-drawn map of Cherokee Cave, 1949 (inset). After the Lemp brewing empire collapsed during Prohibition, Cherokee Cave was mostly used as a trash dump before quick-thinking entrepreneur Lee Hess turned it into a tourist attraction in 1945. Cherokee Cave remained open until 1960, when it was demolished for Interstate 55.

1871:
KEEPING THE
TAPS RUNNING

Even with the mighty Mississippi flowing beside the city, it took over a century before St. Louisans could expect reliable running water in their homes and businesses. The city's first water reservoir was built on top of a Native American mound in 1831, providing twelve street-corner spigots for St. Louisans to use. It was undersized from the start, and the strain would only worsen as St. Louis averaged more than 6,000 new residents a year throughout the 1840s. A new reservoir that could hold 40 million gallons was added at Benton and Seventeenth streets in 1849, but St. Louisans were still on short allowance. New problems were also arising. Factories had spread north of the waterworks—then near the present-day Eads Bridge—which meant the waste they dumped into the river circulated back into the city by way of citizens' drinking water.

By 1863, St. Louis was among the nation's largest cities, and it was living in a near-constant state of water emergency. That year the desperate city authorized $3 million worth of bonds to create new waterworks. It would take nearly a decade to choose a site and build the plant, but in 1871 the Bissell Point Waterworks opened at the foot of Angelica Street on St. Louis's north side. With four enormous purifying basins and a new reservoir at Compton Hill for the city's south side, this new structure could store up to 120 million gallons—at St. Louis's 1871 use rate, it was about a week's supply.

The Bissell Point Waterworks would be surpassed by the Chain of Rocks Waterworks within a few decades, but when its settling basins filled for the first time in 1871, it marked a huge step forward in the city's quality of life. From that point on St. Louisans didn't have to leave their homes for a reliable source of drinking water—even if it was from the filthy Mississippi River.

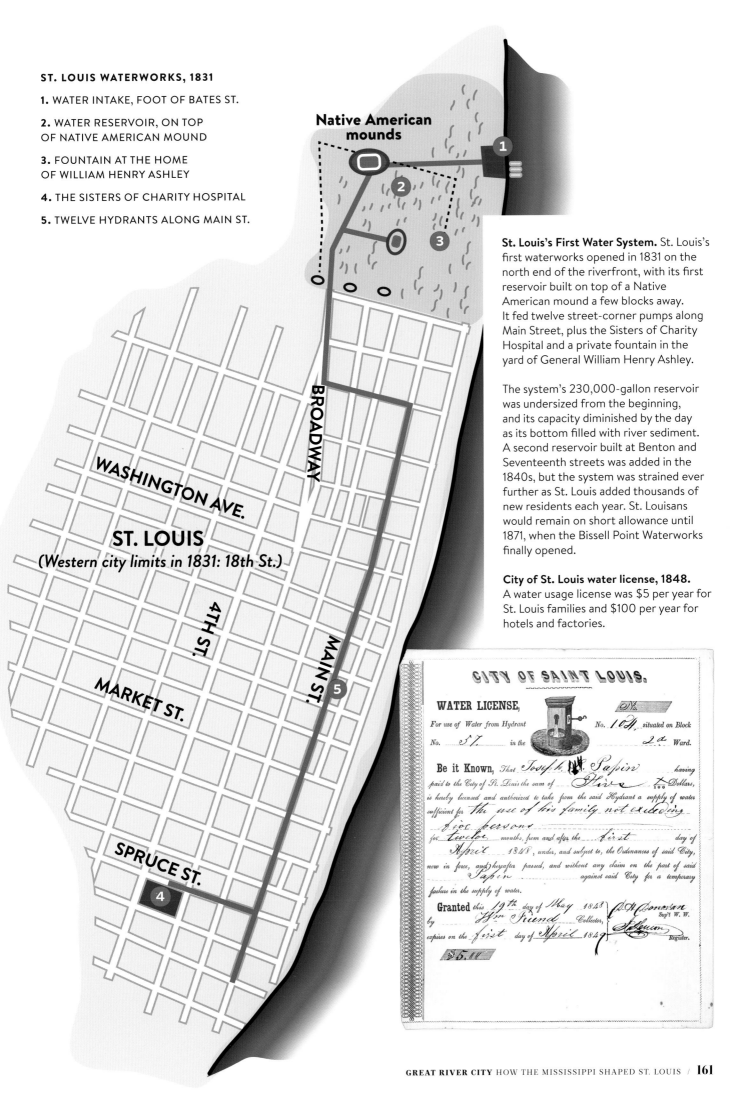

ST. LOUIS WATERWORKS, 1831

1. WATER INTAKE, FOOT OF BATES ST.

2. WATER RESERVOIR, ON TOP OF NATIVE AMERICAN MOUND

3. FOUNTAIN AT THE HOME OF WILLIAM HENRY ASHLEY

4. THE SISTERS OF CHARITY HOSPITAL

5. TWELVE HYDRANTS ALONG MAIN ST.

Native American mounds

WASHINGTON AVE.

ST. LOUIS
(Western city limits in 1831: 18th St.)

BROADWAY

4TH ST.

MARKET ST.

MAIN ST.

SPRUCE ST.

St. Louis's First Water System. St. Louis's first waterworks opened in 1831 on the north end of the riverfront, with its first reservoir built on top of a Native American mound a few blocks away. It fed twelve street-corner pumps along Main Street, plus the Sisters of Charity Hospital and a private fountain in the yard of General William Henry Ashley.

The system's 230,000-gallon reservoir was undersized from the beginning, and its capacity diminished by the day as its bottom filled with river sediment. A second reservoir built at Benton and Seventeenth streets was added in the 1840s, but the system was strained ever further as St. Louis added thousands of new residents each year. St. Louisans would remain on short allowance until 1871, when the Bissell Point Waterworks finally opened.

City of St. Louis water license, 1848. A water usage license was $5 per year for St. Louis families and $100 per year for hotels and factories.

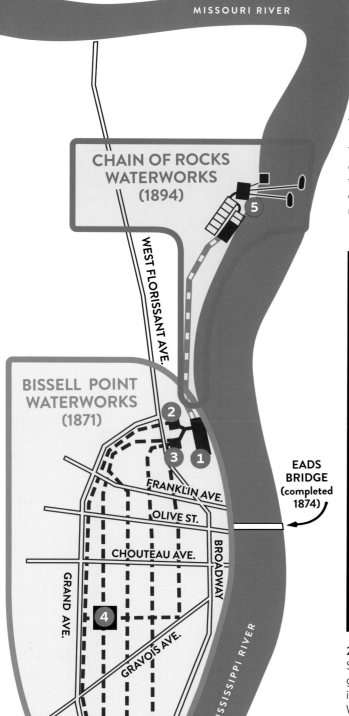

MISSOURI RIVER

CHAIN OF ROCKS
WATERWORKS
(1894)

WEST FLORISSANT AVE.

BISSELL POINT
WATERWORKS
(1871)

FRANKLIN AVE.

OLIVE ST.

CHOUTEAU AVE.

GRAND AVE.

BROADWAY

GRAVOIS AVE.

MISSISSIPPI RIVER

EADS
BRIDGE
(completed
1874)

THE 1871 ST. LOUIS WATER SYSTEM

The 1871 water system marked the first time that St. Louisans could expect reliable running water. The new waterworks and two reservoirs tripled the city's storage capacity. Still, this was only a few days' supply for St. Louis, which was consuming 22 million gallons a day by the mid-1870s.

2. The Grand Avenue Water Tower, 1894. As part of the 1871 St. Louis water system, the Grand Avenue Water Tower used gravity to keep water pressure steady and ensured that St. Louisans saw no surprise blasts or weak trickles from their faucets. When demand grew too high for just one tower, the Bissell Street Water Tower went up two blocks away in 1886.

1. The Bissell Point Waterworks, 1901. Located at the foot of Angelica Street on the north riverfront, the Bissell Point Waterworks pulled nearly 60 million gallons of muddy river water into four massive purifying basins, where it settled for three days before being pumped out to St. Louisans' taps.

Water Works, Station and Park, St. Louis, U. S. A.

5. Chain of Rocks Waterworks, 1911.
A second waterworks opened at the Chain of Rocks in 1894. Safely distant from St. Louis's urban buildup, Chain of Rocks would eventually overtake Bissell Point. In 1915 the Chain of Rocks hosted the largest water filtration plant in the world.

3. The Bissell Street Water Tower, 1894.
A second tower was added to the water system in 1885, built just a few blocks south of the first. The Bissell Street Water Tower was designed by William Eames, whose other works include the Cupples Station warehouses and the Masonic Temple on Lindell Boulevard.

Settling Basin, Compton Heights Looking East, St. Louis, Mo.

4. The Compton Hill Reservoir, 1931.
The new water system added a second massive reservoir to serve the city's south side, but its most famous structure wouldn't rise for another twenty-seven years. The 179-foot-tall Compton Hill Water Tower was built in 1898.

1874:
THE EADS BRIDGE

By the late 1860s train tracks stretched out from St. Louis for thousands of miles in every direction, but the last unconquered obstacle sat right next to the city. A bridge across the Mississippi River was vital if St. Louis were to keep expanding, but it was such a daunting idea that some skeptics refused to believe it was even possible. Between 1867 and 1874, James Eads—a man already familiar with the most unruly and powerful river in the nation—would prove them wrong and give St. Louis a bridge of unprecedented design.

Even on paper the Eads Bridge was shocking. It would bound across the Mississippi on just two piers, with three arches stretching more than 500 feet between them. Even more shocking, those arches would be made of steel, a metal that in the 1860s was still as much alchemy as science. Most shocking of all: The man proposing this radical design had never built a bridge before. James Eads became involved with the most famous project of his storied career thanks to a mix of personal vendetta and pride for his city.

In 1867, Illinois granted Chicago developer Lucius Boomer the exclusive right to build a bridge to St. Louis. James Eads already knew Boomer well. He had built the Gasconade River Bridge, which collapsed in 1855 and killed Eads's close friend and business partner Calvin Case. Besides harboring this personal grudge, Eads felt that a Chicago developer controlling the construction of a St. Louis bridge symbolized the city's future falling "into the hands of enemies of St. Louis." Eads denounced Boomer and began circulating his own bridge drawings. Boomer's engineers tried to publicly discredit Eads, but St. Louisans rallied behind their hometown hero. Boomer eventually gave up on the project, and Eads suddenly found himself with a bridge to build.

The Eads Bridge took seven long years to finish, but it earned James Eads a reputation as one of the greatest engineers in American history. Heralded by poets and architects as a symbol of the city—long before the *Apotheosis of St. Louis* statue or the Gateway Arch—the Eads Bridge was St. Louis's most iconic structure.

The Eads Bridge under construction from below, 1874. Perhaps better than anyone else, James Eads understood the violence, power, and volatility of the Mississippi River. The bridge would have to withstand strong currents, crushing ice floes, and floods that tripled the river's volume.

SECTION OF EAST PIER AND CAISSON

ON LINE AB, PLATE VII.

SHOWING THE INTERIOR OF THE MAIN ENTRANCE SHAFT AND AIR CHAMBER AND THE WORKING OF ONE OF THE SAND PUMPS.

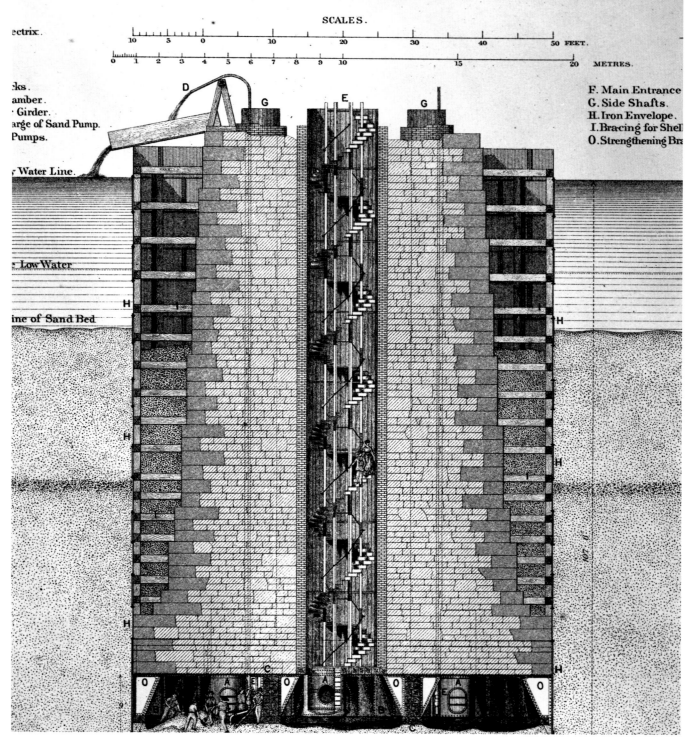

High Water.

ectrix.

cks.

amber.

Girder.

arge of Sand Pump.

Pumps.

Water Line.

Low Water

ine of Sand Bed

SCALES.

F. Main Entrance

G. Side Shafts.

H. Iron Envelope.

I. Bracing for Shel

O. Strengthening Bra

Cross-section of the Eads Bridge pier construction, 1880. Within minutes of climbing out of the caisson's airlock, many workers were left screaming in pain, paralyzed, or worse. The mysterious malady was known as the bends, or caisson's disease. While no one understood what was happening at the time, we do today: The pressurized air inside the pier caissons had three times the nitrogen content of that on the surface. With no way to slowly depressurize, this excess nitrogen became trapped as bubbles inside the workers' bloodstreams.

Building the piers, 1870.
Workers used caissons—open-bottomed iron chambers that are kept watertight by pumped-in air—to build the bridge's underwater piers. Masons stacked the piers' 7-ton limestone blocks on top of the caisson, and the accumulating weight slowly pushed the caisson down to the river's bottom. Once there, workers shoveled away the sand until they hit bedrock.

Building the Eads Bridge, 1873. In material terms, building the Eads Bridge required 2,390 tons of steel, 3,156 tons of wrought iron, 806 tons of timber, and 218,000 tons of limestone block. The final cost was $12 million—equivalent to well over $250 million today.

James Eads, 1860s. When he was thirteen years old, James Eads watched his family's possessions sink to the bottom of the Mississippi River in a tragic steamboat accident. Little did he know that so much of his life would be tied to that same force. Eads worked beneath the river salvaging wrecked steamers, on the river building ironclad gunboats, and above the river constructing the Eads Bridge. He went on to engineer a system of jetties near New Orleans to ensure the river kept a navigable channel and had a proposal in the works for a ship railway to haul oceangoing ships across Mexico's Isthmus of Tehuantepec. Eads died on March 8, 1889, in the Bahamas.

The bridge's opening. On July 4, 1874, 150,000 people gathered in 102-degree heat for the opening of the Eads Bridge. Eads told the crowd, "Yesterday friends expressed to me their pleasure at the thought that my mind was relieved after testing the bridge, but I felt no relief, because I had felt no anxiety on the subject." After a 100-gun salute was fired and General William T. Sherman drove in the bridge's final nail, St. Louisans watched a 14-mile-long parade cross over from Illinois. Library of Congress.

The Eads Bridge is often misidentified as the first bridge built across the Mississippi River, but the Government Bridge at Rock Island, Illinois, used two bridges and Rock Island itself to complete the span in 1856. The Eads Bridge was the first crossing below the entrance of the Missouri River, where the Mississippi's flow intensifies and its water volume increases by 45 percent.

The bridge statues. Many depictions of the Eads Bridge included eight larger-than-life classical statues on top of the bridge's piers, but they were never installed. Some sources claim the finished statues ended up on the roof of the Equitable Building, which stood at Sixth and Locust streets from 1875 until 1955.

Currier & Ives, *The Great St. Louis Bridge, Across the Mississippi River,* 1874

> " . . . a walk over the bridge is one of the most rewarding things that I know of the sort . . . where one looks down 90 or 100 feet on the broad Mississippi and all its steamers, on the broad levee swarming with vehicles of every kind, on the city bordering the shore for miles . . . one can only gaze in wonder, overwhelmed by what the world can scarcely show a second time."

–DR. HERMANN NAGEL, MAY 1875

Crowds on the Eads Bridge observing flooding, 1892

"I have haunted the river every night lately, where I could get a look at the bridge by moonlight. It is indeed a structure of perfection and beauty unsurpassable, and I never tire of it."

–WALT WHITMAN, ON THE EADS BRIDGE, 1879

1879:
THE EXODUSTERS

In the spring of 1879, St. Louisans suddenly found their riverfront host to thousands of refugees. They were the Deep South's Exodusters, and their sights were firmly set on boarding a Missouri River steamboat bound for Kansas. These migrants had suffered through slavery, the Civil War, and a life after emancipation that was nearly as bleak, and now they were taking northbound steamboats to create their own futures. The Exoduster nickname likened their escape from enslavement to that of the Israelites found in the Bible's book of Exodus. For the Exodusters, Kansas represented the promised land beyond the South's racist reach, and St. Louis was the Red Sea–the line separating captivity and freedom.

The first Exodusters appeared on the St. Louis levee in March 1879. While many white St. Louisans simply observed these new arrivals–even mocking their Kansas fever–St. Louis's African American community sprang into action. The Exodusters were carving out their own opportunities, something the St. Louis African American community had been doing for a long time. They sheltered the Exodusters in churches and tenement rooms, caring for them until enough money could be raised to pay their fare to Kansas. It was a daunting task for members of the St. Louis community, many of whom were barely better off financially than the recent arrivals themselves. By the end of April 1879, Rev. Moses Dickson of St. Louis calculated that St. Louisans had provided more than 50,000 meals, 13,000 pieces of clothing, and $4,700 in cash to get 5,169 Exodusters to Kansas.

The St. Louis Colored Refugee Relief Board estimated that as many as 20,000 Exodusters passed through St. Louis during 1879 and 1880. Their story offers a fascinating look at how post–Civil War African American life in St. Louis differed from life in the South. St. Louis's black community understood why these rural Southern migrants would leave their homes, and they had well-established schools and churches where community leaders could grow, build financial wealth, and even play a role in state politics.

The St. Louis riverfront, late 1870s. Between 1879 and 1880 as many as 20,000 Southern migrants appeared on the St. Louis levee, with their sights set on Kansas. The St. Louis African American community fed and sheltered them by the thousands. Prominent St. Louis activist Charlton Tandy even traveled to Washington, DC, to testify on the Exodusters' behalf, using their account books and personal stories to reveal the oppressive situation in the South.

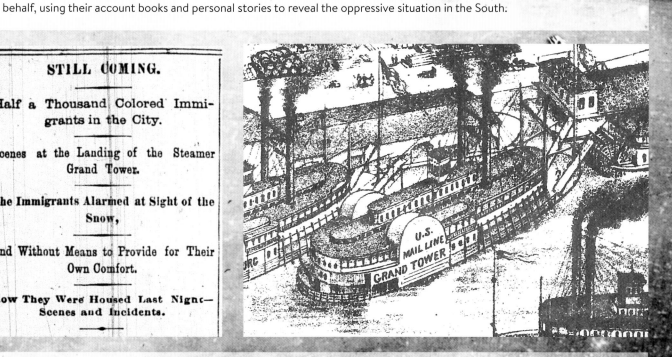

STILL COMING.

Half a Thousand Colored Immigrants in the City.

Scenes at the Landing of the Steamer Grand Tower.

The Immigrants Alarmed at Sight of the Snow,

And Without Means to Provide for Their Own Comfort.

How They Were Housed Last Night—Scenes and Incidents.

Missouri Republican **headline on the Exoduster arrival, March 17, 1879 (left).** *Grand Tower* **steamer, in** *Pictorial St. Louis,* **1875 (right).** The *Grand Tower* brought the first of many groups of Exodusters to St. Louis on March 16, 1879. That morning, St. Louis mayor Henry Overstolz published a warning that the city would offer them no assistance.

The Exodusters' arrival at St. Louis as depicted in *Frank Leslie's Illustrated Newspaper*, April 19, 1879. The Exoduster movement inspired a range of reactions in St. Louis and across America. As Northern reformers applauded the Exodusters' bravery, many Southern whites claimed it was a conspiracy of Northern industrialists who wanted cheap labor. Though many African Americans saw the movement as the embodiment of self-reliance, others—including famous social reformer Frederick Douglass—saw it as running away.

Southern bulldozers, 1870s. White gangs nicknamed "bulldozers" attacked Southern blacks who voiced opinions, educated themselves, or voted. Sometimes the attacks were random, with no apparent motive beyond skin color. As illustrated by this satirical image, law enforcement was often unresponsive or even in cahoots with the attackers.

1. PROCESSION OF REFUGEES FROM THE STEAMBOAT LANDING TO THE COLORED CHURCHES.   2. EMBA

MISSOURI.—REMARKABLE EXODUS OF NEGROES FROM LOUISIANA AND MISSISSIPPI

KANSAS.   3. FEEDING THE REFUGEES AT ONE OF THE COLORED CHURCHES.   4. ST. LOUIS COLORED CITIZENS WELCOMING THE EMIGRANTS UPON THEIR ARRIVAL.

S OF THE ARRIVAL, SUPPORT AND DEPARTURE OF THE REFUGEES AT ST. LOUIS.—FROM SKETCHES BY OUR SPECIAL ARTIST.—SEE PAGE 107.

1880s:
LEAVING THE RIVER BEHIND

To many people in the early 1800s, the idea that a bridge might span the mighty Mississippi River at St. Louis or that a railroad might stretch across the entire United States seemed preposterous. But long before the century's end, both of those visions had become reality. The Eads Bridge conquered the river at St. Louis in 1874, and by 1880 more than 40,000 locomotives crisscrossed the United States on thousands of miles of track. Down by the Mississippi River, life would never be the same.

Steamboats had made St. Louis a metropolis, but their days were numbered. Locomotives glided through the country's vast expanse, and trips that once took long, dangerous weeks on the water now took just days on a smooth, guided track. By the early 1880s less than a quarter of St. Louis's outbound freight traveled by river, and fewer steamboats were showing up on the levee every year. St. Louis's axis of commerce had undergone a permanent shift from north and south along the river to east and west along the rails.

After decades away from the Mississippi, Mark Twain revisited St. Louis in 1883 and couldn't believe his eyes. "Half a dozen sound-asleep steamboats where I used to see a solid mile of wide awake ones," he stated with shock, "the mighty bridge, stretching along over our heads, had done its share in the slaughter and spoliation." Where towering stacks of freight once sat were now only discarded scraps and piles of debris. The levee was but a shell of its former glory, and in the coming decades city leaders would dream of ways that St. Louis could trade in its outdated eyesore of a riverfront for a brighter future.

"Laying Track 600 Miles West of St. Louis, Missouri," 1867. The first transcontinental railroad track was completed in 1869, connecting the huge stretches of America's vast interior. This photograph advertises how far west of St. Louis rails had pushed—for steamboat pilots, those words were an ominous curse. Getty Open Content Program.

Tourist guidebook for the transcontinental railroad, 1878 (right). Uhrig Brewery receipt for a shipment of beer headed from St. Louis to Leadville, Colorado, 1871 (below).

The Handsomest Guide Book
IN THE WORLD!
EVERY TRAVELER NEEDS IT! BUY IT, IT IS THE BEST!

WILLIAMS'
Illustrated Trans-Continental Guide
—OF—
THE PACIFIC RAILROAD, SCENERY OF THE FAR WEST,
Pleasure Resorts, Mines and Lands,
—OF—
California, Colorado, Utah, The Black Hills,
Idaho, Nevada, and the Pacific Coast.

A COMPLETE TRAVELER'S GUIDE
To all Railroads, Stage Lines, and Principal Places of Business
Across the Continent.

300 Pages. Price $1.50, Railroad Edition.

FOR SALE BY NEWS AGENT ON THIS TRAIN.

A. Gardner, Photographer,   511 Seventh Street, Washington.

ACROSS THE CONTINENT ON THE UNION PACIFIC RAILWAY, E. D.

"Westward the course of empire takes its way."—Laying Track 600 miles west of St. Louis, Mo.
OCTOBER 19TH, 1867.

The St. Louis riverfront, 1870s (left) and 1920s (right). Railroad map showing lines from St. Louis, 1881 (background). Seen just as its decline was beginning in the 1870s and long after its decline had set in during the 1920s, the St. Louis riverfront looks like two different worlds. Visiting in 1883, German newspaperman Nicolaus Mohr wrote of the St. Louis levee, "I had imagined the water would be covered with Mississippi steamboats, one next to the other, for miles. . . . But these exciting days have passed and today the river is no longer important. It is the railroads that count." New York Public Library.

L-South From Eads Bridge.

10/4/28

1896:
THE NORTH AND SOUTH RIVERFRONTS

St. Louis's central levee saw important historical moments ranging from the city's founding to the Gateway Arch construction and beyond, but the development taking place off to the levee's sides was often just as important. These factories, rail yards, and industrial sites were rarely glamorous, but they were essential in keeping the city running and workers employed. By the 1890s the north and south riverfronts had become two of St. Louis's biggest industrial powerhouses.

No single industry dominated commerce in St. Louis by the 1890s, and with riverside land at a premium, the north and south riverfronts were home to businesses of all kinds. Breweries smashed against wagon factories, rail yards bumped into gasworks, and stove manufacturers shared space with sugar refineries. Networks of railroads and trolley lines snaked through it all. Across the river in East St. Louis, stockyards, meat-packing plants, and train yards were turning the once-empty Illinois riverbanks into a mirror of St. Louis's crowded conditions.

With St. Louis's population nearing half a million by 1890, people squeezed in wherever they could, working-class families in particular. Tucked among the north and south riverfronts' industrial pandemonium were homes, tenements, churches, and elementary schools. One can only imagine life here, punctuated by shrieking factory whistles and rattling train tracks. In these noisy and active riverside worlds, life went on around the clock.

THE SOUTH RIVERFRONT, 1896

1. City Workhouse (Broadway and Meramec Street). Opened in 1853, the City Workhouse's main function was supplying the crushed limestone needed to pave city streets. Both male and female inmates spent long days breaking and hauling boulders.

2. The Lemp Brewery icehouses. Both the Lemp and Anheuser-Busch breweries produced lager beer, which required thousands of tons of Mississippi River ice—lager only ferments at cool temperatures. Lemp stored its ice in this riverfront row of insulated wooden icehouses. Each could hold more than 5,000 tons.

3. Banner Buggy Company (foot of Rutger Street). Russell Gardner founded the Banner Buggy Company in 1882 and was advertising "100,000 in daily use" by the century's turn. As automobiles replaced horse-drawn buggies, Banner joined with Chevrolet and built the Chevrolet Four-Ninety at the plant until 1920.

4. Laclede Gas Light Company Station A (Second and Rutger streets). Thanks to the St. Louis Gaslight Company, which opened on this riverside site in 1837, downtown streets were aglow by 1847. In 1889 four of St. Louis's biggest gas companies merged under the name Laclede Gas, and this gasworks became one of Laclede's substations.

1. St. Louis Shot Tower. Towering over the tenement houses and factories nearby, the 175-foot-tall St. Louis Shot Tower produced buckshot using a time-tested method. Workers poured molten lead through a copper sieve at the tower's peak, and the free-falling liquid lead formed tiny spherical balls before plopping into a cooling pool below.

2. St. Louis Grain Elevator. Despite its unassuming appearance, the St. Louis Grain Elevator featured cutting-edge technology. Telephone lines connected the building to the Merchants Exchange building and three other local grain elevators so that operators could quote grain prices immediately. Loading both trains and riverboats, the St. Louis Grain Elevator could move nearly 2 million pounds of grain per hour.

3. Belcher Sugar Refinery (O'Fallon and Lewis streets). By the 1850s, William Belcher's St. Louis sugar refinery was the largest one in the United States. In St. Louis, just as popular as Belcher sugar was Belcher water. Searching for a purer water source than the murky Mississippi River, Belcher drilled a well 2,200 feet deep. He found that the well water's mineral content made it unusable for sugar refining, so he opened the well to the public free of charge. Many of St. Louis's finest hotels advertised Belcher water on their menus.

4. Looking north from the Eads Bridge, 1890. Taken during a spring flood in 1890, this image shows how the river affected life along its edge. People wander along the elevated rail tracks—placed up high for just such a flood—surveying the partially submerged buildings below. Although the 1890 flood damaged only a few riverside blocks in St. Louis, it left more than 50,000 people homeless in the lower Mississippi Delta.

1904:
DRINKING THE "MISSISSIPPI RELISH"

For late-1800s visitors to St. Louis, culture shock began with a simple request for a glass of water. Set before them would be the opaque, chocolate-color water of the Mississippi River. One 1858 guidebook reassured visitors that after a short period of feeling "seriously affected" by St. Louis's muddy refreshment, they'd find spring water dull in comparison. Even if they still weren't convinced, they had no other choice. At the time, "purifying" St. Louis's water supply only meant letting it sit for a while so the heaviest mud could fall away.

But that was just fine for many St. Louisans, who claimed the murky river water was not just delicious, it was a boon to the body's immune system. St. Louis doctor Charles Pope was known to keep a jar of river mud in his luggage so he could mix up an instant taste of home while traveling. In between sips Mark Twain found that St. Louis water had a twofold reward: "The land is very nourishing, the water is thoroughly wholesome." St. Louisans and their guests weren't gulping down just mud, but the river's wildlife as well. In 1886 the *St. Louis Globe-Democrat* warned against getting a glass of water in the dark after a downtown office worker discovered an eel squirming around in his sink.

St. Louisans seemed content with their thick, cloudy water, but then came the announcement that the city would host the 1904 World's Fair. City boosters couldn't get over the embarrassing thought of fountains and waterfalls spewing out brown, muddy water to the horror of millions of fairgoers. They scrambled to solve this potential catastrophe, and just weeks before the fair began, "Water Wizard" John Wixford successfully used a mixture of iron and lime to clarify the St. Louis water supply. On March 23, 1904, St. Louisans marveled as crystal-clear water flowed from fountains for the first time. Presumably, the event inspired some St. Louisans to head for the river to collect a nourishing cupful of the old "Mississippi relish."

**MISSISSIPPI RIVER WATER
BEFORE PURIFICATION**

**AS DRAWN FROM TAP
AFTER PURIFICATION**

Water purification, 1916. In 1915 the Chain of Rocks Waterworks opened the largest filtration plant in the world. This image, published in the 1916 report "St. Louis Mayor's Message," purported to show the astonishing difference created by the city's big investment.

St. Louis newspaper advertisements, early 1900s. St. Louisans were haunted by thoughts of what might be lurking in their drinking glasses. Newspapers advertisements for water filters, whiskey purifiers, and bottled spring water played off those fears with horrifying drawings and descriptions of the worms, eels, and microbes that could be found in the water flowing out of the city's taps.

POLLUTED CITY RESERVOIRS!

Their Danger to the Health of the Community—Ways and Means to Protect the Consumer of Germ-Laden Drinking Water.	**Pe-ru-na Is Found the Only Safe Means to Protect the Human System Against the Invasion of Microscopic Enemies.**

Drink This?

Most drinking water holds more solid matter in solution than this. Being in solution, it is not seen, nor can the finest filter take it out; but **it is there**, and is a menace to all who drink it.

These solids in drinking water incite an army of diseases. An excess of mineral salts induces gravel and various kidney troubles, hardening of the arteries, etc.; while typhoid fever, dysentery and a long list of bowel troubles are caused by the invisible filth in drinking water. To be made fit for your use, water **should be purified**.

How We Purify Water

The best way of doing this is by electricity, through the Hydro-Electric Process, which eliminates **all organic impurities and excess of minerals** and yet leaves the water with sufficient life-giving qualities, making a **pure** and **perfect** water for drinking purposes.

Purification by the Hydro-Electric Process is so and so unvarying in its operation and results that take any of the various kinds of water, or a n them all, and submit it to this treatment and get result—water made pure and at the same time f all excess of minerals. The result of this process Diamond Dew. It is simply pure and perfect drink —just water, pure as a diamond, refreshing as th

Diamond De

is sold by the leading grocers in half-gallon bottle for home use. We also supply TILTERS for hom sanitary coolers for the office free, and five-gallon Diamond Dew as needed. The filter is both hand nomical, obviating the expense of icing a special it permits the housewife to draw water from the ice it in her refrigerator as needed.

Diamond Dew is being ma St. Louis hydrant water in dows at Seventh and St. Drop by and see what you h drinking and enjoy a glass

HYDRO-ELECTRIC PROCESS NATIONAL PURE WATER COMPANY

Woman filling a bucket in south St. Louis, 1900s. Street corner spigots were still the main source of water for a large portion of the population in early 1900s St. Louis.

IMPURE WATER

Is the Direct Cause of Typhoid, Malaria, Dysentery, Cholera Morbus, the Fatal Hot Weather Complaints. Duffy's Pure Malt Whiskey is Prescribed by Doctors Ev

GLASS OF DRINKING WATER MAGNIFIED 1.00 TIMES.

Duffy's Pure

ARE YOU DRINKIN

The Horrible, Muddy Water with which our City Fathers are now supplying us? s afford to ruin your health?

DISGUSTING!

The very idea of any sensible person consenting to drink the filthy, muddy water we have at present is almost beyond belief. It is not only disgusting, but is absolutely ruinous to the health. The horrible stuff, muddy as it is, can be made

CLEAR AS CRYSTAL

By using A STEVENS FILTER, the sale of which we control, and we guarantee the perfect operation of them.

SIMMONS HARDWARE CO

uy a Stevens Filter

make the water Clear as which is the only filter made cessfully filter our heavy and water.

HARDWARE C

Mysterious Pink Worm in St. Louis Water

This Illustration, taken from last Sunday's Post-Dispatch, shows the mysterious worm that has made its appearance in St. Louis water. We do not wish to cause alarm, but it is a fact nevertheless that worms, insects, etc., taken into the stomach, often cause serious intestinal disorders and sometimes constitutional disorders. The city authorities are doing all in their power to free the water from these worms, but so far have not succeeded—meanwhile they are being found in hydrants all over the city. Be safeguarded—we carry a line of Filters in various sizes, adapted for all purposes, any one of which will remove not only the pink worm, but all other forms of animal life, from your water supply. Prices range from....

75c to $18.00

We especially recommend our family size Filters at $4.50, $6.00, $7.50 and $10.00.

The Simmons Company Broadway and St. Charles

Cleaning mud from the Compton Hill Reservoir, early 1900s. The 1871 St. Louis water system provided citizens with reliable water, but it still wasn't clean. Periodically the city reservoirs had to be drained and feet of mud scraped from their bottoms.

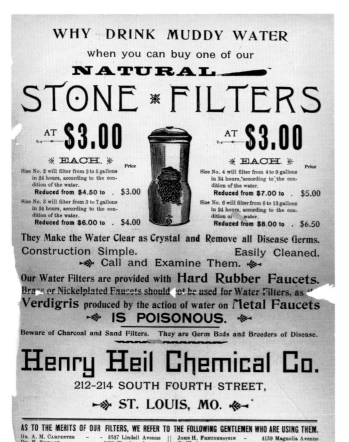

Water filter advertisement, Little Brown Jug water filter, both ca. 1895. Water filters were important home appliances for early 1900s St. Louisans. The St. Louis–made Little Brown Jug was placed in a bucket of dirty water, and impurities were filtered out as the water seeped through the jug's semi-porous surface.

> **Arrived safely in St. Louis on Sunday evening. You God's what a muddy city! I never saw such a richer and more plentiful collection of mud in all my life."**
>
> –JOSEPH MERSMAN, 1849

> **I have seen many filthy places, but I do not think I have ever seen one equal to this."**
>
> –ST. LOUIS HEATH OFFICER DR. WILLIAM GRISSOM, 1867

"If you will let your glass stand half an hour, you can separate the land from the water as easy as Genesis; then you will find them both good: the one good to eat, the other to drink. . . . But the natives do not take them separately, but together, as nature mixed them. When they find an inch of mud in the bottom of a glass, they stir it up, and then take the draught as they would gruel."

—MARK TWAIN, *LIFE ON THE MISSISSIPPI*, 1883

Panorama of the St. Louis Riverfront,
Harper's Weekly, July 1876

1907:
THE RIVER MADE BEAUTIFUL

Beyond the splendor of the 1904 World's Fair, the real St. Louis was a grimy and crowded place–and no part of town looked worse than the Mississippi River. With lumberyards, rail yards, and factories lining its edges, the river was used, abused, and avoided. But in 1907 the St. Louis Civic Improvement League imagined how the river and the city could interact in a totally new way.

By reintroducing nature–particularly the waterways surrounding St. Louis–into daily life, the Civic Improvement League's report "A City Plan for St. Louis" would offer all classes of St. Louisans more healthful, peaceful, and fulfilling lives. The plan's citywide vision called for tree-lined boulevards that ran through neighborhoods and parks, then continued along the Mississippi and Missouri rivers and River Des Peres, which was still a wild river at that time. The Meramec River bluffs, Creve Coeur Lake, Spanish Lake, and the Chain of Rocks Waterworks all became centerpieces for rural escapes from the dense city. The plan's focal point was the St. Louis levee, where blocks of aged buildings would be replaced by a "Riverfront Esplanade" full of trees and grand walkways.

The plan offered an ambitious vision for the city's future, but it was quickly defeated by St. Louis voters who refused to pay its enormous $25 million price tag. However, "A City Plan for St. Louis" did inspire two huge changes that would play out in St. Louis for decades to come. First, it reimagined the city's network of filthy, forgotten waterways as a framework for health, beauty, and civic pride–an idea St. Louisans still pursue through organizations like Great Rivers Greenway. Second, it called for clearing the dense riverfront and replacing it with a green "front door" space for the city–the first foreshadowing of the Gateway Arch National Park we know today.

The riverfront ca. 1910 (top), and the planned Riverfront Esplanade, from "A City Plan for St. Louis." Subtitled "The Riverfront as It Should Be," this image showed the plan to remove the dense urban riverfront for a landscape of grand staircases, arched colonnades, and public green spaces. This esplanade was more than just a pretty space: Hidden beneath was a transportation hub that could serve steamboats, freight trains, and three commuter railways connected to the northern, western, and southern edges of St. Louis. Though they didn't realize it at the time, this plan foreshadowed Gateway Arch National Park.

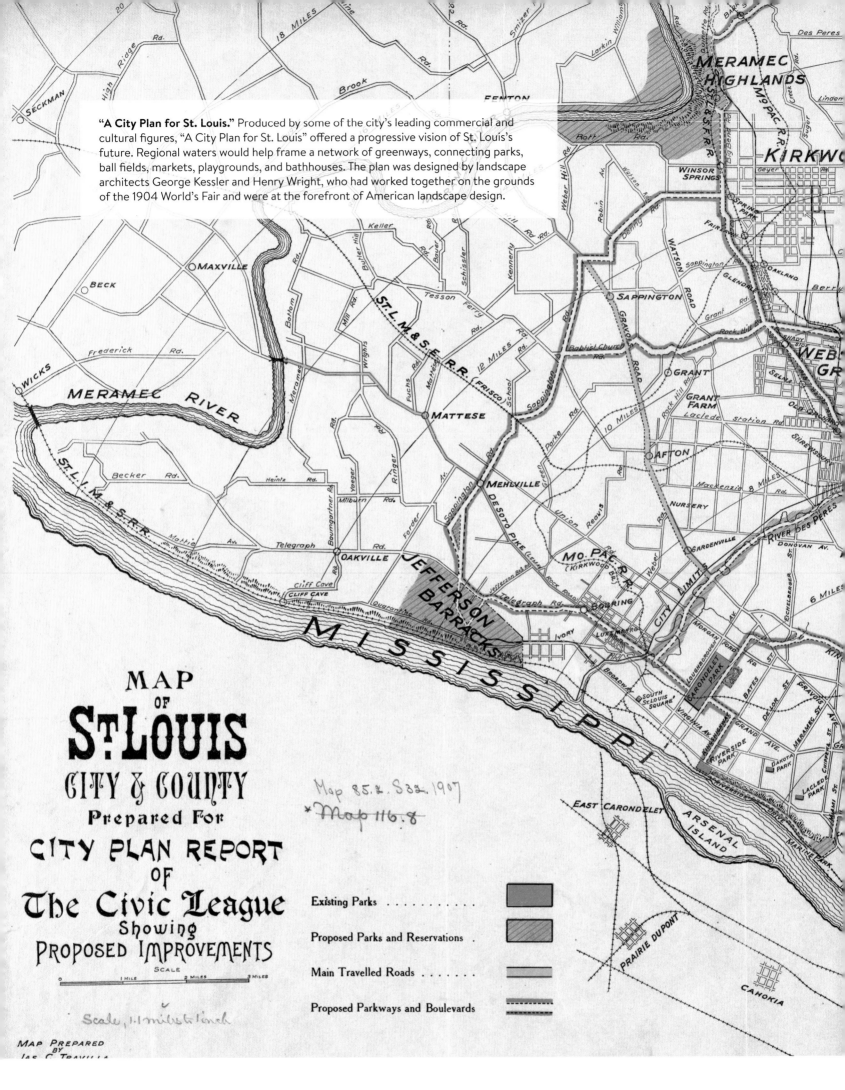

"A City Plan for St. Louis." Produced by some of the city's leading commercial and cultural figures, "A City Plan for St. Louis" offered a progressive vision of St. Louis's future. Regional waters would help frame a network of greenways, connecting parks, ball fields, markets, playgrounds, and bathhouses. The plan was designed by landscape architects George Kessler and Henry Wright, who had worked together on the grounds of the 1904 World's Fair and were at the forefront of American landscape design.

MAP
OF
St LOUIS
CITY & COUNTY
Prepared For
CITY PLAN REPORT
OF
The Civic League
Showing
PROPOSED IMPROVEMENTS
SCALE

Existing Parks . . . .

Proposed Parks and Reservations .

Main Travelled Roads . . . .

Proposed Parkways and Boulevards

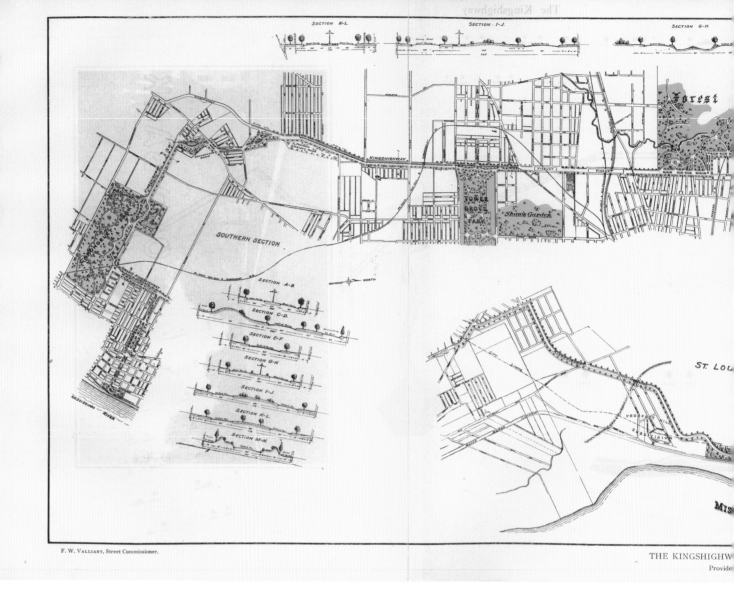

F. W. Valliant, Street Commissioner.

THE KINGSHIGHW
Provide

The Kingshighway, 1907. One of the first pieces of the 1907 City Plan intended to be implemented was for Kingshighway Boulevard. Intended to be the "green necklace" of St. Louis, Kingshighway would connect all of the major city parks, ending with scenic river overlooks at Bellerive Park and the Chain of Rocks. Though the Kingshighway plan made it onto St. Louisans' voting ballots in 1910, it was resoundingly defeated due to its large price tag.

The River Des Peres, 1890s. In 1907 the River Des Peres was untamed, overgrown, and often dangerous. The plan envisioned the "nuisance of which the city would be glad to rid itself" as the centerpiece of a boulevard filled with streetcars, driving trails, sturdy stone bridges, and ornamental greenery.

Bath House No. Six, 2014. The 1907 plan envisioned the region's waters as a symbol for cleansing. The plan called for floating communal bathhouses on either side of downtown. These particular floating bathhouses were never built, but six public baths were built throughout the city. The last, Municipal Bath House No. Six, remained in operation until the 1960s.

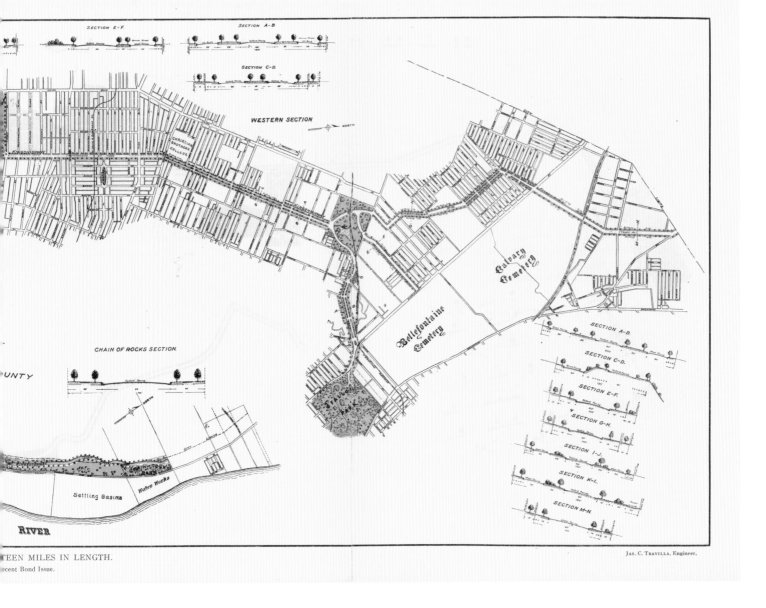

Jas. C. Travilla, Engineer.

TEEN MILES IN LENGTH.

ecent Bond Issue.

Waterworks, Chain of Rocks, St. Louis, Mo.

Chain of Rocks Waterworks, 1930s. The Chain of Rocks Waterworks occupied a large riverfront site north of St. Louis. The 1907 plan called for it to become the centerpiece of a 500-acre park, including a scenic lookout on top of the adjacent river bluffs.

1910:
DAREDEVILS ON THE WATER

Early-1900s St. Louisans gathered by the thousands whenever an airplane took to the skies, so a flight combined with the danger of the Mississippi River was guaranteed to draw a crowd. In 1910 the *St. Louis Post-Dispatch* upped the ante, offering $2,500 to the first pilot daring enough to fly a plane through one of the Eads Bridge's arches. Deciding his *Red Devil* biplane was up to the task, young stunt pilot Thomas Baldwin announced that September 10, 1910, would be a day no St. Louisan would soon forget.

That morning, the streetcars downtown sported blue flags–the signal that winds were right. Some 200,000 spectators flocked to the levee to see Baldwin attempt his stunt, and forty rescue boats took their positions on the river. Five miles upriver near Bellefontaine Cemetery, Baldwin readied the *Red Devil*. He took off heading south, briefly landing in Illinois to check and refuel the plane, then turned around toward the Eads Bridge.

Wind rattled the plane's fabric wings as Baldwin dived toward the bridge. Shaking in his seat, Baldwin trained his focus on the easternmost arch, threading his plane into an opening less than 50 feet high. As Baldwin roared out the other side, the levee erupted into cheers. A smaller crowd watched an emboldened Baldwin repeat his feat upriver, coasting beneath the McKinley Bridge as an encore.

The St. Louis riverfront has never stopped attracting daredevils. Decades after the arches of the Eads Bridge tantalized Thomas Baldwin, a new, much more tempting Arch arose on the riverfront. The first of more than a dozen illegal fly-throughs of the Gateway Arch happened in June 1966, just eight months after the landmark was completed.

Baldwin mid-flight over the Eads and McKinley bridges, September 10, 1910. After successfully coasting beneath the Eads Bridge, Baldwin repeated the stunt upriver at the McKinley Bridge. He landed to a hero's welcome near Bellefontaine Cemetery.

Thomas Baldwin (right). Thomas Baldwin had already entertained St. Louisans at the 1904 World's Fair with his *California Arrow* hot air balloon, piloted by A. Roy Knabenshue (left). The New York Public Library.

Unidentified pilot flying beneath the Eads Bridge, 1920s. Baldwin's stunt inspired riverfront daredevils for years to come, including this unidentified biplane pilot.

1910s:
WAVES OF GARBAGE

Plenty of early-twentieth-century St. Louisans complained about black factory smoke suffocating the city, but few gave much thought to the garbage-clogged Mississippi River. For much of St. Louis's history, the solution to any waste troubles was simple: Just toss trash into the river.

St. Louis's first "night scavengers" began roaming the streets in 1843, collecting carts full of outhouse waste, alley trash, and dead animals before dumping it into the Mississippi. After south St. Louis residents complained of giant rafts of excrement clinging to the riverside, the city enlisted scavenger boats to haul the waste out to the middle of the river and dump it there. As the city's population grew from 75,000 people in 1850 to 575,000 in 1900, trash barges dumped more than 50,000 tons of garbage into the river each year.

As St. Louis industrialized, it was assumed that any new factory would build a waste pipe to carry refuse out to the Mississippi. Heavy metals, bleaches, dyes, and oils dissolved into the poisoned water, but glues, animal offal, wax, and spent grains formed huge floating slicks that tangled into river brush. In the 1930s the city started to grind its garbage into a paste and discharge it directly into the river, and by the 1960s more than 450 tons of waste entered the Mississippi every day. Thankfully, at that critical moment things finally began to turn around.

In 1970 St. Louis opened its first sewage treatment plant, and in 1972 the EPA's Clean Water Act made it illegal for cities and industrial sites to dump raw sewage into the nation's waterways. Downstream water quality has improved ever since, but other sources of river pollution remain that are much harder to battle. The Mississippi has a drainage basin that stretches from Montana to New York, and with each rainfall enormous amounts of pesticides, livestock waste, and pavement grime are carried into the river.

Trash pile beneath the MacArthur Bridge, 1910. The early 1900s riverfront became a no-man's land for dumping. When the river rose, all of this trash would simply disappear.

Girl in a trash-filled alley, 1910s (left). St. Louis trash barge, 1900s (below).
"Scavenger carts" scoured St. Louis alleys each night, collecting trash and taking it to collection points at the river's edge. It was placed on barges, floated out to midriver, and dumped. Beginning in 1904 the city's ever-growing garbage was floated downriver to Chesley and Establishment islands, where the inedible garbage would be piled up, and the organic garbage would be eaten by thousands of pigs. At that time, St. Louis was producing approximately 70,000 tons of garbage and 350,000 tons of coal ash each year.

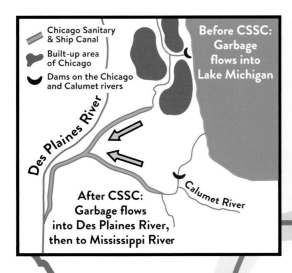

Chicago Sanitary & Ship Canal
Built-up area of Chicago
Dams on the Chicago and Calumet rivers

Before CSSC: Garbage flows into Lake Michigan

Des Plaines River

Calumet River

After CSSC: Garbage flows into Des Plaines River, then to Mississippi River

CHICAGO

MISSISSIPPI RIVER

ILLINOIS RIVER

ST. LOUIS

Chesley Island

Establishment Island

Ste. Genevieve

The Water Wars: St. Louis v. Chicago. Opened in 1900, the 28-mile Chicago Sanitary and Ship Canal reversed the Chicago River's flow, sending the city's sewage to the Mississippi River rather than to Lake Michigan. Nearly 400 miles downstream, infuriated St. Louisans claimed Chicago was infecting them with a wave of typhoid. Missouri filed a complaint with the US Supreme Court, but after years of trying to prove that Chicago's waste was affecting health in St. Louis, the state couldn't produce any legitimate evidence. The Supreme Court dismissed the case in 1906.

St. Louis newspaper excerpts reporting on Chicago sewage, 1900. Journalists reported regularly on the "water war" between St. Louis and Chicago, publishing cartoons and articles about the "visitor" that was headed downriver.

FILTER AND BOIL DRINKING WATER

Health Commissioner Starkloff's Advice in a Proclamat Issued Yesterday Indicates That Chicago Sewage Is in the Mississippi River.

The office boy throws in his line and catches a huge microbe (Chicagoius Typhoidus).

THE VISTOR FROM CHICAGO

SEWAGE STARTS SOUTH---TWO INJUNCTION SUITS.

Flowing Toward St. Louis and Expected to Arrive in Seven Days.

Attorney General Crow Files a Plea in the Federal Supreme Court.

Joliet Finds It a Dirty Blue, but Says It Doesn't Smell Bad—Breaks the Ice at Ottawa— Peoria Worried.

Extended Synopsis Here Given of the Array of Facts Presented by Missouri—St. Louis's Suit in Chicago.

1914:
THE ST. LOUIS BLUES

The Mississippi River connects St. Louis to other places in countless ways, but few can compare to its effects on the city's musical heritage. When musician W. C. Handy was broke and sleeping on the St. Louis riverfront in 1892, he would listen as levee workers belted out haunting songs with "numerous one-line verses." The experience stuck with him for decades, and those tunes and lyrics became the basis of his famous 1914 composition "St. Louis Blues." We now understand the workers' songs to be an early form of the blues, and though Handy's late-in-life recollections may have had some embellishment, there is no doubt that St. Louis's position along the Mississippi River helped make it one of the foremost centers of early blues and jazz music.

St. Louis was the first big industrial city heading north up the river valley, and through the early 1900s the city attracted thousands of southern African Americans looking for good-paying jobs. St. Louis already had a thriving musical scene that stretched back before ragtime, and these new rural migrants would only add to St. Louis's confluence of sound. The city's riverboats, pool halls, taverns, barbershops, and "house rent parties" became breeding grounds for musical experimentation to thrive. St. Louis developed unique styles ranging from ballroom swing to "gutbucket" barrelhouse piano.

Many early studies about the history of the blues have assumed that the urban blues of cities like St. Louis are lesser versions of the "pure" rural blues found downstream in the Mississippi Delta. But on closer look it's clear that the river of music flowed in both directions. The phonograph records coming out of St. Louis featured musicians who had urban and rural origins; that unique sound was studied and copied by musicians downriver who bought the records. The Mississippi River was the connective tie in a flourishing network of music that stretched from the Gulf of Mexico to the Great Lakes. St. Louis was right in the middle of it all.

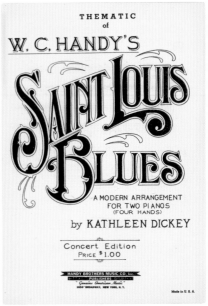

The Mississippi levee, 1903 (above). Sheet music cover for "St. Louis Blues," 1930s (right). W. C. Handy visiting the Old Rock House on the St. Louis levee, 1935 (below). While living on the St. Louis riverfront in 1892, W. C. Handy claimed that he saw a distressed woman stumbling along, mumbling to herself about a man with "a heart like a rock cast in the sea." It became a key line in his masterpiece, "St. Louis Blues." The song now ranks among the most enduring and influential songs in American history.

1917:
REFUGE ACROSS THE RIVER

St. Louis has a long and difficult history of racial conflicts, but in the summer of 1917, it became a city of refuge when East St. Louis erupted in violence and flames. On July 2, 1917, the Illinois city descended into one of the deadliest race riots in United States history. Beneath plumes of billowing black smoke, masses of African American refugees flooded across the Mississippi River on the Municipal (now MacArthur) and Eads bridges. Carrying hastily packed suitcases, they all reported the same story: White mobs were murdering dozens of black bystanders and burning down the city, and no one was stopping them.

The 1917 East St. Louis race riot had its origins in labor tension. East St. Louis had been steadily growing as St. Louis's cross-river industrial center, and southern African Americans were migrating to the city seeking jobs in factories. After 1,700 striking white workers of the Aluminum Ore Company were replaced by black and Eastern European workers in April 1917, the racial tensions that had already existed in East St. Louis hit a new high. On July 2, 1917, the situation exploded when two plainclothes detectives were killed by a group of African Americans who mistook them for the gun-toting white joyriders who had fired at black homes earlier that night.

Over the course of a single day white rioters killed as many as 200 African American citizens, and at least 600 more were left homeless. Rioters also burned more than 200 homes, many prominent East St. Louis structures, and hundreds of loaded railcars. Eleven-year-old Freda McDonald–better known to the world as Josephine Baker–lived near the foot of the Municipal Bridge in St. Louis and witnessed the swarms of refugees escaping across the river. She wrote, "This was the Apocalypse. Clouds, glowing from the incandescent light of huge flames leaping upward from the riverbank, raced across the sky. . . . But not as quickly as the breathless figures that dashed in all directions. The entire black community appeared to be fleeing."

Foot of the Municipal Bridge, 1917. Over the course of July 2, 1917, more than 4,000 black East St. Louisans fled across the Mississippi River to St. Louis. Members of the St. Louis NAACP met the refugees at the foot of the Municipal and Eads bridges and took them to shelter.

East St. Louis, July 2, 1917. As viewed across the river from the Eads Bridge, plumes of smoke rose above downtown East St. Louis on the afternoon of July 2, 1917. Thousands of African American citizens would cross the river that day, seeking safety in St. Louis. From the Collection of the Smithsonian National Museum of African American History and Culture, Gift of Bobbie Ross in memory of Elizabeth Dillard.

THE CRISIS

SEPT 1917   10¢

FRANK WALTS

National Association for the Advancement of Colored People

THE MASSACRE OF EAST ST. LOUIS.

THE NATIONAL ASSOCIATION FOR THE ADVANCEMENT OF COLORED PEOPLE, 70 Fifth Avenue, New York, sent Martha Gruening and W. E. Burghardt Du Bois to East St. Louis, as special investigators of the recent outrages. These two collected in person the facts and pictures from which this article is compiled.

ON the 2nd of July, 1917, the city of East St. Louis in Illinois added a foul and revolting page to the history of all the massacres of the world. On that day a mob of white men, women and children burned and destroyed at least $400,000 worth of property belonging to both whites and Negroes; drove 6,000 Negroes out of their homes; and deliberately murdered, by shooting, burning and hanging, between one and two hundred human beings who were black.

Such an outbreak could not have been instantaneous. There must have been something further reaching even than an immediate cause to provoke such a disaster. The immediate cause usually given is as follows: On the evening of July 1, white "joy riders" rode down a block in Market Street, which was inhabited by Negroes, and began to fire into the houses. The Negroes aroused by this armed themselves against further trouble. Presently a police automobile drove up containing detectives and stopped. The Negroes thinking that these were the "joy riders" returning opened up fire before this misunderstanding was removed, and two of the detectives were killed. Some of the policemen were in plain clothes.

One naturally wonders why should the white "joy riders" fire in the first place. What was their quarrel with the Negroes? In answering that question we get down to

219

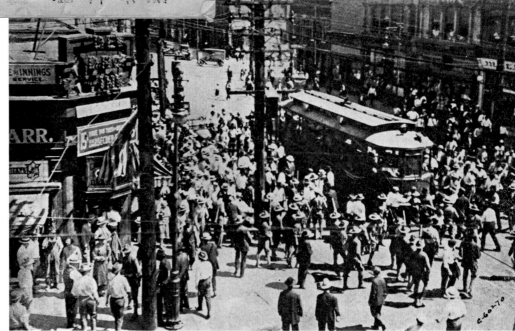

The aftermath. Influential journalist Ida B. Wells, NAACP founder W. E. B. DuBois, and New York social worker Martha Gruening were among the few from outside the St. Louis region who saw the riot's aftermath firsthand. The *Crisis*, the NAACP's magazine, published a twenty-four-page report on DuBois's findings. From the Collection of the Smithsonian National Museum of African American History and Culture, Gift of Bobbie Ross in memory of Elizabeth Dillard.

East St. Louis riot refugees in St. Louis, 1917. The St. Louis NAACP offered free representation to refugees seeking damages for their losses. Nearly 2,000 claims were filed. Department of Special Collections and University Archives, W. E. B. Du Bois Library, University of Massachusetts Amherst.

The Silent Parade, 1917. The riot's shockwave echoed across America's black communities. On July 28, 1917, as many as 10,000 people joined the Silent Parade in New York City in protest of the East St. Louis riot. Historians consider it among the formative events of the twentieth century's civil rights movement.

THE FIRST BLOOD FOR AMERICAN INDEPENDENCE Was Shed By A Negro CRISPUS ATTUCKS

1919:
SOME UNEXPECTED GUESTS

On June 4, 1919, St. Louisans discovered a US submarine chaser naval warship sitting among the levee's normal barges and ferries. The ship's captain had exciting news: An entire flotilla, complete with a submarine, would arrive in St. Louis in just one week's time. On June 12 the K5 submarine, US destroyer *Isabel*, and submarine chasers SC-2 and SC-189 pulled up to the levee amid the wild shouts of cheering St. Louisans.

The visit was meant to inspire St. Louisans to sign up for a tour of duty in the US Navy, and the 245-foot-long *Isabel* wasted no time getting the show started. The boat burned through oil reserves to emit a screen of thick black smoke, and when it cleared, the submarine had vanished beneath the river's surface. But that was just the opening act. Over the next week, the flotilla crew demonstrated naval maneuvers, played military marches, and screened moving pictures of military life. They welcomed thousands of St. Louisans onboard to momentarily hold the wheel or look through the periscope. The crew even repeated the submarine dive, this time bringing along local reporters and distinguished St. Louis guests. But dropping river levels forced the flotilla to head back downriver early, so St. Louisans waved goodbye on June 18.

Though the submarine flotilla thrilled St. Louisans in 1919, they weren't the first (nor would they be the last) strange boats to show up on the St. Louis riverfront. From a replica fifteenth-century sailing ship to a floating fast-food barge, the St. Louis levee has hosted many curious vessels throughout its lifetime.

Flotilla on the St. Louis riverfront, June 1919. With river levels quickly dropping, the flotilla was forced to make a quick departure from St. Louis. Aside from the enormous *Isabel*—which spent a day beached on a sandbar near Cairo, Illinois—the vessels made it back to the Gulf of Mexico without issue.

OTHER UNIQUE ST. LOUIS VISITORS

USS *Inaugural*. After spending World War II patrolling waters off Japan, the minesweeper USS *Inaugural* came to St. Louis as a permanent tourist attraction in 1968. During the 1993 flood the *Inaugural* broke loose and sank after smashing into the Poplar Street Bridge. Every now and then the river will drop low enough to reveal the *Inaugural*'s rusting hull at the foot of Rutger Street. From the Collections of the St. Louis Mercantile Library at the University of Missouri–St. Louis.

The *Matilda*, 1840s. Shipbuilders Emerson and Thomas's 500-ton *Matilda* was the only oceangoing sailing ship built at St. Louis, and its life was racked with problems. Its initial investor went bankrupt, and the lumber company furnishing its parts sold the boat at auction. Launched in spring 1849, the *Matilda* sailed surprisingly well down the Mississippi River but sprang a leak in the Gulf of Mexico and had to dock at New Orleans. It eventually sailed on to San Francisco, where it sank in the harbor.

The McBarge. From 1980 to 2000 the Gateway Arch was joined by the golden arches of St. Louis's floating McDonald's restaurant. Styled in homage to the stern-wheel paddleboats of yesteryear, the restaurant spent two decades serving up floating fast food before declining sales and structural deterioration made it unprofitable. The McBarge quietly closed in 2000.

The *Santa Maria*. In 1969 the St. Louis riverfront stepped five centuries back in time with a full-size replica of Christopher Columbus's *Santa Maria*. The ship was brought to St. Louis from the 1964 New York World's Fair, but just months after its arrival a thunderstorm knocked the boat free. It drifted 2 miles downriver, hit an Illinois dock, and partially sank. It was restored and returned to the levee until 1973, when it was sold to a Florida promoter.

1920s:
THE STRECKFUS EXCURSION BOATS

From the 1910s through the 1930s, St. Louisans took to the levee for nights of dining and dancing, with a soundtrack provided by some of the country's best musicians. Faced with diminishing returns in his freight shipping boats, steamboat owner John Streckfus built a fleet of excursion boats that became the biggest attractions anywhere on the Mississippi River. Headquartered in St. Louis, his boats including the *J. S.*, the *Capitol*, the *President*, the *Sidney*, and the *St. Paul* traveled as far north as St. Paul, Minnesota, and as far south as New Orleans, Louisiana, drawing in crowds wherever they went.

While the segregated excursion boat audiences were unmistakably white (black patrons were only allowed on board on Monday nights) the bands were composed of mostly black musicians hailing from up and down the Mississippi River. Many dreamed of a position with a Streckfus band, but bandleaders like Charles Creath, Dewey Jackson, and Fate Marable only accepted the best. Musicians in Marable's band had to master fourteen new songs every two weeks. Jazz legend Louis Armstrong, who joined Fate Marable's band onboard the *Sidney* from 1919 to 1921, said playing on a Streckfus boat was like "going to the university." Other musicians referred to these excursion steamers as "floating conservatories."

This unique moment of musical history has often been called the era of riverboat jazz, but despite dozens of influential jazz musicians playing in these bands, the genre was often hard to come by: The Streckfus family kept tight control over the music, relying on popular hits, old standards, and novelty tunes that kept patrons dancing. Jazz was far too new and radical, and the captain's orders were final. But once outside the riverboats—in St. Louis's clubs, cabarets, and ballrooms—these musicians produced some of the most exciting and inventive jazz of the era.

SPECIAL RATE COUPON
For Str. Capitol Excursions
USE THIS AND SAVE MONEY

ENJOY SUMMER'S FINEST PLEASURE
Gay, Romantic
Moonlight Excursions
EVERY NIGHT AT NINE

THE CAPITOL
RIVER RHYTHM KINGS
FAMOUS 12-PIECE DANCE BAND
Glorious Nights Afloat — Dancing and Romancing

TOPS IN WEEK-END FUN
Special De Luxe Feature
Sat.-Sun.

Night Cruises at 9
ON THE COOL CAPITOL
The Place to Go for a Glorious Time

ALL-DAY SUNDAY TRIPS
To Hastings Lock — 10 am to 5 pm
Ideal Family Picnic Outings

FOR NIGHT TRIPS **50¢** & SUN. DAY TRIPS
TICKETS ONLY IN ADVANCE
AT LIGGETTS, 7th & HENNEPIN STS., MNPLS.
Show this Coupon at drug store before
6 pm for night trips—day before for

SPECIAL RATE COUPON
For Str. Capitol Excursions
USE THIS AND SAVE MONEY

ENJOY SUMMER'S FINEST PLEASURE
Gay, Romantic
Moonlight Excursions
EVERY NIGHT AT NINE

THE CAPITOL
RIVER RHYTHM KINGS
FAMOUS 12-PIECE DANCE BAND
Glorious Nights Afloat — Dancing and Romancing

TOPS IN WEEK-END FUN
Special De Luxe Feature
Sat.-Sun.

Night Cruises at 9
ON THE COOL CAPITOL
The Place to Go for a Glorious Time

ALL-DAY SUNDAY TRIPS
To Hastings Lock — 10 am to 5 pm
Ideal Family Picnic Outings

FOR NIGHT TRIPS **50¢** & SUN. DAY TRIPS
TICKETS ONLY IN ADVANCE
AT LIGGETTS, 7th & HENNEPIN STS., MNPLS.
Show this Coupon at drug store before

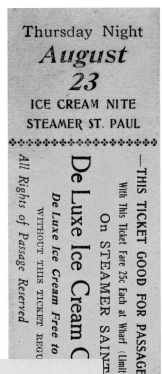

Thursday Night
August
23
ICE CREAM NITE
STEAMER ST. PAUL

—THIS TICKET GOOD FOR PASSAGE
With This Ticket Fare 25c Each at Wharf (Limit 0
On STEAMER SAINT

De Luxe Ice Cream C

De Luxe Ice Cream Free to

All Rights of Passage Reserved

WITHOUT THIS TICKET REGU

25¢ ADULTS **BARGAIN** 10¢ CHILD
WEEK-DAY FARES
STEAMER CAPITOL

HAPPY DAYS on the WATERWAYS
Excursions
To Hastings Lock & Dam—10am to 5pm
• Five Spacious Shady Decks...
• Plenty of Tables, Chairs, Rockers...
• Always Cool and Delightful...
• Everything Under Shelter...
• No Ants—No Flies—No Traffic...
• Modern, Comfort Facilities...
• Amateur Floor Show...
• Two Modern Cafeterias...
Dancing All Day

THIS COUPON entitles you to buy
TICKETS AT JACKSON ST. WHARF FOR
ADULTS 25¢ — CHILDREN 10¢
FOR FOLLOWING DAY TRIPS ONLY

WED.	DAY TRIP	JULY 30
TUES.	DAY TRIP	AUG. 5
FRI.	DAY TRIP	AUG. 8
THUR.	DAY TRIP	AUG. 14
WED.	DAY TRIP	AUG. 20

SHOW THIS COUPON TO TICKET SELLER
AT BOAT — LIMIT-4 TICKETS TO 1 COUPON
All children 12 years or under must
have tickets and be accompanied by
adult. Management reserves right to
M refuse passage to holder of this coupon.

LAST EXCURSION
Wed.
OCT. 14

Largest Sternwheel Passenger Steamer on the Mississippi

CAPITOL
Steamer DeLuxe

ery ight
Moonlight excursions
Every Night at Nine

EXCURSION
ST. PAUL
STEAMER

Streckfus excursion boat flyers and coupons. With St. Louis as its home base, the Streckfus Company dominated the Mississippi River excursion boat business through the 1920s and 1930s. From the Collections of the St. Louis Mercantile Library at the University of Missouri–St. Louis.

The Streckfus family, 1920. "Commodore" John Streckfus first got into the steamboat business with his Acme Packet Company, founded in the mid-1880s. By the 1920s he was operating four of the largest excursion boats on the river, and his whole family was involved. From left to right: Roy, Joseph, "Commodore" John Streckfus Sr., Vern, and John. Murphy Library Special Collections, University of Wisconsin–La Crosse.

Steamer *Sidney*, 1900s. In 1911 the Streckfus family purchased the Diamond Jo Line of packet steamers, introducing them into the St. Louis excursion market. The *Sidney* would be the first of these boats that Streckfus would retrofit into an excursion boat. In this image it still carries the Diamond Jo Line branding near its paddlewheel.

Fate Marable's Capitol Revue, SS *Capitol*, St. Louis, 1920. Fate Marable (seated at piano) had one of the longest careers of any excursion bandleader, lasting from the early 1900s to 1940. Marable was known as a strict, regimented bandleader, and he would nurture some of the greatest jazz musicians of the era, including Louis Armstrong, seen here third from right. Marable also played the calliope, a musical instrument similar to an organ that used the boat's steam to produce sound. From the Collections of the St. Louis Mercantile Library at the University of Missouri–St. Louis.

STRECKFUS EXCURSION BOATS

■ EXCURSION

■ FREIGHT/PACKET/NOT RUNNING

STRECKFUS MOVES TO ST. LOUIS
AFTER BUYING DIAMOND JO LINE

| 1870 | 1880 | 1890 | 1900 | 1910 | 1920 | 1930 | 1940 | 1950 | 1960 |

J. S.

BUILT
1901

BURNED
1910

ST. PAUL

MOVED TO
PITTSBURGH
1936

BUILT
1883

CONVERTED TO
EXCURSION
1918

REPURPOSED
AS WAR BOAT
1939

SUNK
1953

SIDNEY

BUILT FOR
OHIO RIVER
1880

RENAMED
WASHINGTON
1921

DISMANTLED
AT ST. LOUIS
1939

CAPITOL

DESTROYED BY TORNADO
REBUILT AS *DUBUQUE*
1896

BUILT AS
PITTSBURGH
1879

RENAMED
J. S. DELUXE
1919

DISMANTLED
1945

TAKEN OUT OF SERVICE
1936

J. S. DELUXE

BUILT AS
QUINCY
1896

RENAMED
CAPITOL
1919

DISMANTLED AT ST. LOUIS 1939

BOUGHT BY STRECKFUS,
REBUILT AS *PRESIDENT*
1932

PRESIDENT

BUILT AS
CINCINNATI
1924

REMOVED
FROM SERVICE
1999

TOWED TO ST. LOUIS
AND DISMANTLED
1937

ADMIRAL

BUILT AS
ALBATROSS
1903

REBUILT AS
ADMIRAL
1940

DISMANTLED
AT ST. LOUIS
2011

Excursion Boat J. S. on Mississippi River.

AL FRESCO RAINBOW SHADOW BOX DANCING PALACE

STRECKFUS STEAMERS, INC., ST. LOUIS, MO.

EXCURSION STEAMER "CAPITOL" ON THE MISSISSIPPI.

STRECKFUS STEAMERS, SAINT LOUIS.

Photo by Underwood & Underwood, N.Y.

SAINT PAUL

Landing at Fort Madison, Iowa

President steamer, 1930s. The Streckfus packet steamer *Cincinnati* was refitted as the *President*, the first steel-hulled excursion boat in the Streckfus line. The *President* took its maiden voyage in July 1933 and remained based at the St. Louis riverfront until 1940, when it was sent to New Orleans.

Steamer _Capitol_, 1920s. Operating from 1919 to 1936 and based out of St. Louis for most of that time, the _Capitol_ was among the most famous excursion boats on the Mississippi River. The hull of the boat dated to the late 1800s, when it was first built as the packet steamer _Pittsburgh_. From the Collections of the St. Louis Mercantile Library at the University of Missouri–St. Louis.

1926:
THE BRIDGES OF THE MOTHER ROAD

Route 66 offered travelers unique sights all along its 2,400-mile length, but one of the biggest flowed beneath the Mother Road at St. Louis. The Mississippi River was among the most thrilling natural wonders between the road's ends in Chicago and Los Angeles. It became a symbol of St. Louis on postcards and souvenirs, and it was regularly listed as a must-see attraction. But when it came to crossing the Mississippi, tourists had options.

Over the road's official lifetime as a federal highway (1926–1985), five different St. Louis bridges would carry Route 66 across the Mississippi River. The best-known of St. Louis's Route 66 bridges, the Chain of Rocks Bridge, allowed travelers to bypass the city center while the other four–the McKinley, MacArthur, Veterans Memorial, and Poplar Street bridges–dropped travelers into the heart of downtown. The Eads Bridge, St. Louis's most famous Mississippi River crossing, was the only bridge that *didn't* carry Route 66 at some point.

Route 66's time as a major highway had lapsed by 1972, when it was bypassed by interstate highways 55 and 44 in Illinois and Missouri. It seemed the Main Street of America was destined to fade from memory, but travelers kept coming, seeking the highway's slow pace and connection to the landscape. Authors wrote books about the road, historic roadside stops were refurbished and reopened, and museums dedicated to Route 66's history sprang up. That interest has only grown, and today Route 66 attracts thousands of tourists from around the world. Once again, crossing the Mississippi River at St. Louis has become a quintessential part of "getting your kicks" on Route 66.

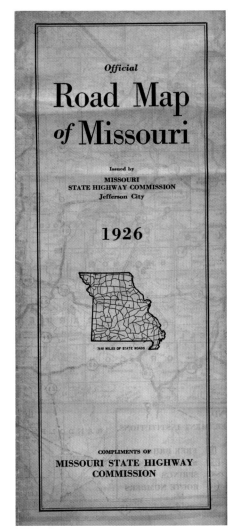

Official

Road Map
of Missouri

Issued by

MISSOURI
STATE HIGHWAY COMMISSION
Jefferson City

1926

7640 MILES OF STATE ROADS

COMPLIMENTS OF
MISSOURI STATE HIGHWAY
COMMISSION

Greetings From
ST. LOUIS
MISSOURI

17,651

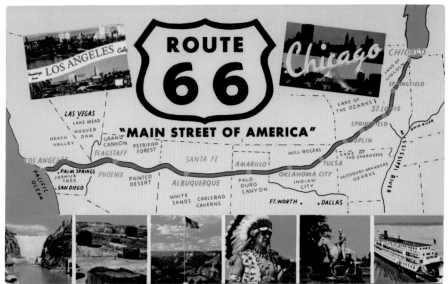

Postcards from Route 66. Route 66 was just one of nearly 100 highways that made up the 1926 United States Numbered Highway System, but it was the only one that went on to become a symbol of America on par with the Statue of Liberty, the Golden Gate Bridge, or the Gateway Arch. As the largest city between the road's ends in Chicago and Los Angeles, St. Louis was a major tourist destination, and the Mississippi River ranked among its most anticipated sights.

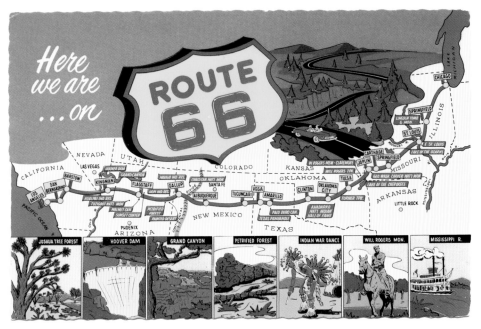

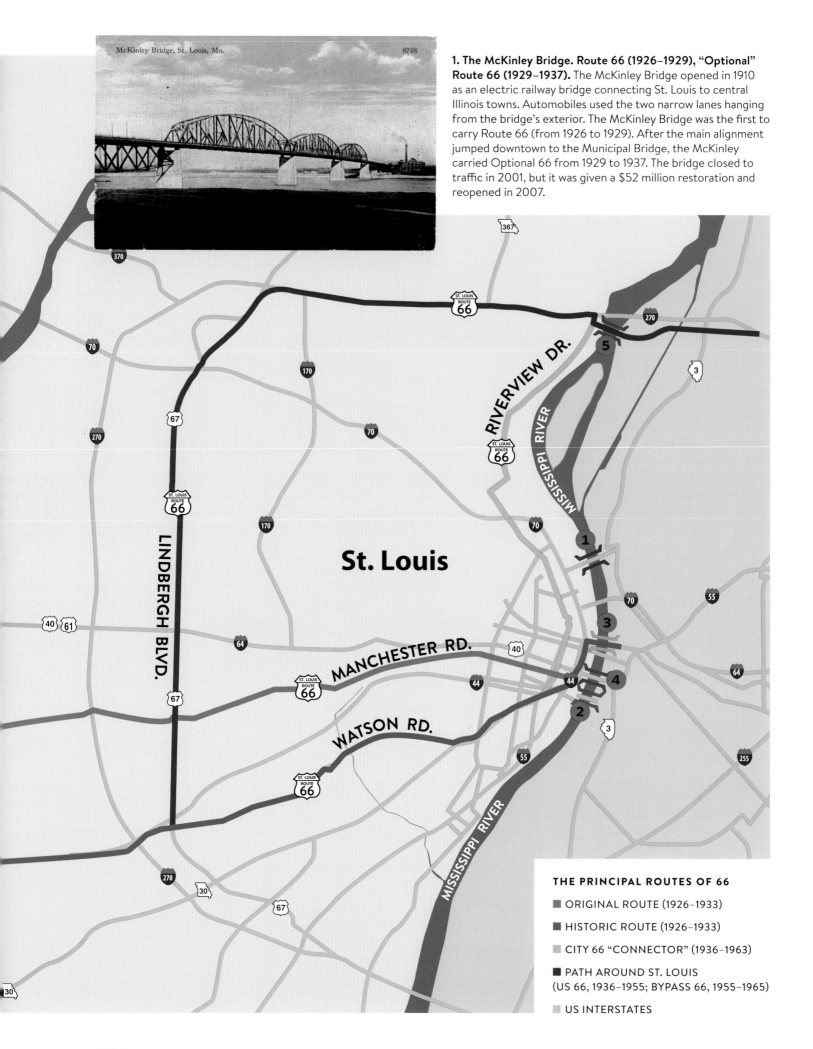

McKinley Bridge, St. Louis, Mo.   8748

1. The McKinley Bridge. Route 66 (1926–1929), "Optional" Route 66 (1929–1937). The McKinley Bridge opened in 1910 as an electric railway bridge connecting St. Louis to central Illinois towns. Automobiles used the two narrow lanes hanging from the bridge's exterior. The McKinley Bridge was the first to carry Route 66 (from 1926 to 1929). After the main alignment jumped downtown to the Municipal Bridge, the McKinley carried Optional 66 from 1929 to 1937. The bridge closed to traffic in 2001, but it was given a $52 million restoration and reopened in 2007.

RIVERVIEW DR.

MISSISSIPPI RIVER

St. Louis

LINDBERGH BLVD.

MANCHESTER RD.

WATSON RD.

MISSISSIPPI RIVER

THE PRINCIPAL ROUTES OF 66

■ ORIGINAL ROUTE (1926–1933)

■ HISTORIC ROUTE (1926–1933)

■ CITY 66 "CONNECTOR" (1936–1963)

■ PATH AROUND ST. LOUIS
(US 66, 1936–1955; BYPASS 66, 1955–1965)

■ US INTERSTATES

3. The Veterans Memorial/Martin Luther King Bridge. "City 66" (1955–1967). The Veterans Memorial Bridge opened in 1951 and began carrying City 66 across the Mississippi River in 1955. When the Poplar Street Bridge opened toll free in 1967, the Veterans Memorial Bridge lost its Route 66 designation and quickly fell into disrepair. It was renamed the Martin Luther King Jr. Bridge in 1972 and given a major renovation in the 1980s.

2. The Municipal/MacArthur Bridge. Route 66 (1929–1935), "City 66" (1936–1955). After years of public outcry for a toll-free alternative to the Eads Bridge, the Municipal Bridge opened in 1917. Renamed for five-star general Douglas MacArthur in 1942, the bridge carried Route 66 from 1929 to 1935, and then the City 66 stretch from 1936 to 1955. It was widely known as one of Route 66's most dangerous spots; newspapers called it "death's diving board."

4. The Poplar Street Bridge. Route 66 (1967–1977). The Poplar Street Bridge opened in 1967 and eventually carried three US interstates (four, counting Interstate 44, which links up a mile before the bridge). The Poplar Street Bridge carried Route 66 during its twilight years, from 1967 until the highway's signs finally came down in 1977.

CHAIN OF ROCKS BRIDGE
St. Louis, Mo.

Where U. S. 66, "Will Rogers Highway", crosses the Mississippi River

5. The Chain of Rocks Bridge, 1929. Route 66 (1936–1955), Route 66 Bypass (1956–1965). The bridge's famous 22-degree dogleg bend resulted from the Corps of Engineers' demands that the bridge face riverboat traffic head on. The Chain of Rocks Bridge closed in 1970, just after the toll-free Interstate 270 bridge opened upstream. In 1981 it served as a backdrop in the dystopian sci-fi film *Escape from New York*. Finally in 1999, Trailnet reopened the bridge as a bicycle and pedestrian crossing.

1934:
HOOVERVILLE

After the October 1929 stock market crash sent the United States spiraling into the Great Depression, many St. Louisans drifted toward the Mississippi's edge. For the penniless, their new home would be the city's Hooverville, built on a piece of disused riverside industrial land. Mockingly named after then-president Herbert Hoover, Hoovervilles were collections of shanties that popped up in the parks, vacant lots, and leftover spaces of every major American city during the Great Depression's lean years. Made up of more than 600 shanty houses that stretched for a mile south of the Municipal (now MacArthur) Bridge, St. Louis's Hooverville was among the nation's largest.

By 1934 unemployment in St. Louis had hit one out of four citizens; three out of four blacks were unemployed. The more than 3,000 Hooverites living along the river's edge tried to preserve a sense of normalcy by electing officials; holding religious services (Hooverville had four makeshift churches); and gathering for twice-a-week bean dinners at the Welcome Inn, Hooverville's improvised city hall. The Mill Creek sewer spilled into the Mississippi River right in the middle of Hooverville, dumping out thousands of gallons of city sewage. Hooverites jokingly called it Mill Creek Bay–Hooverville's "scenic wonder."

As in most cities, St. Louis's elected officials were apathetic to Hooverville's needs, viewing the settlement as only a bother and an eyesore. In 1936 the city received federal funding to acquire and clear riverfront land for the Jefferson National Expansion Memorial (JNEM), including Hooverville. Laborers from the Works Progress Administration–ironically, a Depression-era program created to provide jobs to the unemployed–tore down Hooverville that year. The area remained a haunt for squatters until the construction of the river floodwall in the late 1950s.

The St. Louis Hooverville. Hooverville stretched for more than a mile along the riverfront, just south of the Municipal (present-day MacArthur) Bridge. Today, the area is occupied by the St. Louis floodwall. *St. Louis Post-Dispatch.*

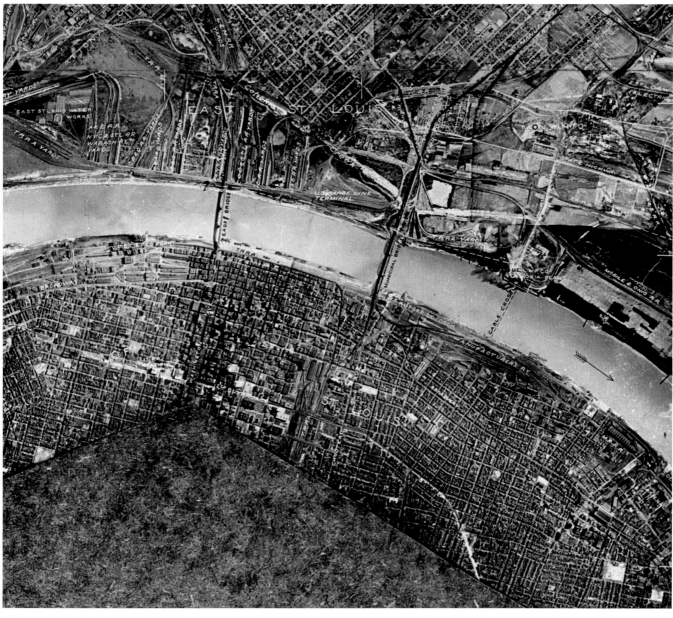

Hooverville children at the Welcome Inn Pool beneath the Municipal Bridge, 1930s. In 1930 charity volunteers started the Welcome Inn to provide food and clothing for Hooverville's residents, as well as a few comforts like this small pool. Its official location was listed as "Under the Free Bridge, Fourth and Chouteau."

Child with a fishing skiff on the river's edge, 1930s. An estimated 300 children lived in St. Louis's Hooverville in 1934. Library of Congress.

Hooverville, 1930s. Flooding was among the biggest threats for Hooverville, sandwiched as it was between the river and the Iron Mountain Railroad tracks. In May 1933 the river rose nearly 7 feet, swamping parts of Hooverville. The *St. Louis Post-Dispatch* reported that many Hooverites were tying down their shacks so that they wouldn't float away.

Works Progress Administration wheelbarrows on the riverfront, 1939. The city's evolving plans for a riverfront memorial brought Hooverville's demise. When federal funding for the Jefferson National Expansion Memorial was granted in 1936, WPA laborers began tearing down Hooverville.

Hooverville, 1933

"Hunger gnawed deeply in,

And some were extremely thin—

But they tightened their belts and with a will

Found the boards and nails to build Hooverville.

So if Old Man River keeps away his flood,

And grafting meddlers are driven out for good,

The folks down here will follow the beacon light,

Leading safely out of this economic plight."

–ANONYMOUS ST. LOUIS HOOVERVILLE POET, *A HISTORY OF THE EARLY ST. LOUIS BAPTIST COMMUNITY*, CA. 1930

1939: THE RIVERFRONT'S BLANK CANVAS

By the 1930s some city leaders were envisioning a new riverfront. In place of hundreds of dirty, outdated buildings, they pictured a massive memorial. It would honor Thomas Jefferson, Lewis and Clark, and St. Louis's role in America's western expansion. They pitched the memorial's benefits as twofold: It would focus national attention on St. Louis's rich history, and it would replace the city's grimy riverfront with a visionary symbol. Boosters lobbied hard and appealed to the federal government to make their vision a reality.

The memorial's footprint–from the riverbank to Third Street and from Washington Avenue to Poplar Street–outlined that of the original village of St. Louis laid out in 1764. Because so few structures from St. Louis's earliest years were left standing, the memorial planners saw no connection between the hundreds of existing riverfront buildings and the story they wanted to memorialize. They saw the structures as intruders, squatting on what one planner called "sacred soil." Their ideal St. Louis–a picturesque, riverside village of fur trappers and explorers–had been swallowed up long ago by the huge city St. Louis had become.

In December 1935 federal funding was approved, and the Jefferson National Expansion Memorial was born. Demolition of nearly forty blocks of the St. Louis riverfront began in 1939, and within two years only the Old Cathedral and a few other scattered structures remained. Among the hundreds of structures destroyed were buildings owned by colonial St. Louisans; buildings that survived the Great Fire of 1849; the first US federal building in St. Louis; and buildings of the fur-trading, banking, and manufacturing companies that powered St. Louis's nineteenth-century economy. The riverfront had been traded in, and soon a massive new memorial would rise in its place. But in 1941 no one knew what that memorial might look like.

Clearing the riverfront: before (mid-1930s; Gateway Arch National Park, National Park Service) and after (1941). Nearly 40 blocks totaling more than 5 million square feet of business space were destroyed for the Jefferson National Expansion Memorial. These demolished streets and structures made up most of St. Louis's original village from 1764 and were among the city's most historically significant.

EARLY TIMELINE OF THE JEFFERSON NATIONAL EXPANSION MEMORIAL

1932
With the Great Depression setting in, St. Louis's already aged riverfront faces even more challenges as property values tumble.

Luther Ely Smith, ca. 1940

St. Louis riverfront, 1932

1933
Looking at the St. Louis riverfront, civic leader Luther Ely Smith envisions a memorial to St. Louis's role in America's westward expansion. He discusses the idea with St. Louis mayor Bernard Dickmann, who is enthusiastic.

1934
The Jefferson National Expansion Memorial Association is promised $22.5 million in federal funds if St. Louis raises $7.5 million on its own. The funding bond passes a city vote, but evidence of extensive fraud is quickly uncovered.

December 21, 1935
President Franklin D. Roosevelt signs an executive order creating the Jefferson National Expansion Memorial. Its boundaries match St. Louis's original 1764 footprint, stretching from the river's edge to Third Street.

Bernard Dickmann, 1939

1936–1938
Condemnation of the riverfront takes place. The Citizens' Non-Partisan Committee finds more than 46,000 false registrations in the 1934 vote, but the Missouri Supreme Court declares the ballots "legally non-existent."

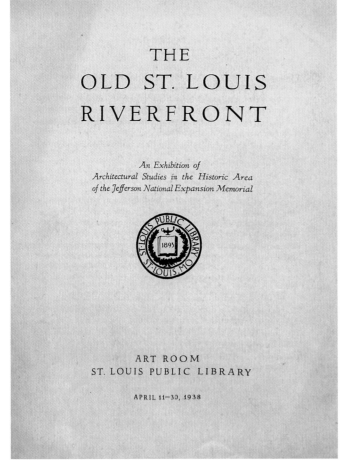

THE OLD ST. LOUIS RIVERFRONT

An Exhibition of Architectural Studies in the Historic Area of the Jefferson National Expansion Memorial

ART ROOM
ST. LOUIS PUBLIC LIBRARY

APRIL 11–30, 1938

"The Old St. Louis Riverfront" Exhibition, 1938. In 1938 the St. Louis Public Library hosted a National Park Service exhibition displaying drawings and photographs of the unique architecture found on St. Louis's doomed riverfront. The irony in the federal government documenting the area's importance while simultaneously funding its destruction gives a glimpse into the era's prevailing mindsets of what constituted "historic significance." The riverfront was viewed as a few important structures lost in an outdated landscape rather than an assembled environment built across more than a century. Gateway Arch National Park, National Park Service.

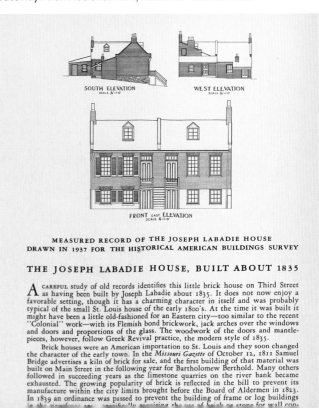

SOUTH ELEVATION

WEST ELEVATION

FRONT EAST ELEVATION

MEASURED RECORD OF THE JOSEPH LABADIE HOUSE DRAWN IN 1937 FOR THE HISTORICAL AMERICAN BUILDINGS SURVEY

THE JOSEPH LABADIE HOUSE, BUILT ABOUT 1835

A CAREFUL study of old records identifies this little brick house on Third Street as having been built by Joseph Labadie about 1835. It does not now enjoy a favorable setting, though it has a charming character in itself and was probably typical of the small St. Louis house of the early 1800's. At the time it was built it might have been a little old-fashioned for an Eastern city—too similar to the recent "Colonial" work—with its Flemish bond brickwork, jack arches over the windows and doors and proportions of the glass. The woodwork of the doors and mantlepieces, however, follow Greek Revival practice, the modern style of 1835.

Brick houses were an American importation to St. Louis and they soon changed the character of the early town. In the *Missouri Gazette* of October 12, 1811 Samuel Bridge advertises a kiln of brick for sale, and the first building of that material was built on Main Street in the following year for Bartholomew Berthold. Many others followed in succeeding years as the limestone quarries on the river bank became exhausted. The growing popularity of brick is reflected in the bill to prevent its manufacture within the city limits brought before the Board of Aldermen in 1823. In 1839 an ordinance was passed to prevent the building of frame or log buildings in the riverfront area, specifically requiring the use of brick or stone for wall con-

October 9, 1939
Demolition begins.
Standing on a flatbed
truck and brandishing a
crowbar, Mayor Dick-
mann pries the first brick
from a Market Street
warehouse. Over the next
year more than 5 million
square feet of building
space is demolished.

1941
The riverfront sits empty.
World War II delays the
memorial's architectural
competition until
1947. In the meantime,
St. Louis's riverfront
becomes a 4,500-car
parking lot.

SOME OF THE LOST BUILDINGS

Simmons Hardware Building
First Street and Washington Avenue (top left)
With more than 1.5 million square feet of warehouse space across six states, St. Louis–based Simmons Hardware's Keen Kutter product line knew no limits. The company's catalogs spanned 5,000 pages and included products ranging from tools and cutlery to iceboxes, tires, and lawnmowers. Simmons lost business with the onset of the Great Depression and went bankrupt in 1939.

The Post Office and Customs House
218 Third Street (top right)
Designed by George I. Barnett (who also designed the Old Courthouse) and completed in 1859, St. Louis's first federal building hosted the US government's western operations during the Civil War. The trials of the Whiskey Ring—a whiskey tax bribing scandal that eventually encompassed a dozen cities but began in St. Louis—brought the building to the nation's front pages in 1875.

The Old Rock House (left)
Unlike the rest of the riverfront, fur trader Manuel Lisa's 1818 Old Rock House was slated for saving. Workers carefully dismantled and numbered every stone, but by the time rebuilding began in 1941, many of the stones had gone missing. The structure sat half-finished and without its back wall. (The original rear wall was made out of the riverfront's natural limestone bluff.) The structure was once again disassembled in the late 1950s to accommodate the relocation of riverfront train tracks, and the rebuilding project was abandoned. In 2018 some of the stones were used to rebuild the front wall of the Old Rock House, which can be seen in the Museum of Westward Expansion beneath the Gateway Arch.

"These buildings should be saved because they will form a real monument to early life and work of St. Louisans. It might first appear that it is not worthwhile, but we can understand their great value when we realize they have no equivalent in other countries. After all, it is the duty of historians to save that which has no equivalent."

–ARCHITECT SIEGFRIED GIDEON, SPEAKING ON THE DESTRUCTION OF THE ST. LOUIS RIVERFRONT, 1939

The St. Louis riverfront before demolition, 1928

" For a mile and a half along the wide brown body of the Mississippi stretches a granite paved, almost deserted wharf. Bordering this was, until very recently, a close-packed belt of empty warehouses, commercial buildings, and factories . . . for many years, the dead belt along the old levee was a problem. A solution has been found however, in plans for a river-front plaza, commemorating Thomas Jefferson and national expansion . . . work has already begun on razing the useless structures. On either side of this cleared area, however, one can still observe the stratification of a century. . . ."

—MISSOURI: *THE WPA GUIDE TO THE "SHOW ME" STATE*, 1941

1940:
FIVE DECKS OF FUN

Few St. Louis experiences could match a river excursion on the SS *Admiral*, but the entertainment vessel that an entire generation of St. Louisans knew so well came from very different origins. The *Admiral* began life in 1907 in Vicksburg, Mississippi, as the *Albatross*, a single-deck railcar transfer boat. When Vicksburg's railroad bridge across the Mississippi River opened in 1930, the *Albatross* was suddenly jobless. Joe Streckfus, the owner of St. Louis's biggest excursion boat company, saw opportunity in the modest *Albatross*. He towed it to St. Louis and stripped it down to its steel hull. A boat like no one had ever seen before would soon take shape.

Setting out twice daily from 1940 to 1979, the *Admiral* felt more like an ocean liner than a boat for the river. Gone were the gingerbread railings and tumbling wooden paddle-wheels of the typical Mississippi steamboat. In their place were art deco brushed steel, white leather trimmings, and air conditioning. Its sleek interior design sprang from the mind of Mazie Krebs, a fashion and advertising illustrator for Famous-Barr. Thousands of first dates, birthday outings, Sunday cruises, and last dances took place on its five decks. In 1962 the *Admiral* became racially integrated, and African Americans were finally allowed to join in the festivities.

Interest in river excursions started to fade by the 1970s. In 1979 a hammer-wielding US Coast Guard inspector checking for weak spots knocked through the boat's hull, and excursions ground to a halt. The *Admiral* spent decades as a docked night club and then a casino, which finally closed in 2010. With no interested buyers stepping forward to keep the *Admiral* afloat, the boat's owners sold it for scrap. In July 2011 a small crowd gathered to watch the *Admiral*–its top deck already ripped away–make its final voyage from the St. Louis riverfront.

The SS *Admiral*, 1950. The *Admiral* could carry up to 4,400 passengers on each of its twice-daily excursions.

The *Albatross* on the St. Louis riverfront, late 1930s (above). The *Admiral* under construction, 1938 (below). Constructed in 1907 in Dubuque, Iowa, the *Albatross* had rails built into its deck so that train cars could be moved one at a time across the Mississippi River. Streckfus bought the *Albatross* in 1935, after it had sat unused for five years on the Vicksburg riverfront. The Streckfus Company kept the details of its new boat under wraps, refusing to reveal even its name during the construction process. A Streckfus family legend tells of Roy Streckfus hanging different letters over the boat's side each day just to tease the eager reporters watching from the levee.

The SS *Admiral* opening season brochure, 1940. The *Admiral* set off on its maiden voyage on June 12, 1940. At that time it was the world's largest river cruise ship and the first Mississippi riverboat to be fully air-conditioned.

Dining on the *Admiral*. The *Admiral's* dining tables were the setting of first dates, birthday parties, or weekend nights out for thousands of St. Louisans.

Top deck. On the top deck, known as the Lido, passengers sat beneath bright umbrellas, watching St. Louis pass by as a narrator pointed out sights on the shore.

STRECKFUS STEAMERS
PORT OF ST. LOUIS

Flashes from the Flagship
S·S·ADMIRAL

Dancing and romancing in the Blue Salon
Cocktails in the swank Club Admiral
Cool as Maytime in the Mountains . . . .
Gay "brellers" on the Lido Deck . . . .
Ahoy! You're in for a circus on the Main Deck

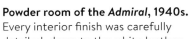

Powder room of the *Admiral*, 1940s.
Every interior finish was carefully detailed, down to the white leather-wrapped stools and music-note-shaped mirrors of the powder room.

Lowest deck. The lowest deck was likew a floating carnival, complete with popcorn stands, pinball machines, and skill-testers. From the Collections of the St. Louis Mercantile Library at the University of Missouri–St. Louis.

Ballroom. The second and third decks housed the Blue Salon Ballroom and its mezzanine, known as the Club Admiral. The excursion band played from the ship's starboard side to thousands of passengers dancing the days and nights away. From the Collections of the St. Louis Mercantile Library at the University of Missouri–St. Louis.

The *Admiral* leaving for an excursion, 1956

"**Thousands of curious motorists cruised back and forth on the levee several hours before leaving time. . . . Heading downstream to the bluffs, every house flashed welcoming light signals to the new boat . . .**"

—THE WATERWAYS JOURNAL, REPORTING ON THE *ADMIRAL'S* MAIDEN VOYAGE, 1940

1947:
ST. LOUIS'S FUTURE FRONT DOOR

It's almost impossible to imagine anything but the Arch standing on the St. Louis riverfront today, but in May 1947, it was just one of 172 possibilities for the riverfront's future. The design of the Jefferson National Expansion Memorial (JNEM)—already a decade in the making—was to be decided by an architectural competition, and architects from around the world sent in their best ideas. Some of the proposals were graceful, others lackluster, and still others bizarre. Among the designs were elevated expressways, aquariums, planetariums, public housing, obelisks, and even a hot air balloon port.

Before submitting his entry (No. 144), a young architect from Michigan named Eero Saarinen had experimented with dozens of arch concepts. He had sketched out a semi-circular arch, an arch standing in the river, and even an arch that jumped over the river with one leg in Missouri and one in Illinois. Hundreds of drawings later he finally landed on a catenary curve, the shape a rope naturally makes when hung by its two ends. Friends stopping by Saarinen's studio all made the same remark: It looks like a gateway.

Eero Saarinen's Gateway Arch thrilled the architectural competition's seven-member jury. On February 18, 1948, the Gateway Arch was unanimously chosen as the winner in the competition's second round. The Gateway Arch's clean-lined silhouette seemed to announce a new future for St. Louis. It celebrated abstraction, technology, and modernity, and it stood in raw contrast to the dense and aged industrial city surrounding it. When ground broke more than a decade later in June 1959, everyone was eager to watch this stunning new monument rise on the riverfront.

Eero Saarinen with Gateway Arch model, 1960 (above). Billboard advertising the coming Jefferson National Expansion Memorial, 1956 (below). By winning the JNEM competition, Eero Saarinen stepped out from the shadow of his more famous father, architect Eliel Saarinen, who had a competition entry of his own. Sadly, Eero Saarinen never saw his masterpiece completed. Suffering from a brain tumor, he died on September 1, 1961. Library of Congress.

Eero Saarinen, 1940s.

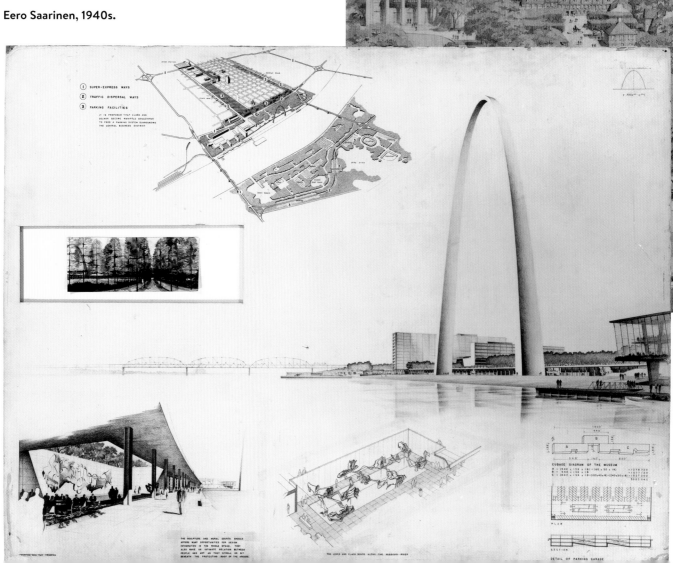

Eero Saarinen's entry, No. 144: The first (left) and second (above) rounds. Saarinen's first-round drawings show that he initially planned for many buildings and sculptural pieces surrounding the Arch, including a teahouse, two restaurants, a "frontier village," a historic arcade, and a campfire theater. The Arch itself would have four sides and be made of concrete. In the competition's second round, Saarinen streamlined the arch's outline to three sides and unveiled plans for its glistening stainless-steel skin. On February 18, 1948, the jury unanimously chose it as the winner. Gateway Arch National Park, National Park Service.

As great designs often do, the Gateway Arch drew varied responses at its public debut. A *New York Times* article called it "fitting, beautiful and impressive," while a St. Louisan quoted in the *Globe-Democrat* referred to it as a "stainless steel hitching post." The most aggressive criticism came from architect Gilmore Clarke, who thought it looked like a threatening symbol that might have been created by an authoritarian regime.

OTHER JEFFERSON NATIONAL EXPANSION MEMORIAL ENTRIES

Some of the era's most prominent architects entered the Jefferson National Expansion Memorial competition, including Louis Kahn; Walter Gropius; Edward Durell Stone; Charles Eames; and the firm Skidmore, Owings & Merrill. Minoru Yamasaki, who later designed St. Louis's Lambert Airport terminal and the infamous Pruitt-Igoe public housing complex, was dismissed in the competition's first round. Gateway Arch National Park, National Park Service.

Second Place: Phillips, Eng & Associates

Third Place: Breger, Hornbostel, Lewis & Associates

Harris Armstrong's first-round entry. All seven competition jurors chose to advance the first-round design of St. Louis architect Harris Armstrong. Its sweeping design drastically reshaped the levee's edge, which broke the rules that had been laid out in the competition guidelines. Forced to rework his bold design, Armstrong's second-round entry—featuring a hulking, rectangular monument in the center of the landscape—was dismissed by the jury.

1965:
BUILDING THE GATEWAY ARCH

On February 21, 1961, an excavator plunged into the soft riverfront dirt where the Gateway Arch's south leg would soon rise. With more than 60 feet to dig through to reach bedrock, the small load of dirt it extracted would be the first of thousands. For the next four years and eight months, St. Louisans would watch the Gateway Arch's two legs come closer to joining.

The Arch's construction required precision from the start. If measurements were off by even a fraction of an inch at the base of the legs, the top could have been disastrously mismatched. There were many challenges. Construction engineers relied on basic surveying equipment to calculate the Arch's difficult angles, and obtaining those measurements was complicated by St. Louis's blistering summer heat, which distorted and expanded the stainless steel. The two leg teams–nicknamed Yankee on the north and Rebel on the south–developed a healthy rivalry as they pushed toward the inevitable meeting.

City leaders hoped the Gateway Arch would link up in time for St. Louis's bicentennial in 1964, but building such an unprecedented structure was fraught with setbacks and delays. The completion date was finally set for the morning of October 28, 1965. Thousands of people gathered on the riverfront, and thousands more watched from living room television screens. Squinting up at the tiny gap separating the two massive legs, the public was about to witness either a climactic joining or a catastrophic failure.

The last piece, known as One North, was more than 8 feet wide, and the opening between the legs was fewer than 3 feet. As St. Louis Fire Department hoses kept the legs' bases cool under the creeping morning sun, a hydraulic jack thrust against the structure's legs, slowly widening the gap. Over thirteen tense minutes, the final piece was carefully positioned into the narrow opening. Workers released the hydraulic jack, and for the first time, the Arch's two legs rested against each other. After thirty-two years in the making, St. Louis could finally celebrate its monument on the Mississippi River.

The Gateway Arch's anatomy, 1965.
The Gateway Arch's 142 triangular stainless-steel segments narrowed as they rose, ranging from 54 feet wide at the base down to just 17 feet wide at the top. When work reached a height of 533 feet, a truss was added to support the precariously tall legs.

Working on the Gateway Arch, 1963.
Wind speeds near the top of the Arch often reached 60 miles an hour, and workers risked their lives on a daily basis. Although an actuarial firm predicted that thirteen workers would be killed during the Gateway Arch's construction, there were no deaths.

Fourth of July on the Archgrounds, 1964. City leaders tried desperately to get the Arch completed in time for St. Louis's bicentennial in 1964, but building such an unprecedented structure came with many delays. That Fourth of July, thousands of St. Louisans gathered around the half-finished Arch legs to watch fireworks over the river.

CORE protests, July 1964. St. Louis civil rights activists publicly protested that almost no African Americans had been hired on the Arch's construction teams. On July 14, 1964, Committee of Racial Equality activists Percy Green and Richard Daly climbed 125 feet up the Arch's north leg, refusing to come down for over four hours. The incident was one of several that spurred the US Department of Justice to file the first "pattern or practice" case under Title VII of the Civil Rights Act of 1964, claiming the AFL-CIO had a pattern of discriminatory hiring.

October 28, 1965. The Gateway Arch's final piece was inserted on October 28, 1965. Architect Eero Saarinen had since died, but his widow Aline Saarinen watched from the crowd. She told a newspaper reporter that the Arch was "the climax of my husband's career— the thing that meant the most to him." *St. Louis Post-Dispatch.*

1969:
THE MISSISSIPPI RIVER FESTIVAL

Every summer from 1969 to 1980, one of St. Louis's best places for live music appeared in a natural clearing along the river bluffs near Edwardsville, Illinois. This clearing was quiet and empty the rest of the year, but when summer nights settled in, a makeshift musical city formed around a massive white circus tent. Over those eleven summers, the Mississippi River Festival brought together more than 350 musical acts that played before some 1.5 million attendees from around the region.

The festival began when Southern Illinois University Edwardsville invited the St. Louis Symphony Orchestra to hold an outdoor summer season on its campus. To appeal to a wider audience, more performers were added on nights in between the symphony's shows. Acts covered a broad musical range, from the National Dance Troupe of Zambia to shock–rocker Alice Cooper.

Aside from the high quality and variety of musicians, the festival drew much of its magic from the Mississippi River bottoms. There were few permanent structures, creating an intimate and secluded environment. The stage sat at the bottom of a natural amphitheater in the sloping river bluff, surrounded by a dense ring of trees. A massive white circus tent sheltered nearly 2,000 seats, and beyond that a lawn had blanket space for thousands more.

For local young adults the drive across the Mississippi River was like an at–home road trip. Meeting friends in the parking lot, finding space on the lawn, and watching popular musicians beneath the stars became an annual tradition that signaled summer's arrival in St. Louis. Though it was a beloved and well–attended event, the Mississippi River Festival struggled under mounting financial difficulties as the 1970s passed. Promoters experimented with outside management from 1978 to 1980, but on August 23, 1980, a concert by ZZ Top marked the Mississippi River Festival's final show.

The Mississippi River Festival tent. The main performance tent at the Mississippi River Festival housed over 350 musical acts across the festival's eleven years of operation, from 1969 to 1980.

Mississippi River Festival schedule, 1977. By 1977 the festival was so popular that organizers were struggling to control the enormous crowds that often showed up.

Lawn crowd gathered to see the Who, 1971. The Festival's popular rock acts attracted enormous crowds. The Who's 1971 appearance brought in over 31,000 attendees, and concerts by Emerson, Lake & Palmer; Seals & Crofts; Chicago; Dave Mason; the Beach Boys; Yes; the Marshall Tucker Band; and the Eagles would all attract more than 20,000 attendees.

1974:
SAVING WHAT REMAINED

While the city was still celebrating its new riverfront national park in the early 1970s, some St. Louisans were noticing just how much of St. Louis's river heritage had been lost in the process. The Gateway Arch razed St. Louis's most historic area, and more downtown buildings were succumbing to "urban renewal" with each passing year. The modern historic preservation movement was gaining steam, and it soon became clear just how vulnerable the city's riverfront heritage was.

Laclede's Landing, as the levee's remaining original blocks were nicknamed, had survived by chance. The small area was sandwiched between the Eads and the Veterans (now Martin Luther King Jr.) bridges, which kept it from being absorbed into the Jefferson National Expansion Memorial's footprint and from being demolished for parking lots and industrial yards, like the historic riverfront farther north had been. Though the Landing's buildings still stood, the area was so dilapidated by the early 1970s that many assumed it was beyond saving.

In 1974 the Laclede's Landing Redevelopment Corporation (LLRC) was created to coordinate revitalization efforts in the district. Together, the LLRC and building owners worked tirelessly, rehabbing more than a dozen historic structures that amounted to nearly 1 million square feet of space. Life gradually filtered into Laclede's Landing, but with a split personality: tourists by day and revelers by night. Laclede's Landing never quite became the "neighborhood" that planners had initially hoped for, but its revival continues, and its future looks bright. The two-block-long parking garage that cut off Laclede's Landing from the Arch grounds was removed in 2016, and new offices and residential units are continually being built.

Though it largely goes unnoticed by those heading into one of the Landing's night-clubs or restaurants, the district offers something quite valuable to St. Louisans and their guests. It's all that remains of St. Louis's original streets, and it's among the last places where authentic buildings tell St. Louis's origin story: that of a trading center bound to the side of the Mississippi River.

Laclede's Landing, 1990s. The three square blocks of Laclede's Landing are essentially all that's left of the original, three-block-wide street grid of St. Louis, laid out by Pierre Laclède and Auguste Chouteau in 1764. In the late 1970s, St. Louis entrepreneurs began restoring and opening businesses in its remaining historic structures. Library of Congress.

Raeder Place Building, 727 N. First Street, 2018. Built in 1873 as a tobacco company headquarters, Raeder Place is St. Louis's finest surviving cast-iron-front building. Cast-iron façades allowed for much larger windows and increased the brightness of the building's floors. The riverfront contained dozens (if not hundreds) of similar buildings, all lost during the creation of the Jefferson National Expansion Memorial.

Profile St. Louis article on Laclede's Landing restoration, 1977.

The Greeley Building during renovation in the late 1970s, Second and Morgan streets. In 1976, Laclede's Landing became St. Louis's first historic commercial area listed on the National Register of Historic Places. As buildings were brought back to life, the Landing turned into a popular weekend destination of music venues, bars, and restaurants.

Mississippi Nights, 914 N. First Street, demolished in 2007. From its opening in 1979, Mississippi Nights was one of the Landing's most beloved spaces. Starting as a country & western bar, it quickly evolved into one of St. Louis's premiere music venues. In 2007, Mississippi Nights was forced to close and was demolished for the Lumière Place Casino & Hotel. The closing was universally mourned by St. Louis artists, many of whom had played its famed stage.

700 block of N. First Street, 1976. Even after the push to preserve the Landing began, buildings were still in danger of being lost. Only the closest three buildings in this image still stand as of 2019. The hulking former headquarters of the Switzer Candy Company (seen in the distance) suffered a collapse during severe weather in the summer of 2006.

1981:
A CELEBRATION FOR ALL ST. LOUISANS

Over the Fourth of July weekend in 1981, the inaugural VP Fair transformed the Jefferson National Expansion Memorial into one of the country's largest birthday parties. Created by the Veiled Prophet Organization–a century-old social society established by St. Louis's elite–the Independence Day celebration was touted as an event that would turn the nation's focus to the St. Louis riverfront. But the VP Fair raised questions about how the national park on the city's riverfront should be treated and how long-standing class and racial divisions kept the city from celebrating as one.

Each summer's VP Fair attracted millions of people, but the event took a huge toll on the Arch grounds. Manicured lawns were trampled into mud, the Gateway Arch's reflecting pools became swimming pools, and upward of 60 tons of garbage littered the park at the end of each year's festivities. As the 1980s went on, the National Park Service worked with fair organizers to provide better trash disposal; beef up security; and push the trucks, tents, and balloons to the streets at the Arch grounds' edges. Still, the VP Fair faced a much deeper issue.

In 1987, Veiled Prophet officials pressured police into closing the Eads Bridge during the fair, calling it a "safety measure" to prevent "east side street gangs" from crossing over from majority-black East St. Louis. The incident exposed the divide between the fair's upper-class organizers and minority communities. The St. Louis riverfront should have been everyone's space, but only some felt welcome to join the city's biggest party.

In 1995 the VP Fair was reborn as Fair St. Louis, and ever since it has focused on creating a spirited, inclusive event "produced by St. Louisans, for St. Louisans and their guests from all over the world." Fair St. Louis has become an integral part of the city's Fourth of July celebrations, and aside from 2014 to 2017 when it was held in Forest Park during the Arch grounds' extensive renovation, Fair St. Louis continues to unite St. Louisans on the riverfront.

Hot air balloon at the 1981 Veiled Prophet Fair. The annual VP Fair would bring hundreds of thousands of St. Louisans to the Arch grounds, but it would also raise concerns. During the 1982 Fair, the Arch grounds' facility manager, Bob Kelly, reported that the lights shook in the Gateway Arch's underground museum as thousands of fairgoers crowded the lawn above. From the Collections of the St. Louis Mercantile Library at the University of Missouri–St. Louis.

The Veiled Prophet Fair, 1981. St. Louis's scorching summer temperatures sent fairgoers seeking relief. For some it came by way of a St. Louis Fire Department truck, for others it came by the Gateway Arch's reflecting pools—to the chagrin of the National Park Service staff. From the Collections of the St. Louis Mercantile Library at the University of Missouri–St. Louis.

1984 Veiled Prophet Parade tokens (left). Crowds beneath the Arch, 1984 Veiled Prophet Fair (above and below). The 1984 VP Fair was the first of three to be nationally televised. It attracted nearly 4 million attendees. From the Collections of the St. Louis Mercantile Library at the University of Missouri–St. Louis.

1993:
THE GREAT FLOOD

Even though humans have now contained the Mississippi River with thousands of miles of levees and floodwalls, it can still break loose, devastating the cities, towns, and farms that line its edges. In the summer of 1993 the river flooded with an intensity that no living St. Louisan had ever seen—or would soon forget.

By June 1993 heavy and persistent rain had bombarded the upper Midwest for months. Some locations had experienced more than six times their normal amount of rainfall. Meteorologists warned that record-breaking floods were on the horizon, and by early July hundreds of gauges on the Mississippi and Missouri rivers read above flood stage. At St. Louis the existing record height—43.23 feet, set in 1973—was passed on July 12, and the water's rise showed no signs of slowing.

Of the eighty-nine levees in the Corps of Engineers' St. Louis District, fifty-one would fall to the river's incredible power. Levees broke at Alton, St. Charles, and Chesterfield, submerging the land beneath 10 feet of floodwater or more and causing thousands to evacuate. In the Metro East, the town of Valmeyer, Illinois, was swept away entirely. The River Des Peres, a small tributary of the Mississippi in south St. Louis, overflowed into Carondelet and Lemay, flooding homes that many families had lived in for decades. Volunteers tirelessly piled sandbags in hundreds of small riverside communities. On August 1, 1993, the river crested in St. Louis at 49.58 feet, more than 19 feet above flood stage and more than 6 feet higher than the previous record.

River levels finally began to drop in mid-August. Evacuees ventured back into their ruined homes and businesses, surveying the swaths of gray mud, rotting carpets, and molding walls. In the countryside the receding water revealed acres of brown, decomposing crops and dead trees. The flooding at St. Louis finally came to an end on September 15, 1993, after seventy-nine consecutive days above flood stage. The Great Flood of 1993 resulted in an estimated $15 to $20 billion in damages across nine states. As of 2019, it ranks among the twenty costliest natural disasters in US history.

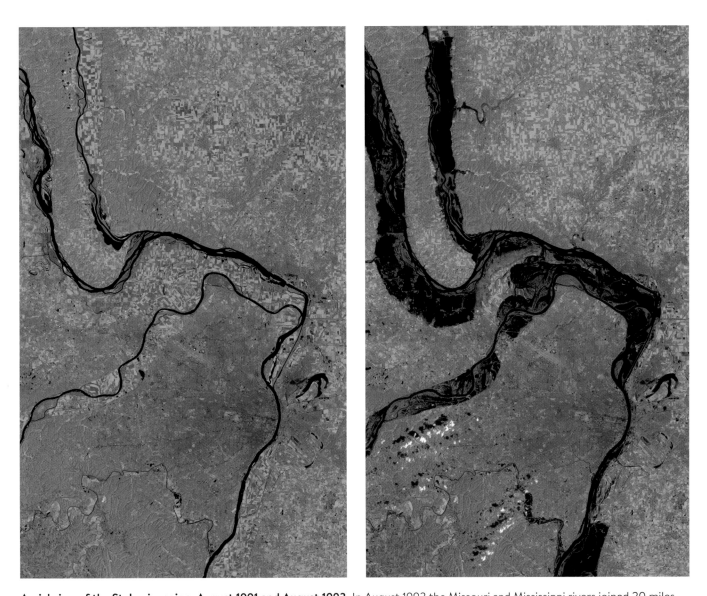

Aerial view of the St. Louis region, August 1991 and August 1993. In August 1993 the Missouri and Mississippi rivers joined 20 miles upstream from their normal confluence. The rivers destroyed levees and spilled into nearby low-lying farmland. Some submerged areas were nearly 5 miles wide. NASA Images.

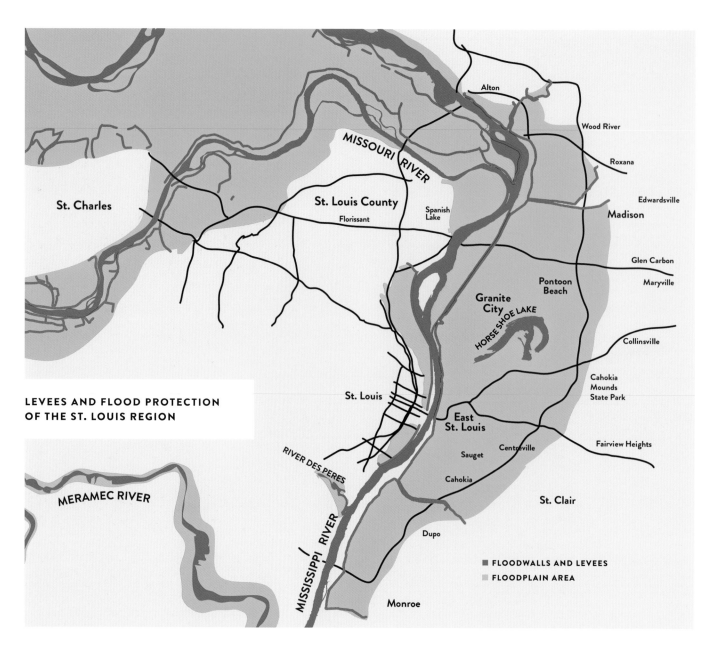

LEVEES AND FLOOD PROTECTION
OF THE ST. LOUIS REGION

St. Charles

MISSOURI RIVER

St. Louis County
Florissant

Spanish
Lake

Alton

Wood River

Roxana

Edwardsville

Madison

Glen Carbon

Maryville

Pontoon
Beach

Granite
City

HORSE SHOE LAKE

Collinsville

Cahokia
Mounds
State Park

St. Louis

East
St. Louis

Fairview Heights

Sauget

Centreville

Cahokia

St. Clair

RIVER DES PERES

MERAMEC RIVER

Dupo

MISSISSIPPI RIVER

Monroe

■ FLOODWALLS AND LEVEES
■ FLOODPLAIN AREA

The St. Louis floodwall. The riverfront system of floodwalls and earthen embankments began in 1959, stretching from Maline Creek 11 miles south to the natural river bluffs near Chippewa Street. During the 1993 flood, this wall—designed for a river height of 52 feet—came within 3 feet of breach.

Canned water and sandbag from the 1993 flood. Donations to help flood victims poured in from around the country. Anheuser-Busch switched some of its beer lines to fill six-packs of drinking water to aid those displaced by the flooding.

St. Louis

IMPACT OF THE GREAT FLOOD OF 1993

April to October 1993

146 days above flood stage at St. Louis

Crested at **46.9 feet** at St. Louis on August 1, 1993

31,000 square miles flooded across 9 states

Federal disaster area stretched across **534 counties**

62 percent of Missouri declared a federal disaster area

1,000+ levees toppled or breached

10,000+ homes destroyed

32 official dead

Over 168,000 people registered for federal aid

$15–$20 billion in damages

Barge traffic shut down on the Mississippi and Missouri rivers

Bridges out for **200 miles**, from Davenport, Iowa, to St. Louis

10 commercial airports flooded

All railroad traffic halted throughout the Midwest

(IMAGES: FEMA NEWS)

Near St. Louis

Chesterfield

Near Ste. Genevieve

River Des Peres

St. Charles

OTHER BIG FLOODS

The 1844 flood and 1993 flood square off as St. Louis's "biggest"—the 1844 flood carried 21 percent more water, but the 1993 flood crested more than 8 feet higher. As a century worth of human-made controls restricted the river and cut off its natural floodplains, the water had nowhere to go but up.

The Great Flood of 1844

The Mississippi River swelled to nearly 12 miles wide during the 1844 flood. Crowds gathered on rooftops in St. Louis to watch the houses and trees of Illinoistown (now East St. Louis) being carried away. Steamboats that were still running on the river reported crashing into chimneys and mill machinery hidden below the water's surface.

The Flood of 1858, St. Louis Levee

With floodwaters creeping up into the storefronts along the St. Louis levee, steamboat workers built makeshift, spare-lumber bridges to access the city. Farther south of St. Louis, the city of Cairo, Illinois, was completely deluged.

The Flood of 1903, along North Broadway

The summer flood of 1903—which rose a foot a day in early June—displaced more than 25,000 people in St. Louis, but the worst of the flooding happened on the Illinois side. This flood event inspired East St. Louis to construct its first levees, which held strong against the Great Flood of 1993.

The Flood of 1973, River Des Peres at Morganford Road

The 1973 flood produced a river crest of 43.23 feet at St. Louis, the highest ever recorded at the time. Through a process called the backwater effect, floodwater pushed up the River Des Peres, swamping low-lying neighborhoods nearby. Among the worst of the 1973 flood's levee failures happened just south of St. Louis, where 6 million acres of Missouri land were flooded.

2008:
THE WELCOME MAT

On October 18, 2008, as many as 100,000 St. Louisans crowded beneath the Gateway Arch to listen to Barack Obama talk about his vision for America. He was touring the nation on his first presidential campaign, and at that point, the St. Louis crowd was the largest domestic audience he had ever received. Just seventeen days later he was elected the first black president of the United States. Though Barack Obama made quite an impression that day, he's far from the only person who has greeted St. Louis from the river's edge.

The Mississippi River has been the backdrop to countless stump speeches, rallying cries, and important announcements going back more than 200 years. On March 9, 1803, St. Louisans watched with mixed emotions as Captain Amos Stoddard arrived to complete the transfer of the Louisiana Territory to the United States, changing St. Louisans' nationality in the process. Known as the Swedish Nightingale, world-famous opera singer Jenny Lind visited St. Louis in 1851. Despite her steamboat arriving on a cold, damp March morning, thousands of people were waiting on the levee to greet her.

While fewer places in St. Louis have been more drastically changed by time, one thing remains the same: If someone wants his or her voice to be heard in a powerful way, the St. Louis riverfront is a great place to do it.

Barack Obama's presidential rally, 2008. Barack Obama's speech was preceded by greetings from local figures, including athlete Jackie Joyner-Kersee, performer Nikko Smith, St. Louis mayor Francis Slay, Missouri attorney general Jay Nixon, US senator Claire McCaskill, and local St. Louis sixth-grade teacher Kennan Morris. The crowd that gathered beneath the Arch was the largest US audience Obama had received at that time. *St. Louis Post-Dispatch*.

OTHER FAMOUS VISITORS TO THE ST. LOUIS RIVERFRONT

1778: George Rogers Clark

As the American Revolutionary War crept closer to St. Louis, Colonel George Rogers Clark helped secure the village's future by capturing the British-held outposts of Kaskaskia and Cahokia. To show his gratitude, Lieutenant Governor Don Fernando de Leyba invited Clark across the river as a distinguished guest of St. Louis. When Clark arrived in late July, there was a riverfront salute, followed by a dinner and dance with prominent St. Louis citizens. Clark was greeted warmly, and some in attendance even collected money to fund Clark's next attack on British-held territory.

1825: Marquis de Lafayette

The Marquis de Lafayette had helped the United States defeat Great Britain during the American Revolutionary War, and in 1824, US president James Monroe invited him on a thirteen-month "grand tour" of the country. On April 29, 1825, St. Louisans gathered on the riverfront, cheering as his steamboat *Natchez* came into view. Lafayette told the crowd he was overjoyed to see fellow "descendants of France" and "American contemporaries" living together. Lafayette stayed just one night, but the city hosted a lavish ball in his honor at the Mansion House Hotel.

1866: Andrew Johnson

On September 8, 1866, a 36-steamboat convoy carrying President Andrew Johnson arrived on the St. Louis riverfront. The visit was part of his multi-city "Swing Around the Circle" campaign—a disastrous goodwill tour that would lead to his downfall. As Johnson began his speech on the St. Louis levee, a loud heckler got the best of him and he launched into a fiery tirade. His speech that day in St. Louis, coupled with a similar outburst in Cleveland a few days earlier, would be used by his congressional opponents as evidence in their calls for his impeachment. Library of Congress.

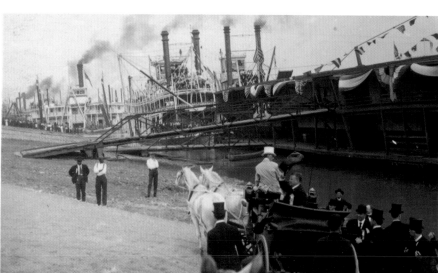

1907: Theodore Roosevelt

In 1907, President Theodore Roosevelt traveled down the Mississippi River to promote transportation investment in the nation's waterways. In St. Louis, one newspaper reported that the screams from the gathered crowd rivaled "the thundering intonations of bursting bombs." Library of Congress.

1909: William Howard Taft

In 1909 the Lakes-to-Gulf Deep Waterway Association lobbied Congress to create a continuous navigation channel on the Lower Mississippi River. To build support they arranged for a massive flotilla to parade downriver from St. Louis to New Orleans, carrying governors, state senators, more than 100 congressmen, and President William Howard Taft. On the evening of October 25, spectators crowded the St. Louis riverfront as Taft boarded the *Oleander*, the head steamer of the sixteen-boat flotilla. The flotilla spent the next five days visiting towns along the Lower Mississippi. From the Collections of the St. Louis Mercantile Library at the University of Missouri–St. Louis.

1979: Jimmy Carter

In August 1979, President Jimmy Carter and First Lady Rosalynn Carter took a goodwill trip on the steamer *Delta Queen*, riding down the Mississippi River from St. Paul, Minnesota, to St. Louis. Arriving in St. Louis on August 24, Carter gave a speech to the large crowd gathered on the Arch grounds. He called the Gateway Arch "tremendous," and he introduced a landmark moment when Bill Bund of Alton, Illinois, became the 10 millionth person to travel to its top.

2015:
A NEW VISION FOR THE GATEWAY ARCH

As the Gateway Arch neared its fiftieth anniversary, concerns about the riverfront were piling up. The grounds felt cut off from the rest of St. Louis, the infrastructure was aging, and some of the landscaping made moving around the site difficult. For people who used wheelchairs, it was sometimes impossible. The Gateway Arch had been losing visitors year after year, and it needed something new to bring its beauty and elegance back to life.

In 2010 a group of regional partners originally known as CityArchRiver (now the Gateway Arch Foundation) opened a competition to redesign the St. Louis riverfront. The guidelines called for remodeled Arch grounds that were easier to access, provided more to explore, and were better connected to downtown St. Louis. Just like the 1947 competition that gave rise to the Gateway Arch, this competition would bring in more than 100 architectural visions from around the world. A successful proposal would not only solve the park's functional issues but would also respect and enhance one of the world's most iconic pieces of modernist architecture.

The winning submission by Michael Van Valkenburgh Associates focused on "framing a modern masterpiece" with intimate spaces amid a wider variety of natural settings. Completed in 2018, the renovations include miles of new pedestrian paths, nearly 1,000 new trees, a children's garden, a skating rink, and a farmers' market. One of the biggest changes was a block-wide lawn extending over Interstate 70 and connecting the Arch grounds to the Old Courthouse and downtown St. Louis for the first time.

While the new Gateway Arch National Park provides a better experience for all visitors, it perhaps offers the most to St. Louisans. For them, the Gateway Arch is more than a national monument or a tourist destination. It is their Arch—the object that represents home—and the new grounds are an invitation for them to revisit the place where their city began.

The new Arch grounds, 2018. After five years of work, the new Arch grounds and Museum of Westward Expansion reopened in July 2018. The grounds offer many more possibilities for daily use, including miles of new bike and walking paths, as well as spaces for a children's garden, skating rink, and farmers' market.

The grounds of the Gateway Arch, 1969 (left) and 2018 (right). The Arch grounds underwent a $380 million renovation that included projects as diverse as planting thousands of new trees, removing a 150,000-square-foot parking garage, building a green bridge over Interstate 44, and raising the riverfront 30 inches. Beneath the Arch, the remodeled Museum of Westward Expansion is focused on six themes: colonial St. Louis, Jefferson's vision for America, the St. Louis riverfront, Manifest Destiny, new frontiers, and the design and construction of the Gateway Arch. *St. Louis Post-Dispatch*.

SELECTED BIBLIOGRAPHY

Blum, Rafaela Ann Amantea. *The Steamer* Admiral *and Streckfus Steamers: A Personal View*. St. Louis: St. Louis Mercantile Library, 2012.

Brown, John K. *Limbs on the Levee: Steamboat Explosions and the Origins of Federal Public Welfare Regulation: 1817–1852*. Middlebourne, WV: International Steamboat Society, 1989.

Campbell, Tracy. *The Gateway Arch: A Biography*. New Haven, CT: Yale University Press, 2013.

Civic Improvement League of St. Louis. *City Plan for St. Louis: Reports of Several Committees Appointed by the Executive Board of the Civic League to Draft a City Plan*. St. Louis: Civic League, 1907.

———. *Disposal of Municipal Waste: Report of the Public Sanitation Committee*. St. Louis: Civic League, 1906.
.
Daily Missouri Republican. Multiple articles.

Fausz, Frederick. *Historic St. Louis: 250 Years Exploring New Frontiers*. St. Louis: University of Missouri–St. Louis, 2014.

Hafen, LeRoy. *The Mountain Men and the Fur Trade of the Far West*. Glendale, CA: Arthur H. Clark Company, 1968.

Havighurst, Walter. *Voices on the River: The Story of the Mississippi Waterways*. New York: Macmillan Company, 1964.

History of Madison County, Illinois. Edwardsville, IL: W. R. Brink & Co., 1882.

Hodes, Frederick A. *Beyond the Frontier: A History of St. Louis to 1821*. Tucson, AZ: Patrice Press, 2004.

———. *Rising on the River: St. Louis 1822 to 1850, Explosive Growth from Town to City*. Tooele, UT: Patrice Press, 2009.

Hurley, Andrew, ed. *Common Fields: An Environmental History of St. Louis*. St. Louis: Missouri Historical Society Press, 1997.

Jack, Bryan M. *The St. Louis African American Community and the Exodusters*. Columbia: University of Missouri Press, 2007.

Kargau, Ernst D. *The German Element in St. Louis*. St. Louis: August Wiebusch & Son Printing Co., 1893.

Kilgo, Dolores. *Likeness and Landscape: Thomas M. Easterly and the Art of the Daguerreotype*. St. Louis: Missouri Historical Society Press, 1994.

McDermott, John Francis. *The Lost Panoramas of the Mississippi*. Chicago: University of Chicago Press, 1958.

Missouri Democrat. Multiple articles.

Missouri Historical Society Bulletin, multiple editions. Missouri Historical Society Press.

Moore, Robert J. *Jefferson National Expansion Memorial Administrative History, 1980–1991: Urban Innovation and Practical Partnership*. Washington, DC: National Park Service, US Department of the Interior, 1994.

National Register of Historic Places Nomination Forms, various districts. Missouri Department of Natural Resources, dnr.mo.gov/shpo/mnrlist.htm.

O'Neill, Karen M. *Rivers by Design: State Power and the Origins of U.S. Flood Control*. Durham, NC: Duke University Press, 2006.

Paine, Albert B. *Mark Twain: A Biography*. New York: Harper & Brothers, 1912.

Primm, James Neal. *Lion of the Valley: St. Louis, Missouri, 1764–1980*. St. Louis: Missouri Historical Society Press, 1998.

Reavis, Logan Uriah. *A Change of National Empire, Or Arguments in Favor of the Removal of the National Capital from Washington City to the Mississippi Valley*. St. Louis: J. F. Torrey, 1869.

Reinhardt, Areola Henrietta. "The Gunboats of James B. Eads During the Civil War." Thesis, Washington University in St. Louis, 1936.

Reps, John W. *Cities of the Mississippi: Nineteenth-Century Images of Urban Development*. Columbia: University of Missouri Press, 1994.

Rosen, Rick. "St. Louis, Missouri 1850–1865: The Rise of Lucas Place and the Transformation of the City." Thesis, University of California, Los Angeles, 1988.

Schneider, Paul. *Old Man River: The Mississippi River in North American History*. New York: Henry Holt and Co., 2013.

Shoemaker, Floyd C. *Missouri and Missourians: Land of Contrasts and People of Achievements*. Chicago: Lewis Publishing Company, 1943.

Smith, Thomas Ruys. *River of Dreams: Imagining the Mississippi Before Mark Twain*. Baton Rouge: Louisiana State University Press, 2007.

St. Louis Globe-Democrat. Multiple articles.

St. Louis Municipal Water Works. *The St. Louis Municipal Water Works System*. St. Louis: n.p., 1949.

St. Louis Post-Dispatch. Multiple articles.

St. Louis Star-Times. Multiple articles.

St. Louis Republican. Multiple articles.

Theising, Andrew. *Made in USA: East St. Louis*. St. Louis: Virginia Publishing, 2003.

Wagner, Allen Eugene. *Good Order and Safety: A History of the St. Louis Metropolitan Police Department, 1861–1906*. St. Louis: Missouri History Museum Press, 2008.

Winter, William C. *The Civil War in St. Louis: A Guided Tour*. St. Louis: Missouri Historical Society Press, 1994.

Woodward, Calvin M. *A History of the St. Louis Bridge*. St. Louis: G. I. Jones & Co., 1881.

Zensinger, Larry, Gary McClure, and Pat Faulkner. *Handbook for a Flood Plain Management Strategy*. St. Louis: East-West Gateway Coordinating Council, 1974.

IMAGE LIST

UNLESS OTHERWISE NOTED, ALL IMAGES ARE FROM THE MISSOURI HISTORICAL SOCIETY COLLECTIONS.

4: *Ribbon Map of the Mississippi River.* Willard Glazier, 1887. From the Collections of the St. Louis Mercantile Library at the University of Missouri–St. Louis.

6: View of St. Louis region, 1999. NASA Images.

9: *Cahokia or "Monk's Mound," Madison Co., ILL.* from *A History of Madison County.* Engraving by W. R. Brink & Co., 1882.

10: Two views of mounds near St. Louis. Watercolor paintings by Anna Maria von Phul, 1818. "Mound City" postcard, ca. 1873.

12: *View of St. Louis.* Lithograph by J. W. Hill, 1852. View of Big Mound. Daguerreotype by Thomas Easterly, ca. 1850s.

13: Three views of Big Mound during its destruction. Daguerreotypes by Thomas Easterly, ca. 1868.

15: *The Founding of St. Louis.* Painting by Carl Wimar, 1860. *Map of the Mississippi River from Pain Court to Cold Water Rock.* Guy Dufossat of Rui, 1767. From the Collections of the St. Louis Mercantile Library at the University of Missouri–St. Louis.

16: Portrait of Pierre Liguest Laclède. Photograph of oil painting, date unknown. Portrait of Auguste Chouteau. Oil painting, ca. early 1800s. Portrait of Marie Thérèse Bourgeois Chouteau. Oil painting attributed to François Guyol de Guiran, 1810. Laclède family home in Bedous, France. Photograph, ca. 1960.

17: *A Plan of the Several Villages in the Illinois Country, with Part of the River Mississippi.* Map by Theo. Hutchins, 1778. New York Public Library Public Domain Digital Collections.

19: Ten-dollar Bank of St. Louis banknote featuring the earliest known view of St. Louis, 1817. Gift of Eric P. Newman Numismatic Education Society. *French Habitation in the Illinois Country.* Engraved print, 1826.

20: Louis Delisle Bienvenue House at Third and Plum streets. Daguerreotype by Thomas Easterly, ca. 1869. Inventory and appraisal of property belonging to Jeanette Forchet, 1790.

21: Old Cathedral, 215 Walnut Street. Photograph, ca. 1900. *The Old Chouteau Mansion, St. Louis, MO.* Lithograph by J. C. Wild, date unknown.

22–23: Ruins of a Creole home. Daguerreotype by Thomas Easterly, ca. 1848.

25: Upper Louisiana transfer document, March 9, 1804. *Transfer of Upper Louisiana at St. Louis, 1804.* Oil painting by F. L. Stoddard, 1906.

27: Portrait of William Clark. Lithograph by John Wesley Jarvis, ca. 1810. Portrait of Meriwether Lewis. Lithograph by Gilbert Stuart, ca. 1800s. Portrait of General Zebulon Pike. Lithograph, artist and date unknown.

29: Broadside advertisement for William Wiggins's *St. Louis* and *St. Clair* ferries, 1842. *Mississippi River Map No. 1.* United States Army Corps of Topographical Engineers, 1822. From the Collections of the St. Louis Mercantile Library at the University of Missouri–St. Louis.

30: *St. Louis in 1832* from *Pictorial St. Louis.* Lithograph copy of painting by Leon D. Pomarede, 1875. Ferryboat *Alonzo Church.* Photograph from the Swekosky–Notre Dame College Collection, 1915.

31: *Map of Rail Lines Owned and Operated by Wiggins Ferry Co.* from *The City of St. Louis and Its Resources.* The *St. Louis Sunday Star-Sayings*, 1893. Ferryboat *Julius S. Walsh.* Photograph, ca. 1920s. Image courtesy of Murphy Library Special Collections, University of Wisconsin–La Crosse.

32–33: Ferryboat *Samuel B. Wiggins.* Photograph, ca. 1920s. Image courtesy of Murphy Library Special Collections, University of Wisconsin–La Crosse.

35: Advertisement for the arrival of the steamboat *Zebulon M. Pike* at St. Louis. *Missouri Gazette*, July 26, 1817.

36: Sketch of the steamboat *Zebulon M. Pike*, ca. 1964. Depiction of the arrival of the *Zebulon M. Pike* during *The Pageant and Masque of St. Louis.* Photograph, ca. 1914.

37: *Steamboat* Maid of Orleans *on the Mississippi River, Going to St. Louis.* Illustration, 1820. Bill of lading for the steamer *Maystown*, signed by R. Buchanan, February 24, 1823. Portrait of Henry Shreve from *Political Portraits with Pen and Pencil.* Engraving by Samuel Treat, 1848.

39: View of a dilapidated Creole home near the Mississippi River. Watercolor painting by Anna Maria von Phul, 1818.

40: Portrait of Anna Maria von Phul, 1817. *A View of a Cave 2 Miles from St. Louis.* Watercolor painting by Anna Maria von Phul, 1818. *Map of St. Louis and Vicinity.* Engraving by J. Melish, 1818.

41: Depictions of fisherman on the St. Louis levee, St. Louis residents and a cart, and a Creole St. Louis street. Watercolor paintings by Anna Maria von Phul, 1818.

42–43: Clockwise from top left: Depictions of a St. Louis belle, a Native American woman, a boy in a beaver hat, a Creole woman, a Creole cart and driver, a young man, and a Creole woman with a boy. Watercolor paintings by Anna Maria von Phul, 1818.

45: *One of the Views from the Top of the Mound.* Watercolor painting by Anna Maria von Phul, 1818.

46: *Map of the City of St. Louis, Missouri and Vicinity.* J. H. Fisher, 1853.

47: Portrait of Benjamin Gratz Brown. Carte de visite photograph, ca. 1870. Missouri's Anti-Dueling Statute, 1822. View of the East St. Louis riverfront. Russell Froelich Collection, ca. 1920s.

48: Portrait of Dr. Bernard Gaines Farrar. Photograph of a painting, date unknown. Portrait of Major Thomas Hart Benton. Daguerreotype by Thomas Easterly, ca. 1840s. Portrait of Joshua Barton. Painting, date unknown. Portrait of Thomas Biddle. Lithograph, ca. 1818. Portrait of Charles Lucas. Painting by William Lucas, 1815.

49: Agreement regulating the terms of a personal agreement between Thomas H. Benton and Charles Lucas, August 11, 1817.

51: *View of St. Louis.* Oil painting by George Catlin, 1832. Advertisement for the Ashley and Henry expedition. *Daily Missouri Republican*, March 27, 1822.

52–53: *Map of the American Fur Trade, as Conducted From St. Louis*, 1807–1843. Library of Congress Images. Portrait of James Beckwourth. Photograph, ca. 1860. Wikimedia Commons. Portrait of Jim Bridger. Photograph by C. O. Zimmerman, date unknown. Portrait of Robert Campbell. Photograph of painting, date unknown.

54: Map of St. Louis. Lewis C. Beck, 1822. Portrait of Manuel Lisa. Photograph of painting, date unknown. Manuel Lisa's Old Rock House. Photograph, ca. 1940s.

55: Advertisement with engraving for J. Murphy Wagon Company, *St. Louis City Directory*, ca. 1840. Advertisement with engraving for J. & S. Hawken Rifle Company, *St. Louis City Directory*, 1847.

57: *Flatboatmen Relaxing on Their Cargo.* Hand-colored engraving by Alexander Anderson, ca. 1820. *Barge on the Mississippi.* Colored lithograph by A. St. Audelaire, 1832.

58: *Keelboat on the Mississippi River.* Daguerreotype by Thomas Easterly, 1848.

59: *The Mississippi Raft near Port Gibson.* Colored lithograph by Nat. Kinsey, 1956. *Bayou Sacre, Louisiana.* Colored lithograph by Henry Lewis, 1848.

61: Portraits of James Seward, Amos Warrick, Madison Henderson, and Charles Brown. Engravings from *Trials of the Madison Henderson Gang*, 1841. Broadside advertisement for an excursion on the regular steam packet *Eagle.* July 7, 1841. *Map of the City of St. Louis.* Rene Paul, Esq., 1844.

62: Broadside advertising a reward for the capture of runaway slaves. Wm. Russell, October 1, 1847.

63: *Map of St. Louis Showing the Burnt District of May 1849.* Julius Hutawa, 1849. *Burning of McIntosh at St. Louis, in April, 1836.* Engraving from from *Illustrations of the American Anti-Slavery Almanac*, 1840. Library of Congress Images. *The Pro-Slavery Riot of November 7, 1837. Death of Rev. E. P. Lovejoy.* Engraving, 1838.

64: List of rules from Bernard Lynch's slave pen. B. M. Lynch, ca. 1850s. Lynch's slave market, 104 Locust Street. Daguerreotype by Thomas Easterly, 1852.

65: Petition of Winny, a free woman of color, to the St. Louis Circuit Court, May 16, 1825. Portrait of Dred Scott. Daguerreotype by J. H. Fitzgibbon, 1857. Portrait of Lucy Delaney. Engraving from *From the Darkness Cometh the Light*, 1891.

67: *Map of the Harbor of St. Louis.* US Corps of Engineers, 1837. Portrait of Lieutenant Robert E. Lee. Photograph of a painting, 1838.

68: St. Louis, Missouri. Dike No. 107.8, Crain's Island. Photograph by US Engineer Office, ca. 1940s. From the Collections of the St. Louis Mercantile Library at the University of Missouri–St. Louis. Dike on the Mississippi River. Photograph by David Lobbig, 2012.

69: Mississippi River Lock and Dam No. 27, Granite City, Illinois. Photograph by US Corps of Engineers, date unknown. *Map of the Upper Mississippi River Canalization Improvement and Connecting Waterways.* Map featured in *Streckfus Scenic Waterway.* US Engineers Office, 1937.

71: *View of the First Presbyterian Church, Fourth Street, St. Louis MO.* Colored lithograph by J. C. Wild, 1840.

72: *View of Front Street, St. Louis, Missouri.* Colored lithograph by J. C. Wild, 1840. *Views of St. Louis, Missouri and Its Vicinity.* Cover page of lithograph portfolio by J. C. Wild, 1840. Cover page of *American Notes for General Circulation.* Charles Dickens, 1842.

73: Engraved illustration of Charles Dickens, 1842. Wikimedia Commons.

74–75: *South East View of St. Louis from the Illinois Shore.* Colored lithograph by J. C. Wild, 1840.

77: *Missouri Leviathan.* Lithograph by George Tytler, 1842. Mastodon bones from Kimmswick, Missouri. Photograph by George Stark, 1901.

78: Cover page of *Description of the Missourium, or Missouri Leviathan.* Prentice and Weissinger, 1841. University of Pittsburgh Library System.

79: Mastodon skeleton at the Natural History Museum, London, England. Photograph by Andrew Wanko, 2018. Engraving of *Koch's Hydrarchus, Composed of Portions of the Skeletons of Several Zeuglodons* from *Animals of the Past*, 1900.

81: *Sub Marine No. 7. Eads & Nelson's Steam Wreck Boat.* Engraving, 1858.

82: Portrait of James Eads. Photograph, ca. 1860s. Wreck of the steamer *Calypso.* Daguerreotype by Thomas Easterly, 1865.

83: *Government Snag-boat Removing Obstructions from the Channel of a Western River* from *Harper's Weekly*, November 2, 1899. Colored lithograph by Schell and Hogan, 1899.

85: Ruins on the St. Louis riverfront following the Great Fire of 1849. Daguerreotype by Thomas Easterly, 1849.

86: *The Great Fire on the 17th and 18th of May, 1849.* Colored lithograph by L. Gast, 1849. Portrait of Captain Thomas B. Targee. Oil painting by Mat Hastings, 1902.

87: Fire engine Dinkey, Union Fire Company. Daguerreotype by Thomas Easterly, 1852. *Parade Uniforms of the St. Louis Volunteer Fire Department, 1840–1860.* Painting by C. W. Hoffman, ca. 1905.

89: *Map of the City of St. Louis, Missouri and Vicinity.* J. H. Fisher, 1853.

90: Advertisement for "Dr. McGowan's Essence of Tar." *St. Louis Dispatch*, October 3, 1856. *Portrait einer Cholera Praservativ-Frau.* Engraving by P. C. Geissler, 1850. Library of Congress. Scanning electron microscope image of *Vibrio cholerae* bacteria. Photograph by T. J. Kirn, M. J. Lafferty, C. M. P. Sandoe, and R. K. Taylor, 2000. Wikimedia Commons.

91: Chouteau's Pond after it was drained. Daguerreotype by Thomas Easterly, 1852. Tombstone of Pierre Chouteau at Bellefontaine Cemetery. Photograph by Cary Horton, 2018. Receipt of H. D. Meyer for goods bought from Nulsen & Mersman, February 15, 1865.

93: *View of St. Louis from Lucas Place.* Colored lithograph by Edward Buehler, 1854.

94: Residence of John How, 1515 Lucas Place. Photograph, date unknown. Residence of Sarah Collier, 1603 Lucas Place. Photograph by Boehl & Koenig, 1868. Residence of Henry Kayser, 1420 Lucas Place. Photograph by J. C. Strauss, ca. 1890s. Residence of Robert Campbell, 1508 Locust Street. Photograph, date unknown.

95: *View on Lucas Place.* Engraving, 1860. *View of the City of St. Louis.* Lithograph map by J. H. Colton and Company, ca. 1850s. *The Broadway, St. Louis.* Engraving, 1858.

97: Advertising card for the passenger steamer *Hibernia*, 1853. Advertisement for the steamboat *Eagle.* Alton Telegraph Office, 1840. Advertisement for the steamboat *Gladiator.* The *Missouri Republican*, 1852. Circular advertisement for the steamboat *Belle of Pike*, 1870. Circular advertisement for the steamboat *Iron City.* M. S. Mepham & Bro., 1866.

98: Interior of the steamboat *Great Republic.* Photograph, 1875.

99: Ticket for the excursion steamboat *Grand Republic.* McLean and Tomkins Printing, 1892. Flyer advertising roller-skating on the steamboat *Grand Republic*, ca. 1870s. Bill of fare for the steamboat *Missouri*, 1847.

100: The steamer *Charles P. Chouteau* transporting cotton. Photograph, 1870s. Passengers on the lower deck of the *Great Republic.* Lithograph by American Photolithograph Company, ca. 1870s.

101: *Unloading a Mississippi Steamboat in East St. Louis, Illinois.* Lithograph by G. Upham, 1882. The steamboat *Trudeau* in St. Louis. Photograph by William Swekosky, date unknown.

102–103: *High Pressure Steamboat* Mayflower, *First Class Steam Packet Between St. Louis and New Orleans.* Colored lithograph by Nathaniel Currier, 1855.

105: From top left: *Explosion of the* General Brown, *Explosion of the* Ben Franklin, *Explosion of the* Glencoe, *Explosion of the Steamer* Louisiana. Engravings from *Disasters on the Western Waters* by James T. Lloyd, 1856.

106: Kate Kearney, *St. Louis & Keokuk Packet Co.* Daguerreotype, 1853. Image courtesy of Murphy Library Special Collections, University of Wisconsin–La Crosse. *Explosion of the* Moselle. Engraving from *Disasters on the Western Waters* by James T. Lloyd, 1856.

107: "Steamboat Boiler Under Construction." Photograph, ca. late 1800s. Image courtesy of Murphy Library Special Collections, University of Wisconsin–La Crosse. The steamboat *Sultana*, filled with passengers. Photograph by Thomas W. Bankes, 1865.

109: *Carondelet or Vide-Poche, Missouri* from *Das Illustrirte Mississippithal*. Lithograph by Henry Lewis, 1857. *St. Louis*, from *Das Illustrirte Mississippithal*. Lithograph by Henry Lewis, 1857.

110: Broadside advertising Banvard's panorama, February 9–13, 1852.

111: Portrait of John Banvard. Lithograph by Charles Baugniet, 1849. Flyer advertising John Egan's *Monumental Grandeur of the Mississippi Valley*. The Mercury Office, 1850.

112–113: John J. Egan, American (born Ireland), active mid-19th century; *Panorama of the Monumental Grandeur of the Mississippi Valley*, c.1850; distemper on cotton muslin; 90 in. × 348 ft.; Saint Louis Art Museum, Eliza McMillan Trust 34:1953.

115: View of the St. Louis levee. Daguerreotype by Thomas Easterly, 1852.

116: View of entrance gate to Schnaider's Beer Garden. Photograph by Emil Boehl, ca. 1880. *St. Patrick's Day Procession in St. Louis*. Illustration by G. Lehr, 1874.

117: Nameplate of the *Weekly American* newspaper. J. M. Julian and Company, 1846. "Sam's Principles!" Political broadside, 1853. Boarding advertisement from *Greene's St. Louis Directory*, 1845. Mullanphy Emigrant Home. Photograph by Emil Boehl, 1867.

119: *Map of Sewer Districts: For Sewer Report of March, 1949*. St. Louis Board of Public Service, 1949. From the Collections of the St. Louis Mercantile Library at the University of Missouri–St. Louis.

120: Detail of *Map of the City of St. Louis, Missouri and Vicinity*. Edward Charles Schultse, 1852.

121: Mill Creek Sewer under construction near Tenth Street. Daguerreotype by Thomas Easterly, 1868. Mill Creek pumping station. Photograph by Cary Horton, 2019.

123: *Ice Bridge Over the Mississippi at St. Louis* from *Harper's Weekly*. Colored lithograph by E. A. Abbey, 1873. From the Collections of the St. Louis Mercantile Library at the University of Missouri–St. Louis. *Destruction of Steamers at St. Louis*. Engraving by A. Gordon, 1877.

124–125: Steamboat *John Trendley* stuck on an icy river. Photograph, 1887. *The Winter Carnival at St. Louis* from *Frank Leslie's Illustrated Newspaper*. Engraving by G. B. Ellsbury, 1864. Photographer taking pictures on the frozen Mississippi River. Photograph by Michael Sheridan, 1913. Woman standing the frozen Mississippi near the Eads Bridge. Photograph by Michel Sheridan, 1913. "Ice Gorge on the Mississippi River, St. Louis, Missouri." Postcard, ca. early 1900s.

126–127: Bridge at St. Louis over the Mississippi. Photograph, 1875.

129: View of the St. Louis levee from the south elevator. Photograph by Robert Benecke, ca. 1860s.

130–131: *Our City (St. Louis, MO.)*. Colored lithograph by A. Janicke & Co., St. Louis, 1859.

133: *Map of St. Louis Showing East St. Louis*. Julius Hutawa, 1870.

134–135: Floodwater over railroad tracks in Madison, Illinois. Photograph, 1903. *A Tale of Two Cities*. Pamphlet, ca. 1910. Mississippi River flood, looking from St. Louis toward East St. Louis. Panoramic photograph, 1903. *Washington Park Lots in East St. Louis*. Map by Conrad P. Curran Printing Company, ca. 1920s.

137: Steamboat pilot's certificate of Samuel Clemens, 1859. Portrait of Samuel Clemens at fifteen years old. Daguerreotype by G. H. Jones, 1850. Wikimedia Commons. Mark Twain with David Rowland Francis at the dedication of the Eugene Field House. Photograph, 1902. "City Harbor Boat 'Mark Twain,' St. Louis, Mo." Postcard, ca. 1900s.

139: *Scott's Great Snake.* Lithograph by J. B. Elliott, 1861. *United States Mississippi Gun-Boats Being Built at Carondelet, Near St. Louis, Missouri.* Hand-colored engraving from *Harper's Weekly.* Alexander Simplot, 1861.

140–141: *New Topographical Map of St. Louis County, Missouri.* Schaerff and Company, 1867. The former Union Marine Works shipyards in Carondelet, Missouri. Photograph by D. C. Humphreys, 1885. "U.S. Hospital Ship *Red Rover.*" Photograph by William R. Wells, 1864. *The Interior of a Sanitary Steamer.* Engraving by Alexander Simplot, ca. 1860s.

142–143: USS *Cairo.* Photograph, 1863. *Bombardment of Island "Number Ten" in the Mississippi River.* Colored lithograph by Currier & Ives, 1862. *The Bombardment and Capture of Fort Hindman, Arkansas Post.* Colored lithograph by Currier & Ives, 1863. *Admiral Porter's Fleet Running the Rebel Blockade of the Mississippi at Vicksburg.* Colored lithograph by Currier & Ives, 1863.

145: Cover of *Central Magazine*, January 1874. Accompanying Mr. L. U. Reavis's Work Entitled *St. Louis: The Future Great City of the World.* R. P. Studley and Company, 1870.

146: Cover page of *A Change of National Empire.* J. F. Torrey, 1869. *A Map of St. Louis and Its Environs,* Portrait of Logan Uriah Reavis. Lithograph, ca. 1870. Cover page of *St. Louis: The Future Great City of the World.* L. U. Reavis, 1875.

147: *St. Louis Mercantile Library Hall.* Illustration by August Gast and Company, 1854. The Million Population Club at the National Balloon Races at the Indianapolis Motor Speedway. Photograph by Bretzman Photographers, 1910.

149: *Scene on Almond Street* from *A Tour of St. Louis.* Engraving by Dacus and Buel, 1878. The Social Evil Hospital. Photograph, ca. 1910s.

150–151: *View of St. Louis, Missouri.* Lithograph by Emile B. Krauss, 1854. *Selling Her Picture.* Engraving from *Theatrical and Circus Life*, 1882. *A Scene at a Free-Love Meeting.* Engraving from *Joker's Budget*, 1855. *An Orgie in the Wine-Room.* Engraving from *Theatrical and Circus Life*, 1882.

153: Detail of *Pictorial St. Louis, the Great Metropolis of the Mississippi Valley.* Map by Camille Dry, 1875.

155: Men gathered around a large sinkhole. Photograph from the Swekosky–Notre Dame College Collection, ca. 1910. Detail of *Pictorial St. Louis, the Great Metropolis of the Mississippi Valley.* Map by Camille Dry, 1875.

156: Detail of *Map of the City of St. Louis, Missouri and Vicinity.* Edward Charles Schultse, 1852.

157: Painting of English Cave, 1840. Portrait of Captain Ezra English. Photograph, ca. 1850s. *Wm. J. Lemp's Brewery.* Wood engraving, 1883.

158: Picnic at Cliff Cave Park. Photograph, 1891. A boat in a lake in Carondelet Park. Photograph by W. C. Persons, ca. 1920s.

159: Beer garden at Uhrig's Cave. Photograph by Robert Benecke, ca. 1860s. *Map of Cherokee Cave.* Drawing by L. M. Shaw, ca. 1940s. Dr. N. N. DeMenil row houses remodeled as the Cherokee Cave Museum. Photograph by William G. Swekosky, ca. 1950s.

161: City of St. Louis water license granted to Joseph L. Papin, 1848.

162: The Grand Avenue Water Tower. Photograph, 1894. "Water Works, Station and Park, St. Louis, U. S. A." Postcard by Erker Brothers Optical Company, 1901.

163: The Chain of Rocks Waterworks. Photograph by Oscar Kuehn, 1911. The Bissell Point Water Tower. Photograph, 1894. The Compton Hill Reservoir. Photograph by Sievers Studio, 1931. "Settling Basin, Compton Heights Looking East, St. Louis, Mo." Postcard, ca. 1909.

165: A view of the Eads Bridge under construction. Photograph, 1874.

166: *Section of East Pier and Caisson.* Engraving by Julius Bien, 1880.

167: Sinking of the East Pier during construction of the Eads Bridge. Photograph, 1870. View of the Eads Bridge under construction, from the second pier looking east. Photograph by Boehl and Koenig, 1873.

168–169: Portrait of James Eads, ca. 1860s. *The Bridge at St. Louis.* Colored lithograph by Compton and Company, 1875. Library of Congress.*The Great St. Louis Bridge, Across the Mississippi River.* Colored lithograph by Currier & Ives, 1874. The Mutual Life Insurance Building (formerly the Equitable Building). Photograph, 1875.

170–171: Crowds on the Eads Bridge observing the flooding on the Mississippi River. Photograph, 1892.

173: The levee at St. Louis as seen from the Eads Bridge. Photograph, ca. 1870s. Newspaper article detailing the arrival of exodusters. *Missouri Republican*, March 16, 1879. Detail of *Pictorial St. Louis, the Great Metropolis of the Mississippi Valley.* Map by Camille Dry, 1875.

174: *Missouri—Remarkable Exodus of Negroes from Louisiana and Mississippi, Incidents of the Arrival Support and Departure of the Refugees at St. Louis.* Engravings published in *Frank Leslie's Illustrated Newspaper,* April 19, 1879.

174–175: Cartoon showing bulldozers attacking black civilians. Engraving by C. Hamilton and Company, ca. 1879.

177: Receipt of the Uhrig Brewing Company for a shipment of beer from St. Louis to Leadville, Colorado, 1871. Advertisement for *Williams' Illustrated Trans-Continental Guide,* 1878. *Across the Continent on the Union Pacific Railway.* Photograph by A. Gardner, 1867. Digital image courtesy of the Getty Open Content Program.

178–179: St. Louis levee looking south from the Eads Bridge. Photograph by Boehl and Koenig, 1879. St. Louis levee looking south from the Eads Bridge. Photograph by St. Louis Sewer Department, ca. 1920s. *Transportation Lines Tributary to the Commercial Interests of St. Louis and New Orleans.* Map by Joseph Nimmo Jr., 1881. New York Public Library Public Domain Digital Collections.

181: Detail of S*aint Louis in 1896.* Colored engraving by Graf Engraving Company, 1896. William J. Lemp's Western Brewery Complex's ice houses. Engraving, 1883. City Workhouse quarry. Photograph by William G. Swekosky, ca. 1940s. Banner Buggy Company. Photograph by Charles Clement Holt, ca. 1910s. Laclede Gas Light Company. Photograph by W. C. Persons, ca. 1930.

182–183: Detail of *Saint Louis in 1896.* Colored engraving by Graf Engraving Company, 1896. Luther M. Kennett's Shot Tower. Daguerreotype by Thomas Easterly, 1850. Belcher Sugar Refinery. Photograph by Emil Boehl, 1866. View of the St. Louis riverfront north of the Eads Bridge. Photograph from the Swekosky–Notre Dame College Collection, 1890.

185: Comparison of unfiltered and filtered Mississippi River water. Photograph from the *St. Louis Mayor's Message,* 1916.

186: Various advertisements for water purification devices published in the *St. Louis Republican* newspaper, 1901–1905. An unidentified woman uses a water pump in a south St. Louis neighborhood. Photograph by Richard Gruss, ca. 1910.

187: Cleaning mud from the Compton Hill Reservoir. Photograph by William G. Swekosky, ca. early 1900s. Henry Heil Chemical Co. advertisement for stone water filters, ca. 1895. Little Brown Jug water filter, ca. 1895.

188–189: *Panorama of the St. Louis Riverfront* from *Harper's Weekly,* July 8, 1876. Colored engraving by Schell & Hogan, 1875.

191: The St. Louis levee. Photograph by Emil Boehl, ca. 1910. *The Riverfront Esplanade: The Riverfront as It Should Be.* Lithograph published in "A City Plan for St. Louis." T. Humphry Woolrych, 1907.

192–193: *Map of St. Louis City & County Prepared for City Plan Report of the Civic League Showing Proposed Improvements.* Map published in "A City Plan for St. Louis." Jas. C. Travilla, 1907.

194–195: *The Kingshighway, Nineteen Miles in Length.* Map published in "A City Plan for St. Louis." Jas. C. Travilla, 1907. "River Des Peres near Old Manchester Road." Photograph by John W. Dunn, ca. 1890. The former Municipal Bathhouse Number Six. Photograph by Cary Horton, 2013. "Waterworks, Chain of Rocks, St. Louis, Mo." Postcard by St. Louis News Company, ca. 1930s.

197: Thomas Baldwin flying over the Mississippi River near the Eads Bridge. Photograph, 1910. Thomas Baldwin mid-flight near the McKinley Bridge. Photograph by Kaut Studio, 1910. Thomas Baldwin and A. Roy Knabenshue. Photograph, 1904. New York Public Library Public Domain Digital Collections.

198–199: Unidentified pilot flying beneath the Eads Bridge. Photograph by Russell Froelich, ca. 1920s.

201: Men looking through trash south of the Municipal (MacArthur) Bridge. Photograph, ca. 1910.

202–203: An unidentified girl eats an apple in a St. Louis alleyway. Photograph, ca. 1910. St. Louis rubbish cart unloads waste onto a barge. Photograph, ca. 1910s. Chicago Sanitary and Ship Canal under construction. Photograph, ca. 1890s. Wikimedia Commons. Selection of newspaper stories discussing the issue of Chicago sewage in the Mississippi River. *St. Louis Republican Newspaper*, 1900.

205: "The Mississippi Levee St. Louis, Mo." Postcard by George Stark, 1903. Sheet music cover for W. C. Handy's "St. Louis Blues." Kathleen Dickey, ca. 1943. W. C. Handy at the Old Rock House on the St. Louis levee. Photograph, ca. 1935.

207: Looking across the Mississippi River at East St. Louis during the riot of July 2, 1917. Photograph from the NAACP's Crisis magazine, 1917. Collection of the Smithsonian National Museum of African American History and Culture, Gift of Bobbie Ross in memory of Elizabeth Dillard. Welcome to St. Louis sign at the foot of the Municipal (MacArthur) Bridge. Photograph by St. Louis City Planning Commission, 1917.

208: Selection of images from the coverage of the 1917 East St. Louis race riot from *Crisis* magazine, September 1917. Collection of the Smithsonian National Museum of African American History and Culture, Gift of Bobbie Ross in memory of Elizabeth Dillard.

209: East St. Louis riot refugees in St. Louis. Photograph by *St. Louis Star* photographer, 1917. Department of Special Collections and University Archives, W. E. B. Du Bois Library, University of Massachusetts Amherst. Citizens reporting property losses in connection with the East St. Louis riot. Photograph, 1917.

210–211: The Silent Parade in New York City in protest of the East St. Louis riot. Photograph by Underwood & Underwood, 1917.

213: A crowd on the riverfront greets US Navy anti-submarine flotilla for a demonstration visit. Photograph, 1919. A Navy sub chaser docked at the foot of Market Street. Photograph by William J. Peters, 1919. A hydroplane floats on the Mississippi River near downtown St. Louis for a 5th Liberty Bond promotion. Photograph by William J. Peters, 1919. A Navy sub chaser near a dock at the foot of Market Street. Photograph by William J. Peters, 1919.

214–215: USS *Inaugural* docked at St. Louis. Photograph, 1969. From the Collections of the St. Louis Mercantile Library at the University of Missouri–St. Louis. The *Matilda*. Daguerreotype, 1849. The floating McDonald's on the St. Louis riverfront. Photograph from Mac Mizuki Photography Studio, 1980. View of a replica of the *Santa Maria* in front of the Gateway Arch. Photograph, ca. 1969.

217: Coupons for excursions on the steamer *Capitol*, 1941. From the Collections of the St. Louis Mercantile Library at the University of Missouri–St. Louis. Advertisement for the final annual excursion of the season on the steamer *Capitol*. From the Collections of the St. Louis Mercantile Library at the University of Missouri–St. Louis. Pamphlet advertising moonlight excursions on the steamer *St. Paul*. Streckfus Steamers, 1938.

218: Roy, Joseph, John Sr., Vern, and John Streckfus. Photograph, 1920. Image courtesy of Murphy Library Special Collections, University of Wisconsin–La Crosse. "Steamer 'Sidney' on the Mississippi River." Postcard by Adolph Selige, ca. 1910s.

219: Fate Marable's Capitol Revue band on the steamboat *Capitol*. Photograph, 1920. From the Collections of the St. Louis Mercantile Library at the University of Missouri–St. Louis. Dancers on the second deck of the steamer *Capitol*. Photograph by William F. Carroll, date unknown. From the Collections of the St. Louis Mercantile Library at the University of Missouri–St. Louis.

220–221: The *President* steamboat on the Mississippi River. Photograph by Pierce W. Hangge, date unknown. "Al Fresco Rainbow Shadow Box Dancing Palace." Postcard by Streckfus Steamers, date unknown. "Excursion Boat *J.S.* on Mississippi River." Postcard, ca. 1900s. "Excursion Steamer 'Capitol' on the Mississippi." Postcard by Underwood and Underwood, 1926. "Landing at Fort Madison, Iowa." Postcard by C. U. Williams, ca. 1910.

222–223: Steamer *Capitol*, lighted for the American Legion Convention. Photograph by Streckfus Steamers, 1935. From the Collections of the St. Louis Mercantile Library at the University of Missouri–St. Louis.

225: *Official Road Map of Missouri*. Missouri State Highway Commission, 1926. "Greetings from St. Louis, Missouri." Postcard, date unknown. "Route 66, 'Main Street of America.'" Postcard by Curt Teich & Company, ca. 1964. "Here We Are . . . on Route 66." Postcard, date unknown.

226–227: "McKinley Bridge, St. Louis, Mo." Postcard, ca. 1910s. The Veterans Memorial (Martin Luther King) Bridge. Photograph, date unknown. The Municipal (MacArthur) Bridge. Photograph, ca. 1920s. The Poplar Street Bridge. Photograph, ca. 1960s.

228–229: The Chain of Rocks Bridge. Photograph by W. C. Persons, 1929. "Chain of Rocks Bridge St. Louis, Mo. Where U. S. 66, 'Will Rogers Highway', crosses the Mississippi River." Postcard by Curt Teich & Company, 1935.

231: The St. Louis Hooverville. Photograph by *St. Louis Post-Dispatch* photographer, ca. 1930s. Image courtesy *St. Louis Post-Dispatch*. Aerial view of St. Louis. Photograph, 1936.

232: Hooverville children at the Welcome Inn Pool beneath the Municipal (MacArthur) Bridge. Photograph by Isaac Sievers, 1931. Child with a fishing skiff on the edge of the Mississippi River. Photograph by Isaac Sievers, 1931.

233: The St. Louis Hooverville, from across the Iron Mountain railroad tracks. Photograph, 1931. Works Progress Administration wheelbarrows on the riverfront. Photograph by Works Progress Administration, 1939.

234–235: Hooverville houses on the St. Louis riverfront. Photograph by Isaac Sievers, 1934.

237: The St. Louis riverfront prior to clearance for the Jefferson National Expansion Memorial. Photograph, Gateway Arch National Park, National Park Service. The St. Louis riverfront after clearance for the Jefferson National Expansion Memorial. Photograph by Papin Studio, 1941.

238: Luther Ely Smith. Photograph, ca. 1940. Aerial view of the St. Louis riverfront. Photograph by Ted McCrea, 1932. Mayor Bernard Dickmann. Photograph by Richard Moore, 1939.

239: View north up Third Street from Olive Street. Photograph, ca. 1911. Exhibition guide, "The Old St. Louis Riverfront." Gateway Arch National Park, National Park Service, 1938.

240: A view north on Second Street from Market Street during demolition in preparation for the Jefferson National Expansion Memorial. Photograph by Richard Moore, 1940. Aerial view of a parking lot on the cleared St. Louis riverfront, 1954.

241: Simmons Hardware Building. Photograph by William Swekosky, ca. 1930s. The US Post Office and Customs House. Photograph by Hoelke and Benecke, 1870. The Old Rock House. Photograph, 1916.

242–243: St. Louis riverfront and skyline from Illinois. Photograph by W. C. Persons, 1928.

245: Boy Scouts from New York embarking on the SS *Admiral*. Photograph by *St. Louis Post-Dispatch* photographer, 1960.

246: The steamer *Albatross* on the St. Louis riverfront. Photograph, ca. 1930s. The SS *Admiral* under construction on the St. Louis riverfront. Photograph, 1938.

247: Brochure advertising the inaugural season of the SS *Admiral*. Streckfus Steamers, 1940.

248: Forward lounge of the steamer *Admiral*. Photograph, ca. 1940. Passengers on the top deck of the *Admiral*. Photograph, ca. 1950s. "Flashes from the Flagship, S.S. *Admiral*." Illustration, ca. 1960. Flyer for excursions on the SS *Admiral*. Streckfus Steamers, date unknown.

249: Lower deck concession stand on the SS *Admiral*. Photograph, ca. 1950s. From the Collections of the St. Louis Mercantile Library at the University of Missouri–St. Louis. Powder room on the SS *Admiral*. Photograph by Paul Piaget, 1940. Nuns seated on the top deck of the SS *Admiral*. Photograph by Edward Goldberger, 1955. A dance in the SS *Admiral*'s ballroom. Photograph, ca. 1942. A children's recital in the SS *Admiral*'s ballroom. Photograph, ca. 1950s. From the Collections of the St. Louis Mercantile Library at the University of Missouri–St. Louis.

250–251: View of the SS *Admiral* on the Mississippi River. Photograph by Dorrill Studio, 1956.

253: Eero Saarinen behind a model of the proposed Jefferson National Expansion Memorial. Photograph by Balthazar Korab, 1960. Library of Congress. Billboard advertising the Jefferson National Expansion Memorial. Photograph by Dorrill Studio, 1958.

254–255: Architect Eero Saarinen. Photograph by Gateway Arch National Park, National Park Service, ca. 1940s. Eero Saarinen's first-round entry drawing for the Jefferson National Expansion Memorial Architectural Design Competition. Gateway Arch National Park, National Park Service, 1947. Eero Saarinen's second-round entry drawing for the Jefferson National Expansion Memorial Architectural Design Competition. Gateway Arch National Park, National Park Service, 1948.

256: Phillips, Eng & Associates entry drawing for the Jefferson National Expansion Memorial Architectural Design Competition. Gateway Arch National Park, National Park Service. Breger, Hornbostel, Lewis & Associates entry drawing for the Jefferson National Expansion Memorial Architectural Design Competition. Gateway Arch National Park, National Park Service.

257: T. Marshall Rainey & Associates entry drawing for the Jefferson National Expansion Memorial Architectural Design Competition. Gateway Arch National Park, National Park Service. Harris Armstong's first-round entry drawing for the Jefferson National Expansion Memorial Architectural Design Competition. Gateway Arch National Park, National Park Service.

259: Children look at a safety net near the top of the Gateway Arch. Photograph by Floyd Bowser, 1965.

260: Construction workers on scaffolding at the base of the Gateway Arch. Photograph by Arteaga Photo Studio, 1963. Fourth of July festivities on the grounds of the partially completed Gateway Arch. Photograph by *St. Louis Post-Dispatch* photographer, 1964.

261: Aerial view of laborers at work on the Gateway Arch. Photograph, 1963.

262: Percy Green and Richard Daly climb a leg of the Gateway Arch. Photograph by James Rackwitz, 1963. CORE protests in front of the Old Courthouse. Photograph by Lloyd Spainhower, 1964.

263: The final piece of the Gateway Arch is lifted. Photograph by *St. Louis Post-Dispatch* photographer, 1965. Image courtesy *St. Louis Post-Dispatch*.

265: The St. Louis Symphony plays the main tent of the Mississippi River Festival. Photograph by Henry T. Mizuki, 1969.

266–267: *Profile St. Louis* feature on the Mississippi River Festival. *Profile St. Louis*, 1977. Grounds of the Mississippi River Festival at night. Photograph by Henry T. Mizuki, 1969. A crowd at the Mississippi River Festival. Photograph by Henry T. Mizuki, 1969. A crowd gathered for a performance by the Who at the Mississippi River Festival. Photograph by James Carrington,

August 16, 1971. The Mississippi River Festival ticket booth. Photograph by Henry T. Mizuki, 1969. The main tent at the Mississippi River Festival. Photograph by Henry T. Mizuki, 1969.

269: The Gateway Arch as seen from Laclede's Landing. Photograph, 1990.

270: The Greeley Building amid renovations. Photograph by Henry T. Mizuki, 1980. Raeder Place Building. Photograph by Cary Horton, 2018. *Profile St. Louis* feature on the redevelopment of Laclede's Landing. *Profile St. Louis*, 1977.

271: Mississippi Nights. Photograph by Kevin Hartnell, 2007. Wikimedia Commons. View of the 700 block of North First Street. Photograph by Henry T. Mizuki, 1976.

273: Hot-air balloon at the Veiled Prophet Fair. Photograph by *St. Louis Globe-Democrat* staff, 1981. From the Collections of the St. Louis Mercantile Library at the University of Missouri–St. Louis.

274: People wade in the Gateway Arch reflecting pools at the 1981 Veiled Prophet Fair. Photograph by *St. Louis Globe-Democrat* staff, 1981. From the Collections of the St. Louis Mercantile Library at the University of Missouri–St. Louis. A St. Louis firefighter sprays crowds with a water hose at the Veiled Prohpet Fair. Photograph by *St. Louis Globe-Democrat* staff, 1981. From the Collections of the St. Louis Mercantile Library at the University of Missouri–St. Louis.

275: Crowds beneath the Gateway Arch at the Veiled Prophet Fair. Photograph by *St. Louis Globe-Democrat* staff, 1984. From the Collections of the St. Louis Mercantile Library at the University of Missouri–St. Louis. Crowds along Leonor K. Sullivan Boulevard at the Veiled Prophet Fair. Photograph by *St. Louis Globe-Democrat* staff, 1984. From the Collections of the St. Louis Mercantile Library at the University of Missouri–St. Louis.

277: Comparative aerial views of the St. Louis region in August 1991 and August 1993. NASA Images.

278: The St. Louis floodwall. Photograph, Flickr Commons, 2018.

279: Unloading canned water for flood relief in Alton, Illinois. Photograph by FEMA, 1993. FEMA News Photos.

280–281: Clockwise, from top left: Views of the 1993 Mississippi River flood at St. Louis, Chesterfield, River des Peres, St. Charles, near Ste. Genevieve, and near St. Louis. Photographs by FEMA, 1993. FEMA News Photos.

282: Flooding on the Mississippi River from *Harper's Weekly*, May 4, 1859. Engraving, 1859. Flooding on the St. Louis levee. Photograph by J. H. Fitzgibbon, 1858.

283: 1903 flooding along North Broadway. Photograph from the Swekosky–Notre Dame College Collection, 1903. Flooding on the River des Peres near Morganford Road. Photograph by Henry T. Mizuki, 1973.

285: Presidential rally for Barack Obama beneath the Gateway Arch. Photograph by Emily Rasinski, 2008. Image courtesy *St. Louis Post-Dispatch*.

286: Portrait of George Rogers Clark. Painting by George Catlin, ca. 1820s. Invitation to a ball held for the Marquis de Lafayette at the Mansion House Hotel, 1825. Portrait of Andrew Johnson. Photograph by Brady and Handy Photographers, ca. 1870s. Theodore Roosevelt on the St. Louis levee. Photograph, 1907.

287: The steamer *Oleander*. Photograph, ca. early 1900s. From the Collections of the St. Louis Mercantile Library at the University of Missouri–St. Louis. President William Howard Taft on his Mississippi River tour. Photograph, 1909. The steamer *Delta Queen* at St. Louis. Photograph by Ralph D'Oench, 1962.

289: The Gateway Arch and surroundings. Photograph by Cary Horton, 2018.

290–291: Aerial view of the St. Louis riverfront. Photograph by Ted McCrea, 1969. Aerial view of the St. Louis riverfront. Photograph by David Carson, 2018. Image courtesy *St. Louis Post-Dispatch*.

ABOUT THE AUTHOR

Andrew Wanko is Public Historian of the Missouri History Museum. He worked extensively on the Museum's *250 in 250* exhibit, which celebrated St. Louis's 250th anniversary in 2014, and served as the exhibit lead on *Lost Buildings of St. Louis and A Walk in 1875 St. Louis*. He also directed the Museum's feature-length documentary *Show Me 66: Main Street Through Missouri*, which won the 2017 Midwest Regional Emmy for Best Historic Documentary Film.

ACKNOWLEDGMENTS

Thank you to everyone who helped me create this book. Dozens of people from the Missouri Historical Society and multiple other institutions have contributed to the finished product by providing images, editing text, scanning photos, leading me to new stories, delving into records, or simply sharing their knowledge. Any joy you get from this book is a result of their hard work, and I couldn't have done it without them.

Thanks to Editor Kristie Lein and Director of Publications Lauren Mitchell for making me sound good, and a special thanks to Jody Sowell, who continually provides the vision and excitement for bringing St. Louis history to life for its citizens. Thank you to my family for a lifetime of support, and most of all thanks to my wife, Christa, who constantly encourages me and has patiently listened to more stories about St. Louis history than any one person should ever have to endure.